CHRISTIAN MISSIONARIES, ETHNICITY, AND STATE

CONTROL IN GLOBALIZED YUNNAN

WORLD CHRISTIANITY

Dale T. Irvin and Peter Phan, Series Editors

ADVISORY BOARD:
Akintunde E. Akinade
Adrian Hermann
Leo D. Lefebure
Elaine Padilla
Yolanda Pierce

Moving beyond descriptions of European-derived norms that have existed for hundreds of years, books in the World Christianity series reflect an understanding of global Christianity that embodies the wide diversity of its identity and expression. The series seeks to expand the scholarly field of world Christianity by interrogating boundary lines in church history, mission studies, ecumenical dialogue, and interreligious dialogue among Christians and non-Christians across geographic, geopolitical, and confessional divides. Beyond a mere history of missions to the world, books in the series examine local Christianity, how Christianity has been acculturated, and how its expression interacts with the world at large. Issues under investigation include how Christianity has been received and transformed in various countries; how migration has changed the nature and practice of Christianity and the new forms of the faith that result; and how seminary and theological education responds to the challenges of world Christianity.

OTHER BOOKS IN THE SERIES:

Krista E. Hughes, Dhawn Martin, and Elaine Padilla, eds., *Ecological Solidarities: Mobilizing Faith and Justice for an Entangled World*

Aminta Arrington, *Songs of the Lisu Hills: Practicing Christianity in Southwest China*

Arun W. Jones, ed., *Christian Interculture: Texts and Voices from Colonial and Postcolonial Worlds*

Edward Jarvis, *The Anglican Church in Burma: From Colonial Past to Global Future*

Jifeng Liu, *Negotiating the Christian Past in China: Memory and Missions in Contemporary Xiamen*

Briana Wong, *Cambodian Evangelicalism: Cosmological Hope and Diasporic Resilience*

CHRISTIAN MISSIONARIES, ETHNICITY, AND STATE CONTROL IN GLOBALIZED YUNNAN

Gideon Elazar

The Pennsylvania State University Press
University Park, Pennsylvania

Library of Congress Cataloging-in-Publication Data

Names: Elazar, Gideon, author.
Title: Christian missionaries, ethnicity, and state control in
    globalized Yunnan / Gideon Elazar.
Other titles: World Christianity (University Park, Pa.)
Description: University Park, Pennsylvania : The Pennsylvania State
    University Press, [2023] | Series: World Christianity | Includes
    bibliographical references and index.
Summary: "Explores religious identity and change in China,
    focusing on the activity of non-Chinese Christian missionaries in
    contemporary Yunnan"—Provided by publisher.
Identifiers: LCCN 2023024961 | ISBN 9780271095554 (hardback) |
    ISBN 9780271095561 (paper)
Subjects: LCSH: Missions—China—Yunnan Sheng. | Christianity—
    China—Yunnan Sheng. | Ethnicity—China—Yunnan
    Sheng—Religious aspects—Christianity. | Church and state—
    China—Yunnan Sheng.
Classification: LCC BV3420.Y8 E43 2023 | DDC 266.00951/35—dc23/
    eng/20230630
LC record available at https://lccn.loc.gov/2023024961

Copyright © 2023 Gideon Elazar
All rights reserved
Printed in the United States of America
Published by The Pennsylvania State University Press,
University Park, PA 16802–1003

The Pennsylvania State University Press is a member of the
Association of University Presses.

It is the policy of The Pennsylvania State University Press to use acid-
free paper. Publications on uncoated stock satisfy the minimum
requirements of American National Standard for Information
Sciences—Permanence of Paper for Printed Library Material,
ANSI Z39.48–1992.

To Shuli

Contents

List of Illustrations ix
Map x
Acknowledgments xi

Introduction: Conducting Fieldwork in Yunnan 1

chapter 1 Christianity in Yunnan: Historical Background 20

chapter 2 Ethnicity, Nominalism, and Global Salvation 32

chapter 3 Perceptions of Christian Morality and the Free-Market Civilizing Project 62

chapter 4 The Welfare Option: Yunnan's Faith-Based Organizations 91

chapter 5 Translating Culture: Missionary Linguists and the Construction of Authenticity 119

chapter 6 Out of Space: Christian Deterritorialization and State Space 147

chapter 7 Drawing the Borders of Ethno-Christianity: The Nationalities Village 173

Conclusion: The Future of State Tolerance of Religion in China 201

Notes 215
References 220
Index 240

Illustrations

Figures
1. Samuel Pollard's grave in Shimenkan   129
2. Tourist map of Yunnan   151
3. Miao Village sign   184
4. Miao Village church   186
5. Christian batiks for sale   190
6. Sign in Miao Village church   197

Table
1. Joshua Project Scale   39

Map
1. Yunnan Province   x

Map Yunnan Province.

Acknowledgments

It has been over a decade since I began this project, and I owe thanks to many who have helped me along the way. First and foremost, I am deeply indebted to my advisor, Nimrod Baranovitch, for his invaluable help and guidance from the very early stages of this project to its completion. I would also like thank Tzipi Ivri for inspiring me to engage in ethnographic fieldwork and my teachers at the Asian Studies Department in Haifa University, Rotem Kovner and Yitchak Shichor, for their insights and advice during and after my studies. The dedicated teachers of the Kunming College of Eastern Language provided me with the language skills necessary to conduct fieldwork, while several of my classmates introduced me to Kunming's foreign Christian community. Haifa University provided me with funding throughout my time in China, and the Chiang Ching Kuo Foundation supported me in my final year of writing.

After completing my PhD dissertation, I was fortunate to find an outstanding and inspiring academic home at the Center for the Study of Conversion and Inter-religious Dialogue at Ben-Gurion University of the Negev. I am extremely grateful to Chaim Hames and to Ephraim Shoham-Stiener for their interest in my work and for providing me with the opportunity to return to China for follow-up research. The final stages of writing have taken place under the auspices of the Eastern Research and Development Authority at Ariel University, headed by Miriam Billig, who has enabled me to develop my research in so many different ways. A special thanks is due to my editor, Allison Ofanansky, who has guided me through the long process of turning this manuscript into a book. Like many modern anthropologists, a sizeable portion of my work was written in cafés. Salvador's and the Prague Café in Kunming and Grand Café in Jerusalem have provided much of the ambience and caffeine that enabled me to bring this project to completion.

Most of all, I feel that I owe a huge debt of gratitude to my informants in Yunnan, both foreign and local, who cannot be named and whose voices I have attempted to include in this book. Considering the sensitivity of religious issues in the Chinese context, their willingness to share their stories and beliefs, host me, and engage in multiple conversations simply cannot be taken for granted.

Finally, to my wife, Shuli, whose willingness to move to China with our one-year-old son and unending support through these years of writing made this all possible: there are no words in English, Hebrew, or Chinese to express my gratitude.

INTRODUCTION

Conducting Fieldwork in Yunnan

In the winter of 2006, I was studying Chinese in a language college in Kunming. While I found the studies difficult, monotonous, and uninspiring, I had come to China with the aim of strengthening my language skills, and so, reluctantly, I dragged myself to class every morning. The one redeeming feature of my class was Peter, one of my classmates. Peter was European, in his thirties, making him slightly older than the other students. He was also the only other married student, and his wife, Rebecca, also attended class with us. Outgoing and open, he was the kind of person whose presence would be felt in any context. His interest in China was not entirely clear to me; with his punk-style haircut, I imagined that he might be a biker and wondered how and why he and his wife had come to China. To my disappointment, I learned that Peter and his wife only intended to stay in town for a couple of months and were planning on relocating to a medium-size town in Sichuan.

After a while, Peter and I became quite friendly, and he invited me to his home. Upon entering, I was surprised to a see a prominently displayed ceramic tile with "The Lord's Prayer" written in both English and Chinese. Other Christian quotations, symbols, and verses were spread across the apartment. It turned out that Peter was not a biker at all (the haircut was never explained). He and his wife were dedicated Christians who had come to China to spread the gospel. Peter and Rebecca were missionaries.

I had heard from friends that Kunming had a foreign missionary population, and though there was very little contact between the student expat community and the missionaries, there were a few cafés rumored to be owned and run by missionaries. One bakery in the west of the city that was well-known for having the best bread in town (a rather rare commodity in China) was also known for being a Christian-run establishment with an all-Christian staff. That year, I ran into a middle-aged American in the vicinity of the student cafés. When I asked why he had come to China, he answered, "Let's just say it was *shangdi de anpai*—God's plan."

The missionary presence in Kunming puzzled me. I knew that missionaries had been kicked out of China in the 1950s, following the Communist revolution, and proselytizing was strictly illegal (Spiegel 2004, 45; F. Yang 2006, 101). According to regulations published in 2000 by the State Administration of Religious Affairs, religious personnel invited by state authorities may preach at "lawfully registered sites" (SARA 2000, Article 6; Potter 2003), and all religious activity conducted by foreigners must be authorized by official authorities within China. While the document upholds the policy of "mutual accommodation" initiated by Jiang Zemin in 1993, guaranteeing religious freedom to believers (Duan Qi Ming 1998; Lap 2002, 207; Leung 2005), it clearly states that "aliens may not engage in the following missionary activities within Chinese territory" (SARA 2000, Article 17). According to Article 8 of Decree no. 144, titled "Regulations Governing the Religious Activities of Foreign Nationals in China," "Foreign nationals who engage in religious activities in China must respect Chinese laws and regulations. They are not permitted to establish religious organizations, liaison offices, and venues for religious activities or run religious schools and institutes within China, they are not allowed to recruit believers among the Chinese citizenry, appoint clergy or undertake other evangelistic activities" (State Council 1994). Similarly, worded regulations were posted on the wall of our Chinese language classroom, mentioning explicitly that students are forbidden to engage in missionary work of any kind.

A friend who had been living in the city for almost a decade confirmed, however, that missionary presence was far from small and that missionaries numbered in the thousands. He also asserted that it was a well-known fact that Yunnan was a particularly attractive location for missionaries, as many of them worked among the provinces' many ethnic minorities.

Peter had always been open about what he was doing in China. While he was not giving out missionary tracts on the street, he did not feel the need to conceal the goal of his work and seemed fairly confident that he was in no serious danger. Years later, when I visited Peter in Sichuan, I found out that he was indeed somewhat exceptional in his confidence and straightforward approach. Other missionaries I met were, for the most part, much more discreet. However, when I decided to return to China and research Christian missionary activity in Yunnan, I discovered that my friend was right about the size and nature of the missionary community. Christian presence in Kunming clearly numbered in the thousands, consisting mostly of North Americans but containing a substantial number of Europeans, ethnic Chinese from outside the People's Republic of China (PRC), and a sizable Korean community. Moreover, the missionaries themselves broadly confirmed the information regarding the relative ease of work in Yunnan compared with other Chinese provinces.

When I began doing fieldwork in Kunming, capital of Yunnan Province in the PRC, in the fall of 2009, I knew exactly where to find the city's foreign Christian community. Generally speaking, the city's non-Chinese population is divided in two. Foreign Christian students tend to concentrate in the vicinity of the city's major universities, Yunnan University (Yunnan Daxue) and Yunnan Normal University (Shifan Daxue). The Christian communities of foreigners are concentrated farther out, primarily in the west and north of the city. The existence of Christian-oriented cafés, restaurants, and bookshops selling Christian literature and souvenirs is well known.

With my wife and son, I rented an apartment in a neighborhood with a significant foreign Christian element and enrolled in a language school where most of the students were believing Christians and possibly involved in some form of missionary work. Originally, my plan was to find missionaries in cafés and bars and try to convince them to speak with me and later to introduce me to their Han and minority-group converts. However, I came to discover that missionaries are often easy to spot but difficult to approach. How does one start up a conversation on the clandestine and semi-legal nature of their life and work in China? At the same time, I was apprehensive about being too outspoken about my research. Officially on a student visa, I did not want to attract the attention of local authorities by appearing in places associated with activities of borderline legality. The presence of Christianity was felt quite strongly in the city—calendars with red crosses and Christian insignias and jewelry could be seen in many of the shops and markets around my house. The family who ran the grocery store was Christian, and so were the sisters who sold us fruit in the market. Still, religion was a politically sensitive issue, and I did not feel I could simply ask questions randomly and openly.

Then there was the issue of my own identity. David Aikman, the author of *Jesus in Beijing* (2003, 2006), had been a believing Christian and openly sympathetic to the missionary movement and, as such, was able to open many doors. I, on the other hand, did not have that advantage. I was an easily recognizable Orthodox Jew: a clearly marked outsider. Some people I approached were indeed suspicious of me as a non-Christian. Many others were suspicious of me as an academic: afraid I would be accusing them, as many scholars have, of cultural imperialism or, perhaps more significantly, that I would endanger their work in China. Indeed, many of the missionaries I approached were uninterested in contact and would not meet with me.

However, to my great surprise, it turned out that my specific form of foreignness was actually an asset. Virtually all missionaries in Kunming are evangelicals, and many of them can be cataloged as Christian Zionists with a strong affinity for Israel and a keen interest in Judaism and Jews. Kunming had a small Israeli student community at the time, of which I was the only religious member. My presence in town and my Orthodox Jewish appearance were a rarity that evoked interest among Christians. Before long, both foreign and Chinese Christians began contacting me, wanting to talk about Israel, Judaism, and the Bible. One friend, later to become a major informant, had been to a seminary and was able to read Hebrew. Chances to practice were quite rare in Kunming, and he proposed that we could read some Psalms together. Others were delighted to join us for a Sabbath or holiday meal or spend an afternoon asking me questions. As it turned out, the people I was searching for came to me.

The fact that research was conducted as a dialogue rather than a one-way interview turned out to be of great significance to me. It meant that rather than ask my interviewees to risk their work and well-being to help an anonymous person with his research, I was able to provide something in return that was of interest to them. It also made it possible for me to enter the discussion on the reality of their lives and the nature of their work through the door of theology. Through our discussions on Judaism and Christianity, I was able to discern what their religiosity was like and what they thought of ethnic identity, Chinese culture, and the state. Thus, it was through the mapping of the differences and similarities between us that I was able to understand the nature of their mission.

My relationship with my informants was two sided. On the one hand, there was a feeling of affinity based on a common acceptance of the Bible and the similarities of faith in the context of the vast ocean of Chinese adherents of atheism or non-biblical traditions. There was also a common suspicion of the secular world and the advocates of cold rationalism and materialism. At the same time, there was a vast gulf between us, an ancient unresolved controversy that would, from time to time, reappear. Indeed, much of our theological debate seemed to resemble renditions of very old arguments on the same biblical texts that have been debated by Jews and Christians for the past two millennia (mostly on certain chapters in Isaiah and Psalms). Sometimes I felt that from their perspective, my own religiosity, with its emphasis on laws as well as the sanctity of certain tangible texts and places, was in fact closer to the faith they associated with local Chinese tradition.

At times, I became the target of their missionary efforts. But for the most part, I felt that the exchange of information and ideas was motivated by true and mutual curiosity, and I was happy to allow those whom I came in contact with to conduct their own fieldwork on me. At the end, I felt their curiosity, and a feeling of spiritual kinship had won out. The information provided was always partial and obscured, but as time went by, they were increasingly willing to discuss their intentions and purposes. While the theological content of those discussions on faith and doctrine do not feature prominently in this work, they have been an instrumental element of my fieldwork experience. Indeed, to a large extent, the emphasis placed here on the individual and faith-based nature of evangelical Christianity reflects my own traditional perspective of religion as essentially community based and collective. Likewise, Christian abstraction and open hostility toward concreteness contrasted with my own religious practices. In many ways, these contrasts form the theological outline for this research.

Moving from missionaries to local Han Chinese Christians was fairly easy. The foreign Christians I had come in contact with invariably had many contacts with Han Christians, and these were often more than happy to meet me with the recommendation of a mutual Christian friend. They too were curious about Israel and Judaism and wanted to talk and share their personal story of conversion and their opinions about Christianity and the state. The biggest obstacle of all was in reaching recent minority converts. I emphasize the word "recent" because the older, prerevolutionary Christian communities were fairly accessible. In Wuding, Shimenkan, and Sanyingpan, the Miao and Yi communities dating from the early twentieth century were easily located, and community members were happy to speak to a foreigner (once again, being from the land of the Bible was helpful). Indeed, my presence in areas where minority-group Christians are concentrated did not go unnoticed by local authorities. In several locations, I was stopped by the Public Security Bureau and asked to register in the local office. Yet, while the process made me keenly aware of the state's strong presence and the inability to conceal my own, it was, for the most part, rather straightforward and relatively undisruptive to the purposes of my research. As long as I let the authorities know I was there, no further questions were asked.

The real problem was getting to recent ethnic converts living in cities or in mixed communities. Most attended unofficial "house churches," and meetings had to be arranged through their foreign or Han Chinese church leaders. While some were open to discussion, many were inclined to turn down my request to meet their congregants. Indeed, even close and important informants who became personal friends repeatedly refused to put me in direct contact with members of their churches, and some refused to allow any contact whatsoever. The early stages of fieldwork were full of such disappointments. One missionary, who worked among the Hani in the Red River Valley, was so strongly opposed to the idea that an outsider to the faith would visit his communities that he accused me of harboring covert intention to "write about Christianity from a Jewish perspective."

Clearly, the reason behind the converts' reluctance was largely based on a fear that I might put them into legal danger. While missionaries may occasionally be deported for their activities (Cai 2019), local Christians acting outside the law are at risk of arrest and internment. They wanted to protect themselves and their community, and allowing an outsider in could be dangerous. In addition, several missionaries told me they wanted to distance themselves from their converts and work behind the scenes to avoid giving the impression that the growth of Christianity was not an indigenous process. Others were more concerned that local Christians would misrepresent Christian dogma, providing me with a false impression regarding the true nature and state of Chinese Christianity. Finally, it is hard to ignore the feeling of paternal protection implied in the attempt to represent minority-group Christians, a pattern reminiscent of the position held by missionaries in the nineteenth century as mediators between their often-mistreated minority flock and state magistrates and legal authorities. This sentiment is captured in the words of one young American Christian from Lijiang who tried to explain why she could not help me meet Christians from the local Naxi population: "I guess everyone wants to protect their babies" (Lisa, interview, May 10, 2010). The sensitivity of the topic of proselytizing in the PRC meant that interviews with minority converts were not as widespread as I had hoped, and a significant number of interviews were with foreign and Chinese missionaries. Thankfully, after many months of trust building and a few strokes of luck, I was able to interview several Lisu, Yi, Tibetan, and Naxi converts to Christianity who provided some of the invaluable information presented here.

This research began as an attempt to shed light on what seems to be a paradox: a conflict between rhetoric and reality. The existence of a large missionary community in Yunnan and an expanding church are difficult facts to reconcile with official Chinese state policy and rhetoric regarding the illegality of missionary work. Are Chinese authorities unable to deal with foreign missionary presence? Or has a decision been made to ignore the situation? And why, of all provinces, has Yunnan become the home of so many missionaries? Was it simply an issue of the province's geographic distance from the center, or were their other explanations?

In this book, I argue that China's tolerance of missionary activity is not merely a reflection of state weakness in the global era, as some scholars have written (Kindopp 2004, 139; Madsen 2000, 271). Nor can it be attributed mainly to the state's lack of confidence in its ability to control and contain religion (Spiegel 2004, 41; Tu 1999, 87). Rather, missionary activity is allowed to exist because it serves to promote state goals in Yunnan in a number of ways. In Yunnan, home to twenty-six officially recognized ethnic minorities (*shaoshu minzu*), the existence and nature of missionary work is strongly related to the province's multiethnic character. Employing the term "civilizing projects," coined by Steven Harrell (1996), I attempt to illustrate the way state and missionary activities, previously understood as contradictory in nature, have reached a degree of convergence, specifically with regard to promoting and remolding ethnic identity. Much like the state, the missionaries discussed here are active in a process of a dual nature. On the one hand, they are firmly dedicated to certain forms of cultural preservation. At the same time, they aim to deeply reshape the culture they work to preserve.

Missionary work is examined here in the context of evangelical theology. As others have argued, evangelical Christianity works to downplay many elements of ethnicity, substituting particular ethnic narratives with an emphasis on individualism and a sense of belonging to a global community (Hiebert 2007; McAlister 2005; Poewe 1994; Roy 2004). In Yunnan, missionaries inadvertently aid the state by deemphasizing ethnic identity and replacing it with an ethos of individual faith and an international, deterritorialized identity. These missionaries maintain an extremely positive attitude toward the free-market system, individual entrepreneurship, and the core economic and social values of the reform era (1979–present). They emphasize a code of morality centered on family life, prudent economic behavior, hard work, and good citizenship. As such, missionary Christianity is discussed as a civilizing force, aiding the state in its efforts to modernize and acculturate its ethnic southwestern periphery. The civilizing role played by Christianity is discussed here in reference to a variety of issues, including identity, economic behavior, language, and space.

This book is also an attempt to examine the work of missionaries in the realm of cultural preservation and the subsequent attraction of Christianity for minority converts. As many missionaries I interviewed emphasized, the goal of missionary work is to produce "disciples from all nations" (Luke 24:47; Acts 1:8). As such, some features of ethnicity must be preserved, particularly in the realm of language. For minority converts, Christianity offers a road toward preservation that challenges the perpetual position of minorities as "primitive" others, heading toward a future of Hanization. Through the cultivation of writing systems and connection with a global Christian community providing opportunities for employment and education, minorities are able to rise above their marginal position in Chinese society while still remaining within the confines of the state system.

The state can turn a blind eye to missionary work in Yunnan because missionaries are well aware of the limits of their activity. As such, they do not attempt to challenge state hegemony of space by constructing large church buildings and are careful not to openly defy state policies even when they conflict with evangelical theology. Finally, state tolerance is closely linked to the socioeconomic conditions of reform-era Yunnan, a province experiencing both large-scale development and serious social challenges. In particular, missionaries provide much-valued funds, labor power, and information to deal with Yunnan's social ills, including poverty, drug addiction, and prostitution. As such, missionaries working individually or through organizations play an instrumental role in dealing with the conditions created by the liberalization of the Chinese economy and dismantling of the welfare state.

Following the arguments just presented, I dispute the claim that the spread of Christianity in China should be viewed essentially as a form of resistance to the state and a way in which believers are able to create a nonstate sphere of identity and a rejection of Marxist ideology: "Protestantism . . . is providing millions of Chinese with a frame of reference for their lives that is unconnected to or at least distinct from the state and its ideology" (Dunch 2001, 210–14). Such perceptions are not necessarily shared by local state authorities. The paramount position of the Chinese state and its modernization project or its efforts in the realm of ethnic culture and identity remain unchallenged by evangelicals, despite their attempts at social reform. It is important to note that I do not challenge Ryan Dunch's conclusions about the perspectives of converts. My purpose here is to suggest that what may appear to be a story of diverging and conflicting agendas can in fact be theorized as a convergence of interests and carefully negotiated harmony.

It is difficult to make any sweeping claims about religious policy in China. While the Chinese law stipulates that any "normal" religious activity is allowed (Embassy of the People's Republic of China in the United States of America 1997), the ruling on what constitutes normality is left vague and widely open to local interpretation. As Karrie Koesel (2017) suggests, religious policy in China should be examined on the subnational level, as levels of cooperation and conflict are determined according to local players and interests (see also Reny 2018; Vala 2017). Since ambiguity is part of the system, it would be mistaken to expect total consistency of policy (Spiegel 2004, 47; F. Yang 2006). Thus, confiscation of Bibles and arrest of members of house churches are not unheard of in Yunnan (China Aid Association 2006, 2013). At the same time, during my fieldwork, I heard stories of unofficial churches being suddenly granted official status and of confiscated Bibles later being returned on request, all according to the discretion of the local authorities. And yet, it would be wrong to view religious policy in China as completely arbitrary and circumstantial. As the data presented in this book attest, the accommodation of missionary work in Yunnan is an unofficial policy of a relatively consistent nature.

Since the research for this book was conducted, China has undergone significant changes. In the 2017 CPC National Congress, President Xi Jinping declared that "religions in China must be Chinese in orientation, and provide active guidance to religions so that they can adapt themselves to socialist society" (People's Republic of China, State Council 2017). Following Xi's statement, the state has begun promoting the "Sinicization of religion"—a plan to exert more government control over religion, focusing primarily on religions with connections outside of China, such as Christianity and Islam. As a result, tolerance of unsanctioned religious activity had diminished throughout China. Restrictions on movement beginning with the outbreak of COVID-19 have further contributed to the diminishment of Yunnan's missionary community. Indeed, several of the informants who provided information for this research no longer reside in the region. What the future holds for the post-COVID era remains unclear.

Christianity in Yunnan

Much has been written in recent years about the dramatic growth of Christianity in contemporary China, considered to be one of largest triumphs of contemporary evangelical Christianity (Bays 2003; Dunch 2001; Hattaway 2003; Hunter and Chan 1993; Lambert 1999; Lee 2007; Xi 2010; Lim 2013a; Madsen 2000; F. Yang 2005). The growth of Christianity is in fact part of a greater phenomenon of religious revival in post-Maoist China, which also includes increased interest in Buddhism, Daoism, and other traditions. According to Fenggang Yang, "China may have become one of the most religious countries in the world. All kinds of religions, old and new, conventional and eccentric, are thriving" (2004, 101; see also Lai 2003; Kipnis 2001; Madsen 2011; Ostrov 2005). Protestant Christianity is unique in this context as a recently imported religion, often associated with the era of Western semicolonialism in the late nineteenth and early twentieth centuries and commonly perceived as having been virtually wiped out of China during the Maoist era (Kim-kwong Chan 2005, 96).

Scholars have written extensively on church resurgence as an internal Chinese phenomenon, emphasizing the ability displayed by the Chinese church in pulling itself from the wreckage of the Cultural Revolution, opening a wave of expansion unprecedented in prerevolutionary times. A frequently quoted assessment is that there are probably more Christians worshiping in China on a given Sunday than anywhere else in the world (Bays 2003, 488). David Aikman has even gone so far as to openly ponder whether China is on the verge of becoming a Christian country (2003, 303). In recent years, several scholars have addressed the issue of state cooperation, particularly at the local state level with the house church movement (Koesel 2017; Liu and White 2019; McLeister 2012; Reny 2018; Vala 2017). Yet, while the spread of Christianity in China is well documented, much less has been written about the resurgence of foreign missionary activity. As a result, the disparity between official rhetoric and the legal ban on proselytizing and the de facto tolerance of local authorities toward missionary activity has not been researched in-depth. In fact, several scholars have argued that missionary activity is strictly forbidden and evangelical communities are severely oppressed (A. Yu 2005, 141) and that the resurgence of

Chinese Christianity is "nativist to the core," sometimes even antiforeign (Tu 1999, 91).

Christian writers and missionary scholars, some of whom maintain a close relationship with the missionary community in Yunnan, tend to downplay the issue of foreign involvement in the Chinese church (Covell 1995; Lambert 1999; Hattaway 2000). This is probably because any mention of foreign Christian involvement brings to mind the complicated and traumatic past of colonialism, inequitable treaties, and the opium trade, symbols of China's humiliation in the century prior to the Communist revolution. Indeed, the issue of missionary involvement in the colonial project continues to trouble many Christian scholars and academics (A. Anderson 2004, 141; Covell 1995, 151–52; Dunch 2002). In addition, writing on the subject may jeopardize the work of those missionaries working on the ground. The exception to the rule is David Aikman, who mentions a number of individual missionaries and also refers to Kunming as "something of a Christian missionary base" with four to five hundred foreigners "essentially in some kind of missionary role" (2003, 284–94, 301). However, Aikman does not attempt to explain the particularity of Yunnan in this regard.

In a report on state and church relations in Yunnan, Kathryn Rosenbaum mentions the existence of a clandestine community of missionaries, noting that while missionaries fear deportation, "Yunnan is a very lax province when it comes to persecution of Christians" (2004, 20; see also Forney 2001; UNHCR 2009). Likewise, Miwa Hirono (2008) examines three large, legally registered Christian nongovernmental organizations (NGOs) and compares them to pre-1949 missionary work. However, she does not deal with the many small and officially illegal organizations and the Christian content they offer the people they assist. A more explicit, although still unspecific, mention of missionary work is made by Kim-kwong Chan, who points out that after the PRC joined the World Trade Organization (WTO), an influx of foreigners, including missionaries, have taken advantage of China's increasingly open borders "to proselytize in frontier areas" (2004, 62). Chan's research shows that Chinese officials recognize this potential and that the state has stepped up its efforts against missionaries and its strict adherence to the separation between foreigners and locals when religious activity is involved. However, my fieldwork experience shows that, at least where Yunnan is concerned, local authorities often refrain from strictly enforcing regulations and that much of the missionary activity is ignored.

Similarly, contemporary Christians missions and missionaries are largely absent from Chinese academic writings. In recent years, numerous articles have been published dealing with the history of missionary work conducted before the 1949 Communist revolution and the influence of Christianity on the lives of minority populations. While many of these articles describe the religion as a positive force (in contrast with the Maoist antireligious stance), the phenomenon is discussed with virtually no explicit reference to contemporary foreign involvement. This dearth of Chinese scholarly writing on current missionary work reflects the fact that writing about this illegal act would invariably be perceived as an accusation that official or local governments are failing to uphold the law (for an exception to the rule, see Ma Huechang 2010).[1]

For the most part, Christian organizations working in Yunnan are either clandestine in nature or active in realms that are officially unrelated to conversion, such as welfare and linguistics. While members of the foreign Christian community in Kunming do not hide their religious affiliation, missionary work is rarely displayed publicly. Indeed, working discreetly and privately is an essential element of the delicate coexistence between the missionary community and the local authorities: with very few exceptions, members of the community never use the word "missionary" when referring to themselves. Implying the existence of a certain unwritten agreement between missionaries and local authorities, one missionary referred to "not crossing the line," well aware of the fact that their continued activity is dependent on their ability to maintain a low profile (Simon, interview, October 11, 2012). Accordingly, a number of missionaries I interviewed expressed their uneasiness with Aikman's popular and controversial *Jesus in Beijing* (2003). In the context of his Christian agenda and enthusiasm, his view of the missionary movement is extremely positive. Shortly after his book was published, official policy became stricter, a number of missionaries were deported, books were confiscated, and much of the missionary activity went even further underground (Mark, interview, March 24, 2010). In a later edition of the book, Aikman refuted an accusation that he had not been careful enough with personal identities, insisting that the crackdown was in no way related to his book (2006, 373–79).

Despite the relative tolerance of the Yunnan provincial authorities, government harassment is a permanent feature of Christian life throughout China, particularly after Xi Jinping's rise to power, although its extent is difficult to ascertain. Thus, liberal Christians in the US tend to portray persecution in China as essentially insignificant, while evangelicals overemphasize it (Bays 2009, 6–7). A number of websites dedicated to reporting on worldwide persecution of Christians carry periodical reports on China.[2]

Nevertheless, judging by the information available on one such website (chinaaid.org), events in Yunnan are rare and fairly low key. The only serious trouble with the authorities reported on the website was a 2013 report on an official warrant to close down a house church in the Tibetan town of Deqin, although difficulties have been on the rise in recent years. While actual arrests are relatively few, government control is still quite tight. Indeed, several of my informants claimed to have been under some form of surveillance at one point or another.

Christians in Yunnan are engaged in a variety of different fields, perhaps the most common being English-language instruction (Aikman 2003, 278; Wielander 2013, 6). Indeed, a large number of local Christians I interviewed came to Christianity through an English teacher. According to one source, a high official of the State Administration for Foreign Expert Affairs (SAFEA), responsible for foreign English teachers in China, acknowledged privately that over two-thirds of English teachers are sent to China through Christian organizations. Rather than expressing his concern, the official noted his satisfaction, saying that the Christian teachers were of good quality, well behaved, and willing to go to any destination (P. Anderson 2006, 150).

While English-language instruction seems to be a gateway for missionaries to all parts of China, Yunnan is particular in attracting missionaries of two varieties: those engaged in aid and social welfare work such as orphanages, rehabilitation centers, leper colonies, medical clinics, and rural agricultural projects; and those dedicated to cultural preservation who work among ethnic minorities, often in the realm of language preservation, working with the large Christian NGO the Summer Institute of Linguistics (SIL). A minority of individual missionaries and groups focus on direct preaching rather than on aid work, most notably the Jehovah's Witnesses (Mel, interview, September 26, 2012). As the goal of this book is to elaborate on and add to the explanations provided by local and foreign Christians in Yunnan regarding the missionary presence and the tolerance offered to Christianity at large, I turn now to a short presentation of the reasons provided, corresponding to the chapters of this work.

Following a historical introduction to missionary work in Yunnan in chapter 1, chapter 2 focuses on ethnicity and faith from an evangelical missionary perspective, which encourages the preservation of ethnic markers while attempting to create a form of "pristine faith" (Roy 2004, 28) emphasizing individualism and globalism and diluting ethnic identity. Here I argue that evangelical dilution of ethnicity is compatible with the goal of the state and its ethnic order.

Chapter 3 centers on a common explanation of the expansion of Christianity in China, namely, that favorable attitudes toward Christianity are the result of Christian efforts to provide a moral code for China, thus aiding the state in its goal of achieving social harmony. I describe how morality, social stability, and responsible economic behavior reminiscent of Max Weber's "spirit of capitalism" are used by missionaries to appeal simultaneously to potential converts and to state authorities.

Chapter 4 is dedicated to the role played by missionaries in dealing with Yunnan's social ills. With the rise of the free-market economy, the reform era has seen the effective dismantling of the Chinese welfare state, a reality with grave consequences for a large part of the population, particularly in poor provinces like Yunnan. Owing to its proximity to the opium-producing regions of Southeast Asia, Yunnan has been particularly hard hit by drug addiction, AIDS, and prostitution. To counter these problems, Christian NGOs provide services and knowledge in the realms of aid and therapy, including rehabilitation programs and medical assistance. The activity of Christian NGOs described here further illustrates the ability of foreign Christians to work within the state system without openly challenging it.

In chapter 5, I provide an analysis of Christian activities in Yunnan in the realm of minority language preservation. Here I deal with Christian engagement in the realm of language, translation, and the invention of writing systems, activity that could potentially be perceived as a challenge to the state promotion of Chinese. However, I argue that the strengthening of an ethnic language often serves to help students eventually become proficient in Chinese. Thus, missionary linguists do not threaten the paramount position of Putonghua (standard Mandarin Chinese), rather working to integrate minority people into the state system. Accordingly, linguistic activity may be seen as a form of what Shih Chih-yu has termed "assimilation through ethnicity" (2002, 179). At the same time, translators and linguists attempt to remold ethnic culture by encouraging converts to discard traditional religious practices labeled "superstition" while simultaneously attempting to construct an ethnic identity revolving around a language core.

Chapter 6 is viewed through the lens of Henri Lefebvre's concept of the production of space. Evangelical attitudes toward sacred space and the physical construction of churches reflect a tendency to resign the task of spatial production to the Chinese state. Evangelical concepts of space stand in contrast to current trends among many minority groups who have attempted to re-create a spiritual geography lost in the Maoist era. While evangelical Christianity tends to encourage disassociation from physical space, the sacred space of ethnic minorities is often perceived by missionaries as the domain of local gods or "demons" whose power must be broken to pave the path to conversion. Christian hostility toward ethnic ritual territoriality, including earth gods, sacred mountains, and traditional burial rites, helps weaken the connection between ethnic identity and a specific locality and enhance the authority of the state to relegate and define space according to its own needs and vision.

Chapter 7 focuses on the way Christian minorities negotiate with local authorities over the expression of their ethnoreligious identity. This chapter is centered on a Miao church located in an official "Nationalities Village," a living museum on the outskirts of Kunming. An analysis of the spatial layout and exhibits within the Miao Village and the church reveals the way state authorities enable the parallel coexistence of several narratives regarding ethnicity and religion and the ways ethnicity is both celebrated and subsumed to promote the hegemony of a Chinese monoculture.

Methodology

While this book deals with the delicate relationship between foreign missionaries, minority people, and the state, these three players are not represented equally. As missionary work is officially nonexistent in China, direct interaction with the authorities on the subject was difficult to initiate. Indeed, I feared that attempting to openly contact officials would put my research in jeopardy. For this reason, I decided not to request a letter of introduction from a Chinese academic institution for the purposes of this research. Indeed, my experience throughout my time in Yunnan proved that on issues relating to the confluence of religion and ethnicity, a certain degree of ambiguity is helpful for all those involved. In fact, caution seemed necessary in several ways. For example, virtually all my informants refused to use the term "missionary" unless discussing activists working in Yunnan prior to 1949. It should be noted that such caution was particularly warranted in the Tibetan region of Deqin and Shangrila, where I was specifically told by Christians and other foreigners working in town to conduct my research with caution and not to approach local authorities with research questions. As a result, the state perspective represented in this work relies mostly on Chinese academic writing and the analysis given by converts and missionaries.

Methodologically, this research is based primarily on participant observation fieldwork. The fieldwork described in this book was born out of my first encounters with missionaries in Kunming in 2006, began in earnest in June 2009, and was conducted continuously for fifteen months, until September 2010. It was later supplemented by two shorter visits to the province in the summer of 2012 and again in 2016. The bulk of the work presented here was conducted in the provincial capital, Kunming, where I lived for over a year in a neighborhood well-known for being home to a large foreign Christian population. In addition to my many missionary neighbors, the neighborhood contained several cafés and restaurants catering primarily to the city's missionary population, a foreign-goods store, and a Christian bookshop, all of which I frequented regularly. The neighborhood was also the site of the language school I attended, where virtually all my classmates were Christians involved in various aid and charity projects. Several of them became central informants for this work. While many of the interviews were conducted in Christian-owned cafés and shops, they also took place in my house, where I regularly hosted both Chinese and foreign members of the community.

For the security reasons mentioned earlier, I tried to conduct interviews as informally and casually as possible. I had a strong feeling that using more formal means such as questionnaires and recordings would deter those who had agreed to speak with me despite the risk of incurring unwanted attention from the authorities. Accordingly, all names mentioned are pseudonyms, and many of the locations are obscured. While most of my fieldwork was conducted in the provincial capital Kunming, I followed a multisite method (Marcus 1995), making several field trips to different locations throughout Yunnan, primarily to minority areas where I met non-Han Christians and missionaries working on location. These included trips to meet with representatives of the Miao of the Wuding county, the Yi in Sanyingpan, the Naxi in Lijiang, and Hani in Mojiang and Yuanjiang. Twice, I ventured to neighboring provinces, to Shimenkan, the historical center of Hua Miao Christianity in Guizhou, and to visit missionaries working in Sichuan. My fieldwork ended with a six-week period in the Tibetan town of Shangrila (Zhongdian) among its small foreign Christian community. In these minority Christian communities, I often visited the local church and sought out local pastors and preachers, who were usually willing to spend time with me to explain issues of faith, identity, and historical narrative.

While interviews and life stories are essential to this work, it is also based on observation and analysis of different sites including places of worship, Christian cafés, charities, and officially sanctioned museums. Despite the need for discretion, Christian activists do not refrain entirely from producing and disseminating a certain amount of written material including brochures, calendars, and a limited number of tracts. In addition, they make extensive use of the internet. These written, visual, and virtual resources play an essential role in this research and in my effort to understand the delicate interaction between missionaries, converts, and the state.

Charismatic, Evangelical, Pentecostal: A Typology

Writing about Christianity in Yunnan, I encountered a few problems of terminology. I present them here, in hope that both the problems and the decisions I made may illuminate the issues at the center of this research. Perhaps the most problematic is the definition of "missionary," a term that needs a certain amount of clarification. As mentioned, for security reasons, the word "missionary" is seldom used for self-description. In fact, most of the activists I met simply defined themselves as Christians. But Christians are involved in all kinds of work: they run orphanages and rehabilitation centers, work with the poor and disabled, or simply run a café or restaurant. Often, they cater to all who are interested and in need, Christian and non-Christian alike. Should the linguists of the Summer Institute of Language who are involved in the preservation of ethnic languages be labeled "missionaries," even if they do not engage in direct proselytizing? While some people may argue that aid work provided by Christians in China is merely a front to disguise the "true" agenda of conversion, it is important for me to stress that I make no such claim. The overwhelming majority of the people I interviewed were extremely dedicated to the well-being of those whom they aided, regardless of their faith.

And yet, the people discussed in this book, whether working with drug addicts, teaching English, or compiling a dictionary in an ethnic language, have one common attribute: they all consider their activity a religious duty, often referring to it as their "ministry," and are clearly interested in bringing about personal change among those with whom they work. In fact, those missionaries involved in welfare projects often made no distinction between the physical and the spiritual condition of those whom they had come to help. Accordingly, I have opted to use the term "missionary" throughout. I did so because, reflecting on all the Christians I met in Yunnan, I view the term as a sociological category rather than a role description. Whether or not they are engaged in active proselytizing, the Christians discussed here are not simply expats living in a foreign land—they have followed a calling, or at the very least identify with the calling followed by others.

Christians in Yunnan are diverse. Many of my informants adamantly refused to identify themselves denominationally; others used the terms "Pentecostal" or "charismatic." Some clarification is clearly required. According to Russell Spittler (1994), Pentecostals emphasize ecstatic prayer, healing, visions, "speaking in tongues," and direct personal contact with the Holy Spirit. "Charismatic" is a broader term, defining mainstream Christians who have adopted Pentecostal practices. "Evangelical" is an even broader term, transcending denominational differences. Accordingly, "evangelical" is usually contrasted with being religiously liberal and implies a literal understanding of the Bible, an emphasis on a personal relationship with Jesus, and most importantly in this context, a dedication to the idea of spreading the gospel. In this, I follow Randall Balmer (2004, vii–viii), who defines "evangelicalism" as a movement with a number of manifestations including Pentecostalism, the charismatic movement, and fundamentalism. Accordingly, the people discussed in this book would all come under the category "evangelical." Broadly speaking, these may be divided into two major approaches that I term "Pentecostal/charismatic" and "conservative."

Pentecostal missionaries tended to emphasize experience and strongly deemphasize the text of the scriptures. This is not to say that the Bible was theologically less authoritative, only that the biblical text was seen primarily as the basis for a devotional experience. During my fieldwork, informants who identified with Pentecostalism voiced their criticism of the theological stance of more conservative and dogmatic traditional evangelicals. In contrast, conservative evangelicals had strong reservations regarding Pentecostal missionaries' reliance on experience and revelations. They often emphasized the importance of theological knowledge and the necessity of providing accurate translations and critiqued missionaries who attempted to work without acquiring significant knowledge of local culture.

The emphasis on dogma and sound knowledge is deeply related to the ability to tolerate local customs of a non-Christian origin, a centuries-old part of the missionary experience. Divergent attitudes toward other religious traditions were often determined by personal tendencies and seemed to be largely unrelated to a specific religious ideology. However, for the most part, Pentecostal missionaries seemed far more willing to accept a certain degree of syncretism and the retaining of local belief and myths, often reinterpreted in a Christian light. Once again, Pentecostal tolerance was rooted in the belief that becoming a Christian was first and foremost a personal experience of the divine. Thus, while retaining local customs was clearly not ideal, it was overshadowed by the general turning toward Christ.

These differences can also mark a divergence in how missionaries view the concept of conversion. While Pentecostal missionaries are more likely to take interest in emotional expression as sufficient to convince them of the sincerity of converts, more conservative missionaries view such narratives with suspicion, claiming that Christianity is dependent on a basic understanding of Christian dogma relating to the authority of the Bible, sin, and salvation. Generally speaking, the missionaries I encountered who were working in biblical translation seemed to be overwhelmingly more conservative and at least mildly critical of Pentecostal/charismatic practices.

In general, while differences definitely exist, I do not feel that denominational identity stands at the center of the missionary endeavor, nor do I emphasize it in this research. Therefore, with the exception of the chapter dedicated to language and the significance of "speaking in tongues," in which I make special reference to Pentecostalism, I chose to use the more general term "evangelical" throughout.

Chapter 1

CHRISTIANITY IN YUNNAN
Historical Background

A History of Uneasiness: Protestant Christianity and the Chinese State

To understand contemporary missionary work in Yunnan, we must first examine the history of Christianity in the region and the historical components of its relationship with the Chinese state. First among these factors is the traditional role played by the Chinese state in defining the borders of religious orthodoxy and heterodoxy and control over religious matters. The role of the state in determining the legitimacy of a given religion dates back to Imperial times. Likewise, the state has exercised oppression of religious movements perceived as a threat to social and political stability throughout Chinese history (A. Yu 2005). In traditional China, the legality of religion was decided on the basis of usefulness (*youyong*), from the state's perspective, how it was "sanctioned by tradition, . . . strengthened public morality, . . . and contributed to general order" (Gernet 1985, 67). The need to control and regulate religion has been a defining feature of the encounter with Christianity.

Despite periods of relative success for the missionaries, China was not particularly receptive to the Christian message during the Imperial era. China has had a strong anti-Christian tradition dating back to the Jesuit presence in the seventeenth century. Paul Cohen has explained this anti-Christian tradition through the concept of heterodoxy (*xie*), often defined as ideas in contrast with classic Confucian perceptions (1966,

34–41). However, Christianity was not unique in incurring criticism on the side of the Confucian elite. Buddhism—another foreign import with some distinctly unorthodox ideas from a Confucian point of view—has shared a similar history (A. Yu 2005, 90–134). Objection to Christianity was based in controversy over ritual practice and the Christian denouncement of ancestor worship, as well as opposition to Christian concepts of sin, good, and evil, the practice of celibacy, and a perceived lack of respect for the ancient sages (Gernet 1985, 164–69; Lutz 2001, 182).

A Protestant understanding of church history, particularly in its evangelical form, often views the purity of the early church as having been destroyed when the Roman emperor Constantine turned Christianity into the official religion of the empire. Beginning in the fourth century and up until the Reformation, Christianity was under the yoke of the Roman Empire and had moved far from its early ideals. One of the central conclusions stemming from this understanding is that any contact between religion and the state harbors the potential for religious corruption. This is an account of Christian history that is very much alive today and has been recounted to me several times from both foreign and local evangelical Christians living in China.

Although Christian missions in China date back to the sixteenth century, Protestant missionary involvement only began with the arrival in Canton (Guangzhou) of the English missionary Robert Morison in 1807. The first years of Protestant activity in China saw the translation of the Bible and the publication of a number of Chinese tracts but brought about very few conversions. Initially, missionary work was limited to the coastal area around Canton and was officially prohibited by Chinese authorities. It was only after China's defeat in the first Opium War in 1840 that Protestant missionary work was legalized, and the missionary presence began to increase rapidly (S. Barnett 1972; Barnett and Fairbank 1985; Bays 1996; Overmeyer 2009, 43). By 1865, the first permanent missions were opened in Southwest China. In Yunnan, missionary work became substantial only with the arrival of members of Hudson Taylor's China Inland Mission in the 1870s (Benge and Benge 1998; Zhang Danfeng 2003; Fung 2008).

Significantly, the first major thrust of Protestantism into China corresponds with an era of globalization in the late nineteenth and early twentieth centuries, a time of growing international trade, massive flow of ideas, and the heyday of imperialism. Susan Barnett has described early nineteenth-century missionaries as "part of a cooperative missionary-merchant endeavor to break down China's barriers to Christianity and commerce" (1972, 133; see also Harris 1991). Hostility toward Christianity was greatly enhanced in the nineteenth century as foreign Christians came to be perceived as a political as well as a social danger. In the 1850s and 1860s, the destructive current of the pseudo-Christian Taiping Rebellion confirmed the feelings of Chinese officials that this foreign religion was a potential source of unrest (S. Barnett 1972, 146). As China slipped into a state of semicolonialism, Christians became a target for local hostility, and wild rumors of crimes by missionaries were rampant. Eventually, the relationship between missionary work and the imperialist powers had a devastating effect on relations with the Chinese Communist Party (CCP) (Junio 2017, 299).

Yunnan Province, bordered by regions under direct colonial control since the 1880s (British Burma to the west and French Indochina to the south), held some distinct advantages for missionaries during the late Imperial era. In addition to its convenient location, Yunnan is home to a number of non-Han groups, some of which had been engaged in protracted struggles with Qing Dynasty authorities and the surrounding Han population. As the missionaries would soon discover, a long history of marginalization and the hostile relationship between the ethnic minorities and the Chinese state would contribute greatly to the advance of Christianity in the region.

This potential for conversion was not immediately recognized. Missionaries initially targeted Han Chinese, with remarkably little success, while progress among ethnic minorities was quite slow. However, several waves of conversion among minorities would soon follow. The peak of Christian expansion in Yunnan took place in the first quarter of the twentieth century, as it became one of two provinces (along with Henan) with the fastest rate of growth of church attendance. By 1920, there were as many as 30,000 Christian converts in Yunnan (Ying 2009, 74). A second wave of conversions among ethnic minorities took place during the Second World War and in the years leading up to the 1949 revolution. By the time the missionaries were forced by the CCP to leave China in the 1950s, there were over 133,000 Christians in Yunnan alone (Lambert 2001).

The Maoist years posed great challenges for all of China's religious believers. Christianity's close relationship with the West and association with the degradation of colonialism made its fate particularly dire. After the removal of the missionary presence, the state organized an official "patriotic" organ to unite all Christians under a single roof. The Three Self Patriotic Movement (TSPM: self-government, self-support, self-propagation) was designed to sever all connections between Chinese and foreign churches, including funding, training, and theological influence. Since its establishment, it has been the only legally sanctioned Christian organization in China (Junio 2017, 295; Wenger 2004, 170; Huang and Yang 2005; Whitefield 2009; Xu 2004; Zimmerman-Liu and Wright 2013).

Church-state relations in the early years of the PRC were tense and occasionally violent. Some churches in minority areas wanted to retain their autonomy from the state and refused to join the TSPM, a choice for which they paid heavily (Xi 2010, 200–202). In addition, a number of church leaders voiced their opposition to land-reform policies and to the violent "struggle sessions" held against landlords (Tien 1993, 76–77). Naturally, such opinions made the CCP's need to assert its control over the country's Christians all the more urgent. Official attitudes toward Christianity worsened during the Korean War and the antiforeign sentiment it entailed (Junio 2017, 306–7). Virtually all public religious activity came to a halt throughout China during the Cultural Revolution, leading some observers to the conclusion that Christianity had disappeared from the Chinese landscape (Kim-kwong Chan 2005, 96).

Yet, in what is often referred to by contemporary Christians as the miracle of the Chinese church (Lambert 1994), the reform era has brought about a significant revival of Christianity all over China, much of it outside the official state church. Since the early 1980s, unregistered house churches have been attracting huge numbers of converts (Xi 2010, 205–32). Some observers estimate that they may account for as much as 80 percent of China's Protestant population, numbering as many as one hundred million believers (Bays 2003, 488). As Carsten Vala (2017) has shown, the exponential growth of the house church movement was made possible through the development of extensive informal ties between church leaders and local officials.

According to statistics provided by the Christian Amity Foundation, between one million and three million of the province's forty-five million people are Christian believers (Benewick and Donald 2009, 86). The lack of precise numbers is due to the absence of reliable statistics with regard to Christians involved with house churches, as the official statistics only account for members of the churches registered with the TSPM.

Growth in numbers of Christians has been accompanied by a significant spiritual awakening. The house church movement that has evolved over the past few decades is largely (although not exclusively) evangelical and often Pentecostal in nature, emphasizing personal faith, healing, miracles, and ecstatic prayer rather than the more formal and conservative style of official churches (Bays 2011, 186). Indeed, while evangelical theology is not confined to the house church movement, it plays a particularly significant role in the relationship between house church Christians and the state. Evangelical Christians, including many foreign missionaries, tend to be highly critical of the TSPM and enthusiastic advocates of independent churches, expressing the ideal of "the early church from Roman Times" (Hamrin 2008, 2; see also Hattaway 2003, 14–15; Bays 2009, 7). Indeed, as Lauren B. Homer has observed, some (though not all) house churches would refuse any kind of state registration, even if it were easy and forthcoming (2010, 54).

Protestant Missionaries Among Yunnan's Minorities

Steven Harrell has referred to the missionary endeavor among ethnic minorities prior to 1949 as a "civilizing project": an attempt to enlighten, uplift, and reshape local culture through Christianity. "Civilizing projects" such as the one taken on by the missionaries tend to "develop, sharpen and heighten ethnic identity" and often play a central role in the process of ethnogenesis (Harrell 1996, 6; see also Lim 2013b, 105–19; Scott 2009, 24).

As in other places in the world, it was not uncommon for missionaries in Southwest China to work as ethnographers, providing firsthand accounts of the peoples they came in contact with. These include J. O. Fraser, Isobel and John Kuhn, and the Morse family, who worked among the Lisu (Lambert 2005; Morse 1974); William Young, who converted many of the Wa and Lahu (Covell 1995, 231; Xiao and Liu 2007, 52–56; Zhang Xiao 2002, 27); and many others (Qian 2000; Duan Yunxue 2001; Zhao Wenjuan 2008). However, the missionary "civilizing project," since its inception, has shown complex and ambivalent attitudes toward ethnicity and the missionaries' own role as modernizers. To provide a concise background of the interaction between missionaries and ethnic minorities, I limit myself to two examples of the missionary experience in pre-Communist Yunnan: the conversion of the Da Hua Miao population under James Adam, Samuel Clarke, and Samuel Pollard and the writings of Paul Vial, missionary to the Sani Yi.[1]

In 1896, the English-born Reverend Samuel Clarke began working among the Da Hua Miao, who straddle the border of Yunnan and Guizhou.[2] His work is documented in Clarke's famous book *Among the Tribes in South-West China*, which records Clarke's missionary efforts and the work conducted by Adam and Pollard. First published in 1915, the book is half ethnography, half religious testament. Languages, customs, costumes, and myths are all described, revealing the author's deep interest in mapping and preserving Miao culture. At the same time, it is a firsthand account of Clarke's involvement in a dramatic cultural shift—the abandonment of traditional Miao religion in favor of Protestantism. As such, Clarke's work brings to mind the words of Paul Rabinow: "The missionary... could never be a mere observer. His observation was always observation for change" (1984, 201).

Clarke's and Adam's missionary work among the Miao began with only a handful of converts in the final years of the nineteenth century. The Boxer Uprising (1899–1900) was a major setback: missionaries were ordered by their churches to move from the Chinese interior to the coast, and both foreign and local Christians were in danger all over China (S. Clarke [1915] 2009, 143). Despite the troubles of 1900, conversion rates began to rise dramatically among the Guizhou Miao, with as many as 1,200 believers in 1907 (Covell 1995, 89; Qian 2000). At the same time, Adam met a group of Miao from Yunnan and sent them to his colleague Samuel Pollard, who began converting them. By the time Clarke, Pollard, and Adam died, 1915–16 (strangely, all three died around the same time), they had been able to convert a sizable proportion of the Da Hua Miao, Water Miao, and other Miao subgroups.

To understand how such a mass conversion took place among the Miao, one must consider the marginality, discrimination, and centuries-old struggle between the Miao and the Han Chinese state that has been essential to Miao identity formation (Tien 1993, 7). The historical narrative often cited by the Miao traces their origins to the Yellow River valley, an area also considered the cradle of Chinese civilization. Miao oral history records an ongoing struggle with the Han, leading to one defeat after another and gradual withdrawal down to the rugged southern backwater of China and up to the mountain tops. The "Miao albums" of the Qing Imperial era, depicting people from the Yunnan minority, reflect the prevalent Han conception of the Miao as a group living so far beyond the pale of civilization that their humanity was questionable (Diamond 1995, 100–103). Indeed, discrimination is still well within the living memory of many Miao today (interviews with local Miao pastors, Wuding, November 30–December 1, 2009).

Wars with the Chinese intensified during the second half of the nineteenth century, ending in disaster for the Miao. In the area of the Guizhou-Yunnan border, they were subservient and marginalized by Yi landlords, who were in turn placed beneath the ruling Qing state officials (Covell 1995, 84; Tien 1993, 9). Thus, the Miao that Clarke, Pollard, and Adam encountered occupied the lowest rung of Southwest China's social ladder. This system of discrimination and marginalization made conversion to Christianity an attractive option for many Miao, as the new religion and the contact with foreign missionaries offered a path to overcome their inferior status within the Chinese world. To some extent, the acceptance of the missionary civilizing project may be seen as a rejection the Confucian civilizing project and its drive to assimilate marginal minority people (Tien 1993, 11).

The marginality of the Miao stood in stark contrast with the privileged status of foreign missionaries. According to the inequitable treaties signed between China and the Western powers, missionaries were not subject to Chinese laws. Their legal status gave them considerable influence and enabled missionaries to intervene with the authorities on behalf of their communities in legal disputes, bringing their cases before local magistrates and landlords. They also worked to promote land ownership for the serf-like Miao, gaining many enemies among Yi and Han landowners. As a result, while the number of conversions kept growing, relations with state authorities were often tense and uneasy. Nevertheless, in the missionaries' attempt to maintain their positions, they made a distinct effort to present Christianity to the authorities as a source of social stability rather than discord and instructed their congregants not to take up arms against the Chinese (Covell 1995, 91).

The spread of Christianity in ethnic Southwest China may be seen as part of a larger phenomenon of heterodoxy and rejection of state-sponsored religion, which has been a long-standing tradition among the peoples of upland Southeast Asia. Whether the state to counter was China, Thailand, or Burma, religion, often of a millenarian nature, was often employed as a means toward preserving local independence and constructing ethnicity. Thus, James Scott notes "the good fortune of the Baptist missionaries to have brought the Bible to a people who had long believed in messiahs" (2009, 286). Indeed, when Clarke arrived in the region, he found that, much to his dismay, the Miao identified Jesus as the "Miao King," a messianic hero who was destined to appear and slay the Han (Cheung 1995, 232–35; S. Clarke [1915] 2009, 156; Shu-li 2014, 24).

Perhaps the most significant expression of the role played by missionaries in the process of ethnic transformation can be seen in the missionary invention of scripts for unwritten languages. In the early twentieth century, missionaries invented writing systems for the Lisu, Yi, Jingpo, Lahu, Wa, and Miao minorities (Huang Xing 1992, 75; White 1992; Diamond 1996; Yang Jihong 2013). In the case of the Miao, the task was carried out by

Samuel Pollard. Interestingly, when Pollard first met the Miao, they asked him to teach them Chinese. Clarke noticed a similar interest in Chinese and disinterest in the Miao's own language ([1915] 2009, 137), and Chinese was initially taught by the missionaries and their local assistants. Only later did Pollard begin work on creating a phonetic alphabet for the Miao, based on a writing system used for Native American languages. Creating literacy among previously illiterate ethnic groups was of huge significance for many minority people. This is particularly true within the Chinese context and is in keeping with the link between literacy and culture, implied by the term *wenhua* (culture)—*wen* being the character signifying writing (Ping 1995). Thus, the Pollard script has become a cornerstone of Hua Miao identity and a symbol of past achievements (Lemoine 1989, 7). As the inventor of the Miao script, Pollard is still greatly revered among the Hua Miao, and his elaborate grave can be seen in the former Christian Miao center of Shimenkan, as discussed in chapter 2.

The reshaping of Miao culture brought about by missionary activity enabled the Miao to break out of their age-old marginalization, a change that included the formation of a global identity and frame of reference. After the great wave of conversion among the Miao, reaching fifty thousand converts by 1950 (Lambert 2001), prayers were being offered in Miao villages for poor Han—an unheard-of reversal of social roles. More astonishingly, as Ju K'ang Tien reports, money was collected among the Miao for spreading the gospel in far-flung places like Brazil (1993, 52). Thus, an ethnic group that had historically been on the receiving end of cultural and religious trends found itself taking part in a movement with global span and influence.

This ethnic transformation, however, was a double-edged sword. While missionaries invented writing systems and were genuinely concerned with the cultural survival of their ethnic converts in the face of Hanization, the process of conversion in the late nineteenth and early twentieth centuries invariably contained a strong element of cultural renunciation. Indeed, disassociation from the old religion of spirit worship was a condition for the acceptance of converts. Ralph Covell (1995) highlights the paradox of missionary involvement with ethnic culture: while missionaries set out to save minority ethnic cultures from a process of assimilation, it is precisely that process of assimilation that creates the social crisis enabling them to penetrate an ethnic society. Indeed, the view that a cultural crisis is an opportunity for change is often echoed by Christians today with regard to the ideological vacuum of the post-Maoist era (Hattaway 2003, 12).

Adam and Pollard presided over the burning of spirit-worship paraphernalia, the destruction of idols, and the public denouncement of local shamans. These ceremonies of destruction were presented as an act of freedom, a casting off of old bonds, making way for the new religion. The missionaries also went to great efforts to change previous social norms including what they considered immoral sexuality among unmarried youth and the practice of buying brides. At the same time, they worked to abolish consumption of alcohol and opium by restructuring festivals and celebration to fit Christian monotheism and morality. The centrality of such change can be seen in Clarke's remarks regarding the Miao: "Although they profess themselves Christians, they know very little of Christian doctrine. But they understand that Christianity means no whiskey and clean living" ([1915] 2009, 216). Clarke's praise for "no whiskey and clean living" reveals that attempts to change Miao society were strongly related to missionary efforts to "civilize" their ethnic converts. Indeed, efforts to reduce the use of alcohol and narcotics constitute a central feature of the Christian "civilizing project" to this day, an issue discussed at length in chapters 3, 4, and 7.

At the same time, missionaries, then as now, were dedicated to the principle of an inner, faith-based conversion. Thus, the physical destruction of statues and talismans did not in itself imply a true conversion. Clarke voices the missionaries' concern that locals "would profess themselves Christian if only assistance were given them in their law cases with the Chinese courts" ([1915] 2009, 138). Likewise, Pollard noted that some Miao "knew only the missionary and not Jesus" (Tien 1993, 29). Accordingly, the question soon arose: Was the conversion of minorities based on a true faith experience, or was it simply a reflection of ethnic self-assertion and resistance to the state?

The question became all the more poignant due to the fact that among the Miao and other ethnic groups, conversions were often based on families, villages, and clans rather than on individuals. Indeed, some missionaries were openly criticized for performing mass conversions based on kinship rather than personal faith and were obliged to defend and justify their missionary efforts (Covell 1995, 142; Tien 1993, 25). One such justification can be found in the words of James Fraser, missionary to the Lisu. Fraser responded to critics of mass conversion by claiming that converted families have at the very least "turned from Satan to God" by removing idolatry from their home. He acknowledged that there was much to be done afterward, "but you feel you have, in a sense, already landed your fish when this step was taken" (quoted in Covell 1995, 142n13).

To contain the problem of insincere conversions, missionaries developed a screening system. Typically, the conversion process was accompanied by an examination of a potential convert regarding issues of dogma and faith to assess whether they had "an intelligent faith in the Lord Jesus" (S. Clarke [1915] 2009, 164). While conversions were based on a collective rather than an individual decision, they included an individuation process, culminating in the granting of private, biblical names.

Conversion to Modernity

Since the arrival of the first missionaries, one prominent feature of Protestant missionary work in China has been its connection to capitalism and modernization. Early missionaries like the famous Karl Gutzlaff (1803–1851) saw Western civilization, Protestantism, and prosperity as one and the same. Gutzlaff idealized England and its political and economic system and viewed British prosperity as a blessing from God, corresponding to the true nature of the country's religious and social system (Lutz 2008, 69). Indeed, much like the early Jesuits, Gutzlaff and a number of other missionaries liked to demonstrate their knowledge of science, geography, and history, implying that their deep acquaintance with the natural world was a direct outcome of their faith in Christianity (S. Barnett 1972, 135).

The missionaries to the Miao played a similar role, exemplified in the transformation of the small backwater village of Shimenkan (Stone-gate) on the Yunnan-Guizhou border into an important center of education and health care, with the first hospitals and Western-style schools in Guizhou. Indeed, Shimenkan was built up with the stated goal of becoming a missionary center, a concept expressed by Clarke's remark that "Shimenkan, with its whitewashed chapel and houses, now began to look like a mission settlement" ([1915] 2009, 205; see also Shu-li 2014, 103–8).

The issue of modernization can also be found in the writing of the Catholic missionary Pier Vial, who conducted missionary work among the Sani Yi, a group concentrated east of Kunming and known at the time as the "Gni-p'a."[3] Vial idealized the Sani and their simple, premodern lifestyle, viewing them as a tabula rasa for conversion. At the same time, Vial's distaste for Han Chinese culture is clearly evident in his declared preference for the "headless" Sani over the "heartless" Han (Swain 1995, 154). In Vial's eyes, the Sani (often referred to by the general and somewhat-derogatory term "Lolo") possessed a "love of freedom, non-coercive law and gender equality" (Swain 1995, 151). In a complete reversal of traditional Han perceptions of minorities, Vial often describes the Han as lazy opium addicts and the Lolo as hardworking peasants.

While idealizing the romantic simplicity of Sani culture, Vial was also remarkably self-conscious of his role as modernizer. In his letters, he states that he was "empowering the Sani to deal with the modern world in the face of inevitable change, without the loss of their language and culture" (Swain 1995, 151). Like the missionaries to the Hua Miao, Vial believed that he was helping the Sani survive as a nation by protecting them from the Han and at the same time advocating the destruction of sacred objects as a test of faith for converts. Much like the Communists who came to the region after Vial had left, he believed that modernity and development were inevitable processes and that those who did not join in the global game would not survive. In what Margaret Swain calls "an ironic commentary on competing civilizing projects" (Swain 1995, 175), Vial saw the Sani as a people on the verge of extinction and the civilizing role of Christianity as the savior of their culture.

Conclusion: The Legacy of the Early Missions

Reflecting on the history of missionary work in Yunnan, one can discern a number of major trends, bearing relevance to the contemporary state of Christianity in the province and to the research presented here. The history of missionary work among the Miao and Sani discussed in this chapter reveals the complex and multifaceted attitude of missionaries toward ethnicity and culture. Today, the means for creating cultural change have shifted significantly. Since the decolonization process of the 1950s and 1960s, open attacks on cultural and religious practices and the physical destruction of artifacts have become unacceptable to the public, both in the West and in China. Such activity is invariably met with accusations of cultural imperialism and sometimes even of "ethnocide" (Hvalkof and Aaby 1981; Li Huiyu 2005; Ma Huacheng 2010; Manji and O'Coill 2002; Sun 2013). Well aware of the allegations made against missionaries in the past few decades, missionaries working in contemporary Yunnan and in other parts of China legitimate their work by emphasizing the importance of ethnicity and the preservation of ethnic culture, often quoting the verse from Matthew instructing Christians to "make disciples from all nations" (28:19).

Current trends of cultural preservation and restoration are particularly significant in China, following the mass destruction of the Cultural Revolution (Dreyer 1968). This is true not only of physical but also of cultural phenomena in the broader sense. In recent years, many cultural practices are being promoted in China under the title "intangible cultural heritage," a classification meant to elicit UNESCO recognition and funding.[4] The move toward preservation is especially apparent in Yunnan with its growing tourism industry, based primarily on ethnic-minority regions (Davis 2003; McCarthy 2004). Accordingly, contemporary missionaries must find ways of simultaneously preserving and changing ethnic cultures. The complexity of the relationship between ethnic and Christian identity and cultural continuity has arisen as a central theme of the fieldwork I conducted and is at the heart of my discussion throughout this book.

Finally, the role of Christianity as an agent of modernization is significant both with regard to Christian self-perceptions and in shaping the state's Christian policy. The relationship between Christianity and the Chinese state over the course of the past century and a half has been wrought with discord and hostility. And yet, the analysis of Christian life in Yunnan presented in this book suggests that in the reform era, a delicate understanding and coexistence has been developed between the state and Christianity. The change in Christian-state relations is expressed in a renewed assessment on the part of Chinese academics and government officials of the legacy of early missionaries with regard to the modernization of the region and the "civilizing" of its inhabitants.

Chapter 2

ETHNICITY, NOMINALISM, AND GLOBAL SALVATION

> Many Pubiao customs are directed at preserving their unique culture which makes it difficult for the gospel to penetrate their minds with the message of the savior.
>
> —PAUL HATTAWAY, *OPERATION CHINA*

Examining evangelical attitudes toward ethnicity and ethnic identity reveals a deep ambivalence: evangelical and charismatic Christians often attempt to downplay many elements of ethnicity, substituting communal and territorial attachments with a narrative of individualism and globalism (McAlister 2005, 253; Hiebert 2007, 107–8). Individual-based religions, such as fundamentalist Islam and evangelical Christianity, are essentially hostile toward religion that is ethnically, culturally, and spatially based. They aim to deculturize religion, moving toward the purely spiritual realm of "pristine religion": "Religiosity is in both cases more important that religion. . . . The self and hence the individual, is at the core of the cotemporary religiosity. . . . Religiosity is a personal experience, not a legacy. A born-again believer is by definition skeptical of the religion of his family and forefathers" (Roy 2004, 28–29). Yunnan's minority people are peripheral on both a national and an international level. In this context, deethnicized Christianity offers its believers a new international reference group to replace the old ethnic one. Globalization provides an opportunity to universalize and disassociate Christianity from the cultural context and "to provide a model that could work beyond culture" (Roy 2004, 25; 2010; see also T. Johnson 2010). In ethnic Yunnan, the search for the pristine is reflected in the widespread use of the term "nominal" among contemporary missionaries to describe minority Christians who converted prior to 1949. "Nominal" Christianity is contrasted with "true" Christianity, exemplified in the missionaries' personal salvation narratives.

By focusing on individual rather than ethnic- or tribal-based faith, evangelical Christianity dilutes and diminishes ethnic identity in ways that are beneficial for the Chinese state. Accordingly, missionaries promote an external and folklorized version of culture, focusing on costume, music, and dance—a version of ethnicity that bears a striking resemblance to the one being promoted by the state, while simultaneously working for deep cultural change. Public representations of ethnic identity in China focus almost exclusively on external manifestations such as elaborate architecture and colorful festivals with relatively little attention devoted to minority belief systems and nonmaterial cultural manifestations.

Thus, in contrast to the opinion that missionary penetration into China is viewed by the state as a dangerous threat that must be actively countered (Kim-kwong Chan 2004, 69), with regard to ethnic Yunnan, the international nature of evangelical Christianity may actually be beneficial to the state and its attempt to confine ethnic identity to the realm of folklore. I follow Steven Harrell's definition of ethnicity in the Chinese context as an identity arising out of the need to deal with a center intent on ruling, defining, and educating (1996, 28–29). Harrell presents the differences between the Christian and Communist centers, revealed through their civilizing projects spanning the nineteenth and twentieth centuries. However, in the early twenty-first century, these two civilizing projects have more in common than has been previously assumed in their dealings with the ethnic identity they have helped to create. Indeed, the common ground is extensive enough to enable a relatively peaceful coexistence in present-day Yunnan.

Christ and Culture: Evangelical Perspectives

As a religion with a strong missionary drive, Christianity has dealt extensively with questions of cultural accommodation and ethnicity and the "inherent conflict between Christ and culture" (Niebuhr 1956). In Richard

Niebuhr's thought, Christ represents the universal, absolute, and otherworldly, while culture represents all that is human, circumstantial, and temporary—the "artificial, secondary environment" such as language, habits, ideas, and social organization, which man superimposes on the natural world (Menuge 1999).[1] The conflict holds an essential religious paradox. Christians are asked to reject the worldly and temporary in favor of the all-inclusive and absolute human destiny, while simultaneously, they are required to love the world and its inhabitants.

While the Christ-culture conflict may be present in any context, it is of heightened relevance in the mission field. When attempting to influence a foreign society, an entire culture must be newly evaluated. Thus, the process of conversion invariably contains elements of accommodation and adaptation and elements of change and transformation. Trying to draw the borders between adaptation and rejection is an ongoing process, always in question and constantly redefined.

The Christ-culture question has become increasingly poignant in the global era of rapid and complex cultural change and exchange. Religions, particularly universal ones like Christianity, Islam, or Buddhism, can be conceptualized as globalizing and homogenizing forces, often asserting that humanity is or should be one single community. Religious universalism offers direct and personal contact with God, creating "secularized and privatized religion" (Waters 1995, 127). Similarly, global religion diminishes the importance of locality, tradition, and territory and gives rise to the universal and to an emphasis on the religious self (Giddens 2000, 65). This is particularly true of evangelical Christianity, a religion that attempts "to be all things to all men" (Jenkins 2002, 36). As Elizabeth McAlister notes "evangelical conversion allows for territorial detachment, . . . loosening of nationalist and even familial bonds" (2005, 253). Such trends can be found among Pentecostal Christians in Sweden (Coleman 2000, 63), in Ghana (Meyer 1999, 159), and Chinese laborers in Israel (Kalir 2009, 150).

Thus, the particularity of Christianity is not in the mere detachment from a specific cultural context but rather in the fact that local contexts are replaced with a culturally neutral, global Christian identity. "In the church believers are members of one new people. . . . The Christian's new identity as a member in the family of Christ is eternal and takes precedence over all earthly identities" (Hiebert 2007, 108). The act of withdrawal from local culture, a process of "social disintegration of the link to the past" (Najarian 1982, 94), may be seen as a call on converts to follow the process that the missionaries themselves initiated by detaching themselves from their native cultural context and coming to work in China or elsewhere.

The global nature of Christian identity in China is such that close to 80 percent of Chinese Christians identify first as Christians rather than Chinese, "a finding unlikely to endear them to nationalistic Chinese or to the government" (Yang Zhong 2013, 38). Accordingly, the transethnic nature of evangelical Christianity has led some researchers to emphasize the inherent contradictions and hostility between state authorities and foreign Christian influence (Kim-kwong Chan 2004, 69).

However, with regard to Yunnan, the globalizing and deethnicizing nature of contemporary evangelical Christianity may be a reason for increased state tolerance of missionary activity. Thus, by offering minority people a religiosity based on a globalized community of individuals, ethnic identity is diminished, a process that ultimately benefits the goals of the state. Moreover, unlike Oliver Roy's description of globalized fundamentalist Islam and in accordance with the efforts of the Chinese state, missionaries in Yunnan do not entirely negate expressions of ethnic culture. Rather, they encourage a shift in identity that cultivates ethnicity while simultaneously pushing it to a peripheral position and replacing it with a nonethnic, Christian core.

Introducing Nominalism: Mona and the Missionary Vanguard

The first missionary I met in Kunming was a student in my Chinese-language class in the Eastern Languages College. Mona was an American woman in her forties who had spent nine years in China. When we met, she and her husband were debating whether to return to the US or to continue their work in a Central American country that offered quality, reasonably priced education for their two children. The lack of appropriate educational options was the major reason for their decision to leave China: the Kunming International Academy, the Christian school set up to serve the needs of the expat community, was extremely expensive, and Mona's family could not afford it. As long as Mona's children were young, she sent them to a Chinese public primary school, but as they were nearing adolescence, she was unwilling to expose them to the "atheist indoctrination" in Chinese high schools. Solutions had to be found elsewhere (Mona, interview, August 5, 2009).

The language school that Mona and I attended was located in a neighborhood in the north of the city, one of two major concentrations of foreigners in Kunming and home to a number of Christian-owned cafés, a bakery, and a Christian bookstore/souvenir shop. Unlike the language colleges in the city center catering to young students, my classmates were mostly middle-aged and with families. They were frequently involved in welfare and community work ranging from orphanages to training youth football teams. While the students concentrated around the city's universities were mostly secular, the vast majority of foreigners I met throughout my fieldwork residing in the northern neighborhood were believing Christians. The religious nature of the neighborhood was clearly reflected in the language school's student body; I was the only Israeli and to the best of my knowledge the only non-Christian in my class. Other classes were much the same. In fact, throughout my year in the college, I met only one other student who was apparently not a Christian believer.

Despite being self-conscious about my otherness, I did not expect what happened in my first conversation with Mona. Knowing I was Israeli, Mona asked me if it surprised me that so many Christians felt such a strong connection to Israel and its history. I asked her what she meant. As a Christian, she explained, Jewish history and the Jewish relationship to the past, particularly "with the fathers—Abraham, Isaac and Jacob"—was of paramount importance. As she mentioned the names of the biblical patriarchs, her eyes welled up with tears. Overcome with emotion, she went on to explain that a personal connection with them was so central to her faith that she viewed those who had no such relationship as "not true Christians."

This short conversation with Mona marked two major features of my fieldwork in Yunnan. First, it became clear to me that my personal faith was of great interest to the people I had come to research. Second, Mona first exposed me to what became a recurrent theme among Christians I met—the question of being or not being a "true" Christian. Through the way Mona spoke of her faith, I first encountered the missionary ethos of exemplifying a Christian vanguard—the few believers who "answered the calling" to dedicate their lives to the spreading gospel—and to the opposite of that ethos: the definition of other Christians, including many of the local Christians of Yunnan, as "nominally Christian."

The idea of nominalism became all the more interesting when it began appearing in our conversations regarding Yunnan's ethnic-minority Christians. Mona and her husband had no particular connection with minority Christians but were of course aware of the Christian identity of several of

Yunnan's ethnic groups. After enthusiastically citing the large and increasing numbers of Christians in China, Mona explained to me that those who have identified as Christian for a number of generations usually become "nominal": Christians by name only who have not undergone a personal process of becoming "reborn." In other words, their Christian identity is based on tribal tradition and ethnic categories, such as being a Da Hua Miao or Nujiang Valley Lisu, and not on a personal experience of faith.

In many ways, nominalism is an expression of the difference between foreign missionaries and local Han or minority Christians regarding their attitudes toward their forefathers and pre-1949 conversions to Christianity. While many local Chinese Christians I met boasted of their family being Christian for a number of generations, foreign Christians did not tend to speak of family history. For them, the recurring narrative was not one of inheritance but rather of personal conversion and transformation. Virtually every missionary I met in Yunnan had a personal story of conversion following certain common lines: the dark ignorance of the past, a moment of awakening, and later a decision to dedicate one's life to the cause. Their religiosity was based almost exclusively on the individual, often including an element of open hostility toward traditionalism and identity defined by birth. Thus, the missionary concept of being a "true Christian" implied a clearly marked hierarchy between faith and all other forms of identity.

The ambiguity surrounding "nominal" Christians is expressed in the Joshua Project, an evangelical website dedicated to the worldwide mapping of Christianity among ethnic groups. In the statistical section devoted to each ethnicity, two numbers are given: the percentage of "Christians" and the percentage of evangelicals. A "Christian" is "one who professes to be a follower of the Christian religion in any form, . . . based on the individual's self-confession."[2] The term "evangelical" emphasizes personal faith, the centrality of the Bible, and a belief in the effort to evangelize all of humanity. All nations of the world are categorized as either "reached" or "unreached." An "unreached" group is defined as one that has less than 5 percent Christians and less than 2 percent evangelicals. Thus, while any form of Christianity is recognized, a minimal rate of evangelical Christianity is necessary before the status of "reached" is attained. In the overall progress scale, a group with less than 2 percent evangelicals but more than 5 percent Christians is categorized as being at the stage of a "formative/nominal church." With over 2 percent evangelicals, the group is considered to be at the highest phase of "significant/established church."

While the Joshua Project ascribes some value to "nominal" churches, that is not always the case among missionaries working in the field. Indeed, Joshua Project's data on China is considerably more inclusive than are many of the missionaries active in Yunnan in categorizing people as evangelical. Many of the minority people in Yunnan are considered by some missionaries to be nominal Christians. While Mona thought the Lisu of the Nujiang Valley were mostly nominal, the Joshua Project defines them as 45 percent evangelical and 80 percent Christian.[3]

Apart from Mona and me, our small class consisted of one Brazilian woman and a young Korean student. As the semester was ending and Mona was preparing to leave China, we decided to go out for a cup of coffee. Previously I had not had the chance to speak at length with Lena, my Brazilian classmate (the only language we had in common was Chinese), and I was unaware of her religious identity. During our conversation at the café, I discovered that Lena was also an evangelical Christian. When I asked why she had come to China, she answered, "for religious reasons," and explained how God had instructed her and her husband on a number of occasions, eventually telling them to move to China. She had decided to come, despite the fact that she had a nine-year-old child from a previous marriage who lived with his father in Brazil and whom she had not seen in three years. Mona was clearly moved by the story and their similar life choices. She claimed that while approximately "96 percent of all Christians" entertain the thought of becoming missionaries, only 4 percent actually end up going out to the mission field.[4] The young Korean student was asked when she "knew Jesus." Her answer was, "From my mother's womb," implying that she had been born into a Christian family. Clearly, this was considered insufficient, as it lacked a personal story of faith and conversion. The two women asked again, almost in unison, "But when did you choose [to be Christian]?" Our classmate answered candidly that perhaps she had not yet chosen. She added that in Korea she had not thought about it very much but that in China these issues had become of more interest to her. The two women smiled, wished her good luck, and changed the subject. But the contrast between the two missionary women and the Korean student could not have been clearer. Mona and Lena were part of the elect, the dedicated few who have given their lives to the cause. Our Korean classmate was of a different breed. She had come to China solely for the purpose of studying Chinese. She had not been called to the mission field, and her religion was simply part of her family upbringing. She was a rather nominal Christian.

Table 1 Joshua Project Scale

Stage	Level	Level description
Unreached / least-reached < 2% evangelicals and < 5% Christian adherents	1.1	Very few, if any, known evangelicals; professing Christians ≤ 5%
	1.2	Evangelicals > 0.01% but ≤ 2%; professing Christians ≤ 5%
Formative / nominal church < 2% evangelicals and > 5% Christian adherents	2.1	Very few, if any, known evangelicals; professing Christians > 5%
	2.2	Evangelicals > 0.01% but ≤ 2%; professing Christians > 5%
Significant / established church > 2% evangelicals	3.1	Evangelicals > 2% but ≤ 5%
	3.2	Evangelicals > 5%

Note: The Joshua Project Progress Scale is an estimate of the progress of church planting among a people group or country. This scale is derived from values for percentage evangelical and percentage Christian adherent. However, for a few hundred people groups, the Joshua Project scale settings have been manually assigned and are not derived from religion percentages.

Source: Joshua Project website, https://joshuaproject.net.

Nominalism and Ethnicity: Three Versions of Miao

Despite the criticism implied in the categorization of ethnic Christians as "nominal," the construction of an ethnically based Christian identity was hardly an unintended or surprising outcome of early missionary work. Quite the contrary: it was precisely the appeal to ethnic preservation in the face of discrimination and oppression that appealed to the masses of Miao who turned to Christianity. Ironically, the heightened ethnic identity created through the conversion process conflicts with the contemporary missionaries' end goal of constructing an identity centered around personal faith in Christianity. Thus, the label of "nominalism" reveals an aspect of controversy: what is peripheral to the foreign Christian may be central to some of the converts, who view the preservation of culture and retaining of cultural autonomy as a central motivation for adopting Christianity. Thus, it could be argued that the missionary project has, from an evangelical perspective, backfired. The stepping-stone to conversion in the late nineteenth and early twentieth centuries has become the obstacle to "true" faith in the early twenty-first.

While severe criticism from Kunming's current missionaries regarding mass conversions were quite common, it would be wrong to paint a monolithic picture of present-day missionaries in this regard. Some are extremely critical of "nominalism," sometimes going as far as claiming that it is religiously invalid and even counterproductive, in that an illusion of conversion is created. Others view "nominal" or ethnically based Christianity as an initial stage of conversion, a partial and imperfect Christianity later to be expanded on. These differences seem to be less ideological and more a reflection of personal style and character. However, for the majority of missionaries I encountered, ethnically based Christianity is a source of uneasiness and an incentive for further evangelizing.

The missionaries' discussion regarding ethnically based conversion is related to an analysis of what has been achieved in the past. As far as I could discern, mass conversions of entire villages or ethnic groups no longer take place in Yunnan. While the state tolerates individual conversions, it will not allow conversion movements based on ethnicity or clan. Although such restrictions are not part of official policy (according to which all missionary work is prohibited), the missionaries I spoke to perceived any attempts to proselytize large numbers of people as a clear crossing of the line marking the unofficial limits of tolerance (Simon, interview, May 25, 2010; Michael, interview, June 1, 2010).[5]

Furthermore, missionaries often feel it is prudent to keep their communities of converts relatively small to refrain from drawing unwanted attention. The size varies from region to region; for example, missionaries working among the Yi in Sichuan voiced concern over prayer meetings with over thirty people (Peter and Rebecca, interview, June 6, 2010). A similar limit of twenty to thirty members in an unregistered church was mentioned by David Schak (2011, 92). In the Tibetan town of Shangrila, I was told that a community of over ten would be dangerous and likely to attract unwanted attention (Tom, interview, August 8, 2010). It would seem that even in places where restrictions are more lenient, working with numbers resembling what occurred in prerevolutionary times would be inconceivable (Michael, interview, June 1, 2010).

Nevertheless, missionary criticism of pre-1949 ethnically based conversion reveals that state policy is not the only reason why conversions have become individually based. Mass conversions conflict with evangelical thinking, with its emphasis on individual experience and attempts to limit and contain nonreligious forms of identity. To further explain this uneasiness, I now turn to an illustration of contemporary Miao Christianity through three short case studies of ethnic identity and faith among the Miao of Yunnan and Guizhou.

The Da Hua Miao of Wuding

To witness Miao Christianity today, I decided to take a trip with two friends to the area of Wuding, just north of Kunming. Miao settlement of Wuding is fairly recent. The Miao arrived in 1877 from Guizhou shortly after being badly defeated in a conflict with Chinese Qing forces. The recent arrival of the Hua Miao in the region has led them to populate the highest areas of the mountains. As a local Yunnanese proverb states, "those who came late, went to the top" (Tien 1993, 10), implying that the later waves of immigration were unable to settle in the fertile lower reaches of the mountain and were consigned to endure a harsher life in higher altitudes. Thus, while Wuding city is only an hour or two from Kunming by bus, the underdeveloped and rather poor villages of this mountainous area are quite remote, with some accessible only by foot.

As I rode the bus north of Kunming, the prevalence of Christianity could be seen from the window upon approaching the Miao areas surrounding the city of Wuding. Standing out as dominant structures, each of the villages has its own church covered with white tiles and crowned with a prominent red cross. In Wuding, I cautiously asked about churches in town. Rather than pointing them out, people suggested that we visit the local Public Security Bureau and ask the personnel to show us around, revealing the fact that religion, particularly when foreign visitors are present, is an issue of state concern and monitoring. I decided to decline their offer and proceeded up the mountain to the Christian village of Huapo.

As in other villages, the Huapo church stood out as the largest building. It was locked when we arrived in the late afternoon, but the villagers who came to greet us quickly opened its gates and called for the local minister, who invited us in. The interior of the church was extremely simple, with nothing more than wooden benches, a preachers' pulpit, and the occasional slogan written on the wall.

The pastor, a short, middle-aged man named Zhang, was more than happy to talk with me about the community. We sat in the church, and Zhang related how the people of the area had been converted to Christianity approximately one hundred years ago by an Englishman named "Bolin," Samuel Pollard's Chinese name. Before Pollard arrived, Zhang explained, "we had nothing—no writing and no culture (*wenhua*)" (interview, November

30, 2009). Indeed, the Pollard script is proudly displayed in the church and outside, and signs in the village feature both Chinese and Miao in Pollard script. While the displaying of the script serves as a symbolic sign of Miao culture, it has relatively little practical function. I was not able to discern what percentage of the people in Huapo read it, but they generally study the Bible in Chinese.

To explain the Miao's destitute situation before the arrival of the missionaries, Zhang recited the traditional narrative of Miao history: the continuous war with the Han and the gradual movement from their homeland in central China to southern China and then into Southeast Asia. The connection between conversion and social marginalization was laid out simply: when I asked why the Miao converted, Zhang said they had been discriminated against by the Han, "who didn't think of [the Miao] as human." He stressed the way Christianity provided a sense of self-worth as well as an outlook of universal compassion. The emphasis placed by Zhang on the missionaries as bestowers or revivers of culture and the historical memory of persecution underlines the way Miao ethnicity has been formed in reaction to the Han civilizing center. Thus, Christianity was presented by Zhang as a road to Miao revival—a much valued affirmation of culture and self-respect.

It was getting late in the afternoon, and Zhang invited us to spend the night in one of the rooms on the church roof built to host parishioners from more remote villages who sometimes came in for holidays and events. Zhang was a self-taught man, and his knowledge of Christianity came solely from reading and rereading the Bible. As many of his generation, he had never attended a seminary. I was therefore surprised to discover that he was knowledgeable about my dietary restrictions. He invited us to his home but immediately added that he was aware of my inability to eat pork. He said he would serve us something else but asked about the cooking utensils that had come in contact with lard. I gladly agreed that it would be best for us to eat our own food. Later, he came with a friend to visit us in our room carrying tea and a bowl of baked potatoes.

As we sat together and ate Zhang's potatoes, we discussed the nature of the Miao's faith. Both Zhang and his friend were adamant that their Christianity was not syncretistic in the least—they do not worship their ancestors or hold onto any of their previous deities. In fact, the people I spoke to throughout the Wuding region, including the impressively knowledgeable Zhang, knew virtually nothing about their own religion prior to conversion.

I asked Zhang about the Miao's relationship with other, non-Miao Christians. When we first met, he told us that the Da Hua Miao do not engage in missionary work, as they are too poor to send out missionaries. Later he corrected himself, noting that they do occasionally send people to other Miao groups across the border in Laos and Vietnam, where they are usually known as Hmong. He had not heard of Hua Miao missionaries who have moved beyond the Miao/Hmong community. At the same time, a connection is maintained with other non-Miao Christians. Once or twice a year, a Korean missionary, of which Yunnan has many, arrives at the village to encourage and support their Miao coreligionists. Zhang has been to Hong Kong twice for Christian conferences, funded by a friend of his from Guangzhou. However, despite the affinity and solidarity expressed toward Christians of other ethnic backgrounds, Zhang proudly told me that "like the Jews," the Christian Miao do not marry outside their ethnic group.

Although Zhang did not express particular interest in modern Israel, he was excited about our connection with the Holy Land. He particularly enjoyed when my Israeli friends and I pointed out our cities of origin on the maps added as an appendix to his Bible. Using the words Galilee, Carmel, and Jerusalem in an everyday context seemed to give him great pleasure. As our evening of tea and potatoes was ending, I asked him what he thought were the basic precepts of Christianity. In response, Zhang emphasized faith in a single God "and not in false idols" (*xujia de ouxiang*) as the most important principle of the religion. I later noted that he made no mention of Jesus, humanity's sinfulness, or personal salvation throughout our conversation.

The next day, I met Zhang after breakfast and was given fresh apricots from the tree in his yard for the road ahead. Setting out of Huapo in the morning, we walked on to a number of smaller, somewhat more remote villages, arriving at the first one around noon. Physical conditions in the village were poor, and knowledge of the outside world was scarce. Here too, everybody knew about "Bolin" the English missionary, although the timeline of events was sometimes rather vague. One twenty-five-year-old man who was serving as the church leader of a tiny village, higher up and poorer than Huapo, said he did not know what Miao life was before Pollard, since "he was too young" (Pollard died in 1915; interview with local church leader, December 1, 2009).

When I descended to the village of Manpo, I met Wang, another young preacher, who was undergoing official training in a Bible seminary in the nearby city of Chuxiong. Elaborating on what Zhang had told us about Miao history, he explained how the Miao previously had a complex and comprehensive culture and writing system, but their culture had been destroyed through their long struggle with the Han. Significantly, Wang added that today relations with the Han are good due to the Christian influence; Christianity had taught them about forgiveness, and so they forgive the sins of the past and emphasize the equality of all humans (interview, December 1, 2009). Thus, in Wang's view, while Christianity stands at the center of Hua Miao ethnic identity, it is simultaneously a potential bridge over ethnic divides. Wang's perspective on the matter, very possibly the influence of the state-run seminary he attends, stands in correspondence to the much-promoted official vision of ethnic unity (*minzu tuanjie*).

I had previously heard the idea that Christianity promotes harmonious relations between ethnic groups. Mosi, a Han pastor from Henan whom I met in a Kunming market, told me he often ventured into minority areas to teach people about Christianity. Mosi's explanation for his interest in minorities was that "God loves them, because they suffered oppression from the Han" (conversation, May 20, 2010). Mosi's activity in minority regions was presented as atonement for the troubled ethnic relations of the past and an affirmation of Christianity's transethnic nature. Unlike the ethnically homogeneous Christian communities created by early missionary work among Yunnan's minorities, newer communities in ethnic urban centers such as Shangrila and Lijiang are often ethnically mixed, containing both Han and minority congregants.

Like Zhang, the elderly men in Manpo were happy and welcoming at the sight of visitors in general but truly excited to discover that we came from Israel and shook our hands enthusiastically. After several days in the Wuding region, I began to feel as if the Miao Christians considered us coreligionists. Both ministers I met were clearly aware of the basic difference between Christianity and Judaism (as mentioned, Zhang was fairly well versed in the basics of Jewish law); however, no mention of difference or hint of dispute was ever brought up. The feeling of a shared faith was most pronounced when we decided to make our way out of the area. Pastor Wang decided that we should be escorted from Manpo down the mountain, where we could catch the bus to our next destination, the Yi town of Sanyinpan to the north. One young man volunteered, and we walked together for over an hour, until the town was in clear sight. As we walked down the mountain, we discussed different issues of faith. Like Zhang, his focus was on faith in God, whom he always referred to as "Shangdi" and never as "Yesu" (Jesus). When we parted, he used the blessing that Chinese Christians use with each other: "*Shangdi zhufu nimen*," meaning "God bless you."

The story of Christianity among the Miao of Wuding is closely intertwined with the Miao narrative of history. To the Miao, the message brought by the missionaries working in the early twentieth century was one of cultural resurgence and a way of dealing with harsh discrimination. Ironically, one may argue that the narrative of conversion legitimizes discrimination by explaining it as an outcome of past cultural inferiority. Indeed, both Zhang and Wang placed emphasis on the written script as a major feature of civilization and an important symbol of knowledge and ethnic identity, a point of view that coincides with Chinese notions of *wenhua* (Ping 1995; Poa and LaPolla 2007, 341). The myth of recovering the lost cultural heritage expressed in the Pollard script is accompanied by acute forgetfulness of the pre-Christian past. Zhang's assertion that before the missionaries arrived the Miao "had no culture" expresses that, for him, Christianity has become synonymous with being Miao, relegating the non-Christian past to a vague, unknown, and irrelevant prehistory.

Indeed, while their ethnic identity as Da Hua Miao was central to their conversion, the specifics of Christian theology and the issue of personal salvation were never mentioned. Zhang's ethnic Christianity was revealed through the comparison he offered between the Miao and the Jews. Many Christians of Wuding expressed their interest and emotional connection to us as visitors from the Holy Land. Unlike Mona and other missionaries, Zhang identified with Jewish ethnicity, in particular the prohibition on intermarriage. In stark contrast with the global and ethnically mixed nature of missionary Christianity, Zhang proudly stated that the Hua Miao do not marry outside their ethnic/religious group. While Zhang and Wang identified with the Christian message of universal equality, this did not imply assimilation. On the contrary, the Miao's faith in a single God differentiated between them and other inhabitants of the area.

Shimenkan

Toward the end of my time in Southwest China, I made a visit to the place where the mass conversion of the Da Hua Miao began, in Shimenkan, just across the border of Yunnan in Guizhou. The village is predominantly Hua Miao, although it is also home to some Yi, Hui, and Han. Before the arrival of the missionaries, Shimenkan and the region of Weining were known as "the Tibet of Guizhou," implying a remote and inaccessible region (Shen Hong 2006). However, in the early twentieth century, the village was transformed by the missionaries into an important center for the Miao and one of the most developed areas in Guizhou, boasting the region's first modern schools and hospitals.

The rapid development of the area, sometimes referred to as "the Shimenkan Phenomena," has attracted considerable attention from Chinese scholars in recent years (Zhao Wenjuan 2008; Zhang Shuang 2011). Many consider Shimenkan a model for developing rural ethnic regions, focusing on the advanced, modern educational methods introduced by missionaries (Li Huiyu 2005, 69–70; Huanhuan Li 2013, 37) and on the protection they provided locals against the oppression of authorities (Tian and Wang 2000, 77).

Today, long after the missionaries have left, Shimenkan has largely reverted back to a small, rather dusty, and remote village; though the school remains, the hospital is gone. A few monuments remain to tell the story of pre-1949 missionary presence. The old European-style stone school building is still in use, along with a number of buildings where the missionaries resided. The village also contains a newer church, but unlike the churches in the Wuding region, it is only open on Sundays. Perhaps the most impressive of the sites in Shimenkan is the elaborate grave of Samuel Pollard, adorned with epitaphs in Chinese, English, and his own devised Miao script. To this day, the grave is a site of occasional pilgrimages of devout Christian Miao and the odd foreign visitor (L. Sun 2007).

These, however, are all relics of the past. Indeed, looking for Christianity in Shimenkan felt more like archeology than anthropology. Unlike the villagers of the Wuding region, the men and women of Shimenkan took no particular notice of me (with the exception of the Public Security Bureau), and my origins in Israel did not stir up any reaction, interest, or emotion. People I met were aware of the village's past importance and of the conversion of the Da Hua Miao to Christianity but had little to say about it other than referring me to the appropriate relics.

After encountering some trouble with locating Pollard's grave, I met Ma, a young man who volunteered to show me around. Ma had recently returned from Shenzhen, where he spent six years working as a migrant worker. He had acquired good Putonghua, which made things easier for me, as I was having difficulty understanding the local accent. On our way to the grave, he told me he was a Christian but had not attended church in a long time, adding that many of the farmers in the region found it hard to attend regularly for lack of time (conversation, May 11, 2010). Ma had heard of Pollard and knew the grave site well but had no knowledge about the man (other than the fact that he had come from England) and knew nothing of his religious ideas or the practices he had replaced.

After we visited the tomb, Ma offered to take me to see the school. We hitched a short ride with some people we met at the grave site who had come out for a day trip from the nearby city of Weining. The old part of the school comprises several low stone buildings built by the missionaries in the 1920s. Ma proudly told me that the school was the first in the entire region and was well-known for its high quality before the revolution. In the school yard, two stone tablets in Chinese and Miao tell the story of Shimenkan's glory and the construction of the school buildings. The tablets were quite recent: Ma, who was in his midtwenties, told me they were not there when he attended the school as a child. Their placement is a testament to the growing legitimacy of ethnic culture in contemporary China and of a more positive view of prerevolution missionary work among local authorities.

I left Ma after our visit to the school, as he was pondering the possibility of putting his language skills to use and becoming a tour guide, and walked up the road to find a place to spend the night, finally arriving at a dormitory for transient workers. The teenage girl running the place was Miao, as were many of the guests. When I asked questions about their religion, they shrugged their shoulders and gave me a puzzled look. They were Miao and Christian but had nothing much to say about it.

In Shimenkan, I found nothing of the religious devotion of the Wuding Miao. Among the Hua Miao of Shimenkan, religion has become synonymous with ethnicity to an extent that its theological and doctrinal content is largely irrelevant or unknown. The meaning of Christianity in Shimenkan is focused on the triumphs of the past, the modern facilities brought to this remote corner of Guizhou by the missionaries. Thus, the introduction of Christianity to the region is associated with a short but significant era of glory in which the region was transformed from a remote backwater to a beacon of modernity.

As in Wuding, the Miao alphabet featured prominently in Shimenkan as an ethnic marker of symbolic more than practical meaning. For Ma and other residents of Shimenkan, the true influence of Christianity seems to be their ability to modernize and develop despite their marginalization in the past. This ethnocultural advancement is implied in the introduction of a Miao writing system. Shimenkan preceded the rest of Guizhou (including predominantly Han cities like Guiyang) in the establishment of modern schools and hospitals, a fact portrayed as a Miao triumph over discrimination and inferiority. Thus, the missionary history of Shimenkan has been subsumed by the state narrative of modernization and development.

Ma is a case in point. Since he was a Da Hua Miao, Christianity was part of his identity and ethnicity and was associated with achievements of the past, but it seemed unrelated to issues of theology. Like many young rural men, Ma sought ways to integrate into China's new economic system. Living as a migrant worker in Shenzhen gave him a linguistic advantage, leading him to contemplate whether the tiny tourist industry of Shimenkan could become a possible venue for employment. Thus, while the Miao script, displayed in the school yard, was a source of ethnic pride, my young guide's true asset was his knowledge of standard Chinese, offering the greatest chance for personal advancement.

Anning: A Qing Miao-Han Wedding

About a month after my trip to Wuding, I was invited to a wedding in a Miao village near Anning. The Miao of Anning are the non-Christian Qing Miao also known by the name Hmong Njua.[6] The Qing and Hua Miao are divided linguistically; according to our host in the village (the bride's father), only 30 percent of the Qing and Da Hua Miao vocabulary is identical (interview, December 23, 2009).

In fact, the division between Qing and Da Hua Miao underlines the way in which Christianity has spread along ethnic lines and has come to be associated with specific ethnic subgroups. As our host was driving us from the bus station in the city of Anning to the village, he pointed at two women he recognized as Da Hua Miao from a village across the valley and said, "They are Christian." When I asked what he knew about Christianity, he told me that the people of the Qing Miao village were not acquainted with that religion. To our host and to others at the wedding, Christianity was perceived primarily as a feature of Hua Miao identity.

The wedding was a three-day celebration of which I attended only one. The bride and groom both lived in Kunming as transient workers but had returned to the bride's village to marry. In light of what I had been told by Zhang, the minister from the Hua Miao village in Wuding about intermarriage, I assumed that both the bride and the groom were Miao. As it turned out, the groom was Han. I asked one of the village elders present about intermarriage and was told that in the past, due to discrimination of the Miao, intermarriage with other groups was extremely rare. However, since the reform era began, "everything has changed," and among today's generation, intermarriage is now quite common. Indeed, rates of intermarriage are so high that "today, different groups are hard to differentiate" (discussion with Qing Miao village elders, December 23, 2009).

Between lunch and dinner, the men sat around the tables to drink and smoke. One middle-aged man wearing a turban sang a traditional song and played a flute. Such singing, I was told by the other participants, was becoming increasingly rare. Knowledge of songs and oral history has diminished, now preserved only in the most remote mountain villages. It was, explained the elder, an unfortunate and inevitable consequence of the "opening up and reforms" (*gaige kaifang*) that had begun under the rule of Deng Xiaoping in 1979. Yet despite the diminishment of cultural knowledge, my host stressed that there was nothing to complain about. He pointed out a green, bitter plant boiled in water and said that before 1979, that was virtually all they ate. Today life is much better—a large variety of meat and vegetables are easily available, providing for a lavish wedding feast. The increasing assimilation process seemed like a reasonable price to pay.

One of the elders told a story of how the Hui began the practice of not eating pork: Long ago, some Hui were escaping from the Han and were forced to hide in a cave. Pigs guarded the cave and deceived the Han pursuers into thinking there was no one there. As a token of respect, the Hui vowed to refrain from consuming pork ever again (Qing Miao village elder, December 23, 2009).[7] This story, seemingly unrelated to the Miao, illustrates the ways in which the Miao narrate their perspective on their long and bitter relationship with the Han. Although the story is told of the Hui, it describes common features of Miao legends, including pursuit by a Han enemy and fear of annihilation. It bears resemblance both to the stories conveyed to me by the Hua Miao of Wuding and to similar legends recorded by Samuel Clarke and common among many of the ethnic groups of the region (S. Clarke [1915] 2009, 57; Scott 2009, 24). The cultural result of the conflict described—the taboo on eating pork—is created in the context of this ongoing struggle. Thus, our host was unaware of the fact that the prohibition on eating pork, like most aspects of Hui religious life, reflects a cultural context far removed from China and the Han. Accordingly, the story reflects Harrell's view of ethnicity as a reaction to a coercive "civilizing" center. Moreover, the explanation given for the emergence of this central religious taboo reflects the interdependence of religious and ethnic identities. In this case, the religious practices of the Hui are assumed to be products of the ongoing relationship between a marginal ethnic group and a powerful Han center.

The centrality of an external civilizing mission is apparent in all three case studies described here: the Hua Miao of Wuding, the imagined Hui (as narrated by the Qing Miao elder), and Qing Miao. For the Hua Miao, the focal point of history is the transition from the Imperial/Confucian to the missionary "civilizing mission" with the arrival of Pollard and the invention of the Miao script. In a sense, the story of the Hua Miao, the efforts made by missionaries on their behalf, and their subsequent conversion is similar to the myth of the Hui and the pigs. For the "Hui," as represented by the elder in Anning, religious practice is the product of conflict with the powerful Han. In both cases, religious identity is understood as a form of gratitude toward saviors from the hands of Han oppression. For the Qing Miao at the wedding celebration, the opening of the reform era, initiated within the Chinese center by Deng Xiaoping, is perceived as the defining factor in the reshaping and diminishment of ethnicity. Indeed, the "opening up" of the reform era has a double effect of liberating, in this case from discrimination and prejudice, and at the same time exposing to outside influence, causing the erosion of local culture (Shao 2010, 18).

The comparison between the Hua and Qing Miao reveals an ironic attribute of the relationship between Christianity and ethnicity. As my encounters with the three Miao communities described in this chapter have shown, Christianity and ethnic identity are intimately connected. Thus, according to the Hua Miao clergymen of Wuding, the Hua Miao do not usually marry outside their group. This is clearly not the case among the largely assimilated Qing Miao of Anning. Similarly, the Pollard script is largely limited to the Hua Miao, who display it proudly (although it is not necessarily used on an everyday basis). In Shimenkan, where knowledge of Christianity seems minimal, the Pollard script and the image of Pollard himself are preserved as sources of ethnic pride. According to the head of the Summer Institute of Languages office in Kunming, the same is true with regard to the missionary-devised Lisu script: knowledge of the writing system is considerably more prevalent among the Christian Lisu than among their non-Christian kin (Sean, interview, October 10, 2012). Ironically, while local minority Christians seem more interested in their ethnicity than their non-Christian counterparts, foreign missionaries display ambivalence and at times hostility toward ethnically based Christianity and go to great lengths to emphasize the nonethnic and individual basis of faith.

The Mask of Culture

Shortly after returning from my trip to Wuding, I met with Mark, an American Christian who had been active in China for over a decade. Mark was eager to hear about the way the Hua Miao I met articulated their faith. I relayed the way in which Pastor Zhang had emphasized the monotheistic principle and his attempt to convey a sense of spiritual kinship. To my surprise, Mark expressed deep dissatisfaction with what I had reported. To him, the ideas conveyed by Zhang were evidence of the "nominal" nature of Miao Christianity in the area. The essence of the Christian faith, he explained, was not monotheism but faith in Jesus, an understanding of the sinful nature of all humans, and an acceptance of Jesus as key to salvation. In Mark's interpretation, the fact that Zhang had failed to emphasize Christ, his death and resurrection, is evidence of the Christianity of many minority believers being "traditional": a vague spirituality based on lineage or ethnicity. Christianity as a tradition cannot be considered true Christianity; a real Christian is only one who has experienced a personal change through which they received a "new heart" (Mark, interview, December 12, 2009).

Unlike many of the missionaries I met, whose religiosity was based on experience, for Mark, experience had to be grounded in knowledge of scripture and theology. Lacking either produced "nominal" Christians. He was troubled by the ethnic-traditional nature of Christianity in Yunnan and by the lack of knowledge displayed by many second- and third-generation Christians regarding basic points of Christian theology. For Mark, the dangers of ignorance went beyond nominalism. Lack of theological knowledge has led many Chinese Christians to create a large variety of heterodox groups, often retaining certain elements of their original religious practices (Madsen 2000, 276; Lambert 2006; Xi Lian 2010, 49).

Significantly, Mark's views on "true" versus "nominal" converts were not limited to the Miao or Yunnan's ethnic minorities. Much of his criticism was pointed at the missionary community in Yunnan, particularly the Americans. He repeatedly noted that many Christian missionaries working in China are spreading a shallow and meaningless version of Christianity, "nominal at best" (interview, December 12, 2009). Ignorance of correct doctrine led to superficial conversions, and such ignorance was the result of missionary unawareness of the particular conditions in Yunnan. Thus, the responsibility for nominalism could not be placed wholly on the converts and their motives; it was the inevitable outcome of the form of Christianity they received: "These American missionaries and their cursed naiveté come to China making a whole lot of noise, full of enthusiasm and no understanding of the local culture." Mark added that missionaries arrive with no awareness of the delicate relations between church and state in China. Acting in ways that are inappropriately public, they get in trouble with the authorities and are sometimes deported, subsequently creating a halo of martyrdom around themselves as people who have "paid the price" (interview, March 23, 2010).

Mark observed in his decade in China that many of the locals "play along" with the missionaries, providing the answers expected of them. People often convert for pragmatic reasons, having very little to do with faith. For Mark, such activity is meaningless and potentially harmful. The missionaries feel good about themselves, boasting "hundreds of converts" and reporting inflated numbers to their churches back home, while no real conversion has taken place. Mark claimed that the widely flaunted numbers of Christians in China, in books like the ones written by David Aikman (2003) and Tony Lambert (1999), were largely overblown, aimed at rallying American churches: "because that's what we like in America."[8]

Nevertheless, in Mark's view, the nature of American missionaries was only half the trouble with conversion in China. The larger problem was rooted in certain core elements of Chinese culture. Like many foreign Christians, Mark was critical of certain aspects of Chinese culture and Confucian mores. Metaphors he frequently used for culture were a "mask" or a "crust, formed and hardened over time" (interview, March 23, 2010). Mark equated the "mask" with the Chinese social concept of "face," which in his view was the "sin of pride." The mask covers the faces of the Chinese and is the result of their long cultural tradition of pragmatism and the centrality of the dichotomy between "useful" (*youyong*) and "useless" (*meiyouyong*), which negates the meaning of pure spirituality and makes all conversions suspect. For Mark, the objective of a Christian must be to "break the Chinese mask of 'face' and pride," revealing the hidden self, with its potential willingness to change. Returning to Niebuhr's Christ-culture dichotomy, Mark's declared objective may be seen as an invocation to move beyond culture to create change and a movement to faith, on a personal level.

Mark's long experience in China had only increased his doubts about the ability to create change. Time and again, he came to realize the earthly motives of many spiritual presumptions.[9] The question of Chinese pragmatism in spiritual matters has troubled missionaries since the time of the Jesuits in the seventeenth century. Mateo Ricci and other early Jesuits were accused of the same things Mark claims against the missionaries of today; their converts accepted Christianity externally while inwardly holding onto religious syncretism and materialism. As Ricci remarked, "In China matters of salvation are of little account" (Gernet 1985, 72).

In Mark's view, true Christians were scarce in China, but this did not seem to trouble him. In the choice between quality and quantity, he preferred the former, as he would rather have "a clear mountain stream." In contrast, Mark claimed, after the fall of the Soviet Union, shallow Christianity suddenly appeared in Russia, "like a big, shallow, postmodern lake" (interview, March 23, 2010). The fact that the stream "gets kicked against the rocks" was not necessarily a bad thing. In other words, state control and occasional persecution were a potential for a deeper form of faith (for a similar view of the virtues of persecution, see Hattaway 2003, 12).

Mark was a believer in "gradual, patient work through unconditional love," claiming that "God's work is an oak tree, not a mushroom." Love implies giving charity and doing aid work, caring for local people, especially the socially marginalized. Mark frequently mentioned his wife, Rachel, who ran an orphanage for children from all over Yunnan. The school exemplified Mark's ideology. It was ethnically mixed and inclusive, based on need rather than class, race, or ethnicity. Yet, according to Mark, many locals found Rachel's concern for the children hard to understand, making fundraising difficult even among local Christians. In Mark's opinion, the difficulties were rooted in the cultural tendency toward pragmatism and cultivating social connections as the main incentive for action. With advancement and loyalty to clan and family being so important, "why would somebody help an unknown orphan?"

Often at our meetings, Mark mused on the difference and similarity between China and the US: "We in America are drowning in light. Here in China, they're dying in the darkness." "Drowning in light" is a reference to many Americans' self-definition as Christians (equated by Mark with "light") while they are immersed in worldliness, consumerism, pop culture, and money-making capitalism.[10] At the same time, in "dark" China, the gospel remained essentially unknown. This was not a result of lack of missionary work or printed Bibles but rather a reflection of the cultural mask. Accordingly, both in the US and in China, the road to faith involves overcoming the obstacles of culture, in its different forms.

During a follow-up visit to Kunming in 2012, Mark and I returned to the issue of culture in the context of Yunnan's ethnic minorities. Mark said that while Christianity has not come to replace any specific cultural setting, it can potentially be "a disruptive element." Of course, there is no need for minority Christians to change their style of clothing or language, elements of ethnicity that are highly visible in Yunnan and officially encouraged as part of the tourism industry. Indeed, Mark appreciated the aesthetic value of many elements of ethnic culture: "Some of them are very talented at singing, especially the Miao, and when the missionaries came in the nineteenth century, they taught them how to sing in voices, and you know how pretty that sounds" (interview, October 15, 2012). Nevertheless, culture was only "of middle importance," and conversion does imply certain social changes. The example given was of the Yi, some of whom, according to Mark, still maintain a form of a matriarchic society.[11] Practices of that sort could not be maintained by Christians, as the Yi were sexually promiscuous in a way that contradicts Christian tenets, lacking the biblically based institution of marriage.

Thus, while Mark did not advocate a full-scale rejection of culture and all its manifestations, culture is relegated to a peripheral role and then reexamined and reshaped to fit the new center of identity—the absolute truth of Christ. Mark's concept of cultural preservation and change included a clear division between different forms of ethnic expression. As Mark's reference to Miao singing suggests, song, costume, and other outer manifestations of ethnicity were legitimate attributes of ethnicity, virtually synonymous with those provided by Simon, a missionary whose work among the Bouyei is discussed in chapter 5 (interview, May 25, 2010).

Significantly, Mark and Simon's approach to culture is remarkably similar to contemporary state rhetoric, with ethnicity almost always represented by song, dance, and costume (Blum 2001, 83; Goodman 2009, 75) and to expressions that "foster ethnic pride but do not impede progress": "festivals, costumes—the inevitable dance in a circle" (Harrell 1996, 27). In contrast, social institutions like matriarchal families are clearly marked as unwanted premodern relics of the past (Gladney 1994, 104).

The uneasiness regarding nominalism expressed by Mark and other missionaries seemed to be pointing at minority Christians of the kind I met in Wuding. It would clearly apply to the Miao of Shimenkan. What, then, would be the image of "true" rather than a "nominal" contemporary ethnic Christian? How would their ethnic identity be expressed following conversion?

A Lisu Evangelical in Kunming

I met Zhan, a relatively recent Lisu convert, through Mark's Han Chinese translator Benjamin (Mark spoke passable Chinese but often needed

Benjamin's help to convey complex theological ideas). Benjamin owned a Christian bookstore and at the same time served as the leader of a local house church. It is interesting to note that a hierarchy of sorts existed in this case, headed by Mark, an American Christian, followed by his Han Chinese student Benjamin, and ending with Benjamin's congregant Zhan, a Lisu. Zhan was chosen by Benjamin to speak with me, indicating that his leader believed he was firmly enough grounded in theology to express himself appropriately. For this reason, I present Zhan here, as a convert whose Christian identity was perceived by his missionary leaders as a reflection of "true" Christianity.

Like Benjamin, Zhan was born in Dehong, where there is a sizable Lisu community.[12] The Lisu are a minority in Dehong, where the majority of inhabitants are of the Dai ethnicity, believers in Theravada Buddhism. Unlike the Lisu of the Nujiang Valley, the Lisu of Dehong have not been heavily influenced by Christianity and remain for the most part animists. Zhan, however, comes from a Christian family; his parents converted through the efforts of a Lisu missionary who came to their village from British-controlled Burma before 1949. Such cross-border interactions still play a role in the formation and evolution of Christianity among the Lisu today (Gao and Sha 2014).

According to Zhan, initially the man from Burma was the only Christian in the village, but in time, he was able to convert the entire population (interview, May 5, 2010). In Zhan's perspective, Christianity liberated the people of the village in several respects. For example, the upkeep of religious rites prior to conversion included frequent and expensive sacrifices, a heavy financial burden that Zhan's family was happy to be rid of (Yamamori and Chan 2000, 32; Covell 2001, 277).

After the 1949 revolution, Christianity was severely oppressed, and Zhan grew up in virtual ignorance of the religion. His description of his family is a good example of Oliver Roy's argument regarding the natural skepticism of born-again believers toward their forefathers (2004, 29). Thus, Zhan credits his parents for their conversion but at the same time regards their conversion process as essentially insubstantial; they "know there is a God" but not much else. Zhan's understanding of his parents' faith is reminiscent of Mark's criticism of the Miao Christians I had met in Wuding and their "nominal" faith.

As a young man, Zhan went to Myanmar to work in the jade trade. He came across a Han Chinese church and became a Christian. After four years in Myanmar, he moved back to China, to the border town of Ruili, married a Dai Christian, and met Benjamin, whom he later followed to Kunming. Today, Zhan works at the bookstore and studies the Bible. His goal is to move back to Dehong and work there as a church leader.

Much like Benjamin and Mark, Zhan continuously emphasized the importance of personal faith and presented his faith in strong uncompromising terms: "Only God knows what will happen. He is the sovereign [*zhu*] who runs the world, so faith is the most important thing. It's not enough to say that you're a Christian because of your family. You need to know what Christianity is about and choose it on your own." His identity as a Lisu was clearly important to him, but his relationship with Lisu culture was complex. As a Christian, he would not participate in the traditional Lisu festivals he grew up with, as they contain an element of superstition (he used the common, often officially invoked Chinese word *mixin*), such as the Knife Ladder Festival, in which barefoot Lisu men climb a ladder with knives as rungs. Zhan contended that there is magic involved. "Otherwise, how is it done?" Although Zhan did not elaborate, I was given the impression that he was inferring that the climbers enter a form of trance or hypnotic state enabling them to climb without cutting themselves, marking the ceremony as forbidden for a believing Christian.

Zhan said that he would, in theory, take part in ethnic dances but only if they are "absolutely clean" (*gangan jingjing*), in other words not sexually promiscuous (implying that this is not always the case among traditional Lisu). He does, on occasion, spend Chinese New Year's at the house of his Dai in-laws. Although not particularly devout, Zhan's in-laws identify as Theravada Buddhists and practice some minimal form of Buddhist ritual around the New Year. While the family spends the holiday together, Zhan's Dai family have come to accept that their daughter and son in-law will not participate in any of the ceremonies.

Zhan grew up speaking Lisu, but being married to a Dai woman and living in predominantly Han Kunming, his life was conducted in Chinese. Indeed, Zhan was also literate in the "old Lisu" script, otherwise known as the "Fraser alphabet" after its inventor, the English missionary James Fraser. According to Zhan, everybody in his village can read the script. As with the Miao, the script is taught in church and not in the school system. However, Zhan's young son, at the time five years old, spoke no Lisu or Dai and was proficient in Chinese only. When asked about the issue of language, Zhan seemed to be more interested in English, both for himself and for his child. He expressed admiration for his leader, Benjamin, and his ability to speak English fluently. Interestingly, Zhan felt that knowledge of English could help him further his understanding of the Bible, despite being aware of the fact that the English Bible is a translation. Ideally, Zhan says, he would like his son to speak "Chinese, English, Lisu, and Dai" (listed in that order). In actuality, however, his life in Kunming offers no opportunities to study his parents' native tongues.[13]

Unlike the Miao Christians of Wuding and Shimenkan, Zhan's Christianity was not formed in reaction to discrimination or ethnic survival in the face of a coercive Han center. Rather, his faith resembles that of his foreign and Han teachers, Mark and Benjamin, and is based first and foremost on personal choice. Zhan's conversion process and training to be a church leader took place in an entirely Han Chinese context, first with the Chinese Christians in Myanmar and later with Benjamin in Kunming. Moreover, Zhan's Christianity contains a strong element of criticism regarding ethnic tradition and a call to move beyond culture and toward a global community, expressed in the importance ascribed to the study of English.

Zhan's aspiration to return to Dehong to preach the gospel as a missionary seems the natural outcome of his admiration for his leaders, Benjamin and Mark, and for the early missionary to the Lisu James Fraser, who "had a comfortable life in England, but he chose to come to this primitive [*luohuo*] area." Zhan had not decided where in Dehong he would like to live. Since tolerance of his activities depended on the ethnicity of those whom he attempts to preach to, he saw three options.

The easiest option would be to return to a Lisu community already defined as Christian, like the village Zhan grew up in. There, among "nominal" Christians like his family, Zhan could help spread the faith-based evangelical Christianity he has adopted. As the village was known as Christian since prerevolutionary times, there would probably be no problem with the authorities.

A somewhat more daring option would be to move to a non-Christian Lisu locality. Zhan would be in danger of being identified as a missionary and engaging in officially illegal activity. However, since the Lisu are already perceived as a heavily Christianized minority on the provincial level, Zhan thought that preaching among non-Christian Lisu may be tolerated.

The riskiest and therefore most attractive option for Zhan, who wants to be on the front line of missionary work, would be to preach among the Dai, where the Christian community is extremely small.[14] Since the 1980s, the state has supported Buddhism among the Dai and the revival of Buddhist culture. They limit and control, but do not prohibit, the flow of Theravada monks from Myanmar, Thailand, and Laos to work among the Dai

(McCarthy 2004, 33). Spreading Christianity among the Dai would almost certainly be considered a threat to social stability and could get Zhan into serious trouble. With the Dai's strong Buddhist identity, one may assume that they themselves may not be receptive to Zhan's attempt to proselytize among them.

Zhan's description of the borders of authorized activity reveals how the state has created an unofficial set of classifications regarding the promulgation of Christianity. I have already mentioned the relative lenience of the authorities in Yunnan compared to Beijing or other Chinese heartland areas. According to some Christian activists, the same is true within the province, with a stricter standard and more surveillance for urban Han compared to rural Christian minority people (Boby, interview, February 2, 2010). Minorities who are officially or semiofficially defined as Christian are allowed the largest degree of religious activity. People of the same minority group who have not yet been converted, like many of the Lisu of Dehong, represent a middle case: the Lisu as a whole are well-known for their large Christian population, making evangelism tolerable in the eyes of the authorities even when conducted among non-Christian Lisu.

Working among non-Christian minority groups is the most problematic, particularly when the group is officially identified with another religion, as with the Buddhist Dai. Indeed, recent regulations in Dehong have banned local Dai from converting to Christianity (Yi 2020). However, Zhan is extremely resolute in his faith and is willing to go wherever he is most needed, regardless of the authorities: "You can't recognize a real Christian from the outside; a real Christian is one whose heart is pure. Christians who deny their religion when their tested [referring to those who abandoned Christianity after the Communist takeover] are not real Christians. What's important is to let the government know that they do not make the decision. God does." Our conversations invariably revolved around the center of his life: his faith in Christianity. Despite the importance that Zhan attributes to his Lisu identity, ethnicity does not seem to be a major factor in his personal decision-making beyond the necessity of dealing with state policy. With Zhan being clearly aware of state policy toward ethnic groups in Yunnan, his decision of where to live was presented in light of his ability and willingness to persevere in face of difficulties and state harassment. He never mentioned proximity to his family, issues of ethnic-culture preservation, education, or even familiarity and comfort. Furthermore, Zhan used the language of the state to describe Lisu festivals, referring to them as superstition (*mixin*). Finally, Zhan's personal life choices reflect the reality of ethnic amalgamation. Like other ethnically mixed couples I met in Yunnan, Zhan and his Dai wife spoke Chinese to their son, leading him on the road toward Hanization. The global nature of Christian identity is evidenced in Zhan's interest in English, placing it above Lisu in the priority of languages he would like his son to acquire. This reveals his inclination to place his global Christian identity above his particular ethnicity.

As Zhan observed, Christianity in China is often criticized in two ways: as a Western religion, implying foreignness in the Chinese context, and as a religion of minority people, implying inferiority. As a minority Christian, Zhan must deal with both accusations. His response is that Christianity is neither Western nor Lisu and that it does not belong to any one locality or nation. It is universal, and as such, it is beyond the pale of culture and ethnicity.

Conclusion: Moving Beyond Ethnic Culture

Entering the twenty-first century, Niebuhr's Christ-culture question remains poignant in Yunnan. Some Christians have called for a balance between the two, viewing them as equal and complementary elements of missionary work. A. F. Walls suggests that "the gospel must be both the prisoner of culture" (implying indigenization and expression through local culture) "and the liberator of culture" (implying cultural change) (Bonk 1993, 50). Likewise, Gotthard Oblau stresses that the message of the gospel is "change oriented" and focuses on "the human power of the individual" (2005, 417). Defining change, movement, and rebirth as major aspects of the gospel implies that the lower or negative forces and dynamics are tradition, attachment to the past, and an identity in which the individual is less central than the group.

Contemporary missionaries in Yunnan speak of both change and continuity. However, the overall tendency, as reflected in the interviews presented in this chapter, is to create a clear hierarchy emphasizing Christ and deemphasizing culture and ethnicity. Indeed, in recent years, liberal Christians like John Peale have accused evangelical house churches in China of actively working "against culture," in contrast with the Chinese general public, which is "of culture" (Peale 2005, 106).

Thus, missionaries today express a will to create Roy's "pristine faith," free of ethnic distinctiveness and based almost entirely on individual experience. Oblau's emphasis on change and individuality brings to mind Mark's view of culture as something "of middle importance" when seen in the overall context of personal conversion. Furthermore, the relatively marginal significance of ethnic identity is evidenced in the willingness and indeed enthusiasm of missionaries to live outside their cultural context, crossing ethnic and national lines for the purposes of their missionary work.

I have attempted to illustrate how the complex relationship between Christianity and ethnicity is rooted in the experience of Protestant missionaries in Yunnan since prerevolutionary times. Today, criticism of conversion based on grounds other than individual personal salvation has increased to the point that descendants of pre-1949 converts are looked on by some evangelical Christians as only partially genuine. The tone of criticism can be seen in the words of the "three generations" of evangelical Christians I interviewed. To Mark, the American minister (first generation), "nominalism" is a result of lack of knowledge, overenthusiastic and superficial missionary work, and the ingrained pragmatism of locals. As such, it permeates Chinese Christianity and is the rule rather than the exception. Mark's Han Chinese interpreter (second generation), Benjamin, considers his own conversion in its early stages to have been insufficient, powered primarily by earthly rather than spiritual motives. Finally, Zhan, Benjamin's Lisu student (third generation), is critical of his parents' pre-1949 conversion as reflecting only a minimal God consciousness rather than a full-blown acquaintance with Christian dogma and faith.

The opinions of Mark, Benjamin, and Zhan reflect the gulf between current evangelical Christians and the Miao communities of Yunnan under the "mask" of culture, viewing their religion through the prism of pragmatic ethnicity and empowerment. As my experiences among the Hua Miao Christians in Wuding and Shimenkan and the Qing Miao of Anning reveal, Christianity and religion are closely connected to the markers and symbols of ethnic identity, primarily to the scripts invented by the missionaries and widely displayed as symbols of cultural capital. Ethnic Christians like those of Shimenkan view the successes of the past in the realm of modernization as a validation of their ethnic culture in the face of the Han state center. In the case of the Hua Miao, ethnoreligious identity is strong enough that, at least according to Pastor Zhang, marriage with other ethnic groups is discouraged. Thus, Christian Miao categorized by Mona and Mark as "nominal" seem to ascribe more importance to their ethnicity than do their non-Christian kin, such as the Qing Miao. In contrast, the newly converted Zhan represents a new model of religiosity, one that ascribes only secondary importance to ethnic culture.

In an attempt to balance the drive toward an individually based religiosity and the need to indigenize Christianity and provide room for ethnic expression, missionaries like Mark and Zhan apply what Harrell termed "the hegemony of definition" (1996, 7): an attempt to define the nature and limits of ethnic identity. The elements of ethnic culture they emphasize include costume, song, and language, representations of ethnicity that generally coincide with the image of ethnic minorities produced by the state. In addition to the correspondence between the missionaries and the Chinese authorities on the symbolic level, recent converts like Zhan exemplify the crossing of ethnic lines, a diminished potential for ethnic tension, and indeed a process of rapid Hanization.

Chapter 3

PERCEPTIONS OF CHRISTIAN MORALITY AND THE FREE-MARKET CIVILIZING PROJECT

> BAM [Business as Mission] is not just doing business to generate finances to fund other kinds of ministry. Don't get us wrong. BAM is for-profit business because running a profitable and sustainable business is necessary and glorifying to God.
>
> —BUSINESS AS MISSION WEBSITE

In one of my first meetings with Michael, the director of a drug rehabilitation center in Kunming, he told me a remarkable story. A female leader of a house church community from western Yunnan decided to open a rehabilitation center in her hometown. Having no prior experience, she sought Michael's advice on how to run a rehabilitation program with a Christian emphasis. To Michael's surprise, she told him that the center had been officially sanctioned even though she had not come from within the official Three Self Church system. Local authorities, impressed by her charity work, revoked the official recognition of the Three Self Church in town and gave it to her congregation. To finalize her new official status, she was given the opportunity to attend a brief training and ordination program in Kunming in an authorized Bible seminary, making her an officially recognized minister (Michael, interview, January 6, 2010).

This story reflects the seemingly random and arbitrary way Chinese authorities behave when religious policy is involved. This woman's house church became official because her personal conduct impressed local officials. In contrast to official rhetoric and policy, a Three Self Church arbitrarily lost its official status, for no apparent reason beyond a possible directive that the number of churches in the city should not be increased. At the same time, the story reflects the idea that Christianity may be used to promote social harmony and stability by dealing with social problems (such as addiction) in an age of serious social strife.

In this chapter, I argue that the moral and social role played by Christianity is essential in understanding the way it is being disseminated in Yunnan. Moreover, Christian morality is presented as an agent of the state's "civilizing project" for minorities. Accordingly, this chapter revolves around a recurring set of social and personal attributes, including abstention from smoking and alcohol, economic prudence, and loyalty to spouse and family, presented by converts, missionaries, and Chinese scholars as closely intertwined and interdependent. These are presented as the binary opposites to qualities such as lack of productivity, lack of interest in commercial activity and the accumulation of capital, polygamy or polyandry, low standards of hygiene, and other stereotypes attributed to ethnic minorities. The value system promoted by Chinese and foreign Christians closely corresponds to the conservative neo-Confucian agenda of the state. Thus, Christianity plays the role of civilizer, in ways that are highly reminiscent of the state's own civilizing projects among minority people.

Much has been written in recent years regarding the crisis of meaning experienced by many Chinese in the post-Maoist era. Tu Weiming describes the "profound self-doubt" regarding the relevance of Chinese history and tradition, resulting in "the vulgarization of culture, disintegration of society, especially the family" (1999, 87–89; see also DuBois and Zhen 2014, 4; Lai 2003, 56–58; Mackerras 2003, 113; Ong 1997, 175). Some observers have argued that the pursuit of wealth encouraged by Deng Xiaoping has resulted in the cultivation of selfishness, "which reacts negatively to any attempt at moral guidance," with morality often considered to be "leftist" and reminiscent of Maoist era ideology (Wang 2002, 5). The Chinese search for a moral center in recent decades is closely related to the significant social changes of the reform era, including massive dislocation following internal migration, unemployment, an acute loss of personal security especially when health care is concerned, increasing stress, the breakup of families, and other social problems (Lai 2003, 57).

The moral and spiritual vacuum following China's adoption of a free-market system and the discarding of Maoist ideology is often linked to the flourishing of religion in general (Mackerras 2003,113; Ostrov 2005) and to the growth of Christianity in particular (Bays 2011; DuBois and Zhen 2014, 4; Lee 2007, 282; Palmer 2004; Uhalley and Wu 2001). Like other religions, Christianity offers a moral code and a sense of community in an era of rising individualism and cutthroat competition. However, since the publishing of Max Weber's famous work on the Protestant work ethic ([1905] 2003), Christianity has been widely associated with the economic system of free-market capitalism. The connection between Protestantism and capitalism is emphasized by contemporary Chinese, ranging from young urban professionals (F. Yang 2005) to local civil servants (M. Yang 2004b, 746), including the former head of the Religious Affairs Bureau, Ye Xiaowen (Morgan 1998). In addition to Christianity being perceived as a positive force for the successful integration into the free-market system through its moral strictures, it offers a solution to the social problems that the market system creates. Thus, Christianity is often seen as "progressive, liberal, modern, universal," while at the same time being perceived as an antidote to the dangers of the "chaotic and perilous" reality of the free market by providing a sense of community and belonging (F. Yang 2005, 429).

Business as Mission

The connection between Christianity and the free market features prominently in missionary writing on China, often defining the reform era as "a day of opportunity in China" (P. Anderson 2006, 4; Hamrin 2007; Ma 2011, 189). The marriage of mission and economic activity is exemplified in the Business as Mission (BAM) method, employed by the missionary organization Youth with a Mission (YWAM) and dedicated to "the transformation of people and communities: spiritually, economically and socially—for the glory of God, through a viable and sustainable business with Kingdom of God values, purpose, perspective and impact" to lift people out of physical and spiritual poverty (Nordstorm and Muir 2010).[1]

Christian scholars have argued that the free hand given to Christian aid organizations and NGOs reflects the state's attempts to compensate the "victims of development." This suggests that Christianity may answer the crisis of meaning experienced by many contemporary Chinese, which accelerated after China joined the World Trade Organization (WTO) and was exposed to global flows, by offering a set of "transcendent values" in the face of rising materialism (Chan and Yamamori 2002, 52). In what has been described as "an ironic reversal of the past stance of government vis-à-vis religion" (Bays 2003, 498), the state sometimes facilitates conversion among minority people to counter the harsh conditions of rural Yunnan, a region plagued by poverty, drug addiction, and other social problems.

State efforts in the realm of modernization are closely related with the Chinese civilizing project and the combination of trade, migration, and development work among minorities and beyond China's borders (Dirlik 2002). Modernization is associated with the idea of quality (*suzhi*): "typically including manners, hygiene, discipline, education and competitive and open-minded thinking but which, depending on the context, can also include upright morality, a correct political stand and correct lifestyle and consumption choices" (Nyiri 2006, 86; see also Harwood 2014). Thus, a distinct similarity exists between state and Christian narratives of development and civilization, as Chinese Christians "do not generally view their civilizing project as one opposed to that of the Chinese state but rather as one perfecting it" (Nyiri 2006, 106). I employ this resemblance of development narratives to understand the significance of the widespread dissemination of Christianity in contemporary Yunnan.

Moral Leadership: Following Teachers into the Christian Fold

While this chapter deals primarily with the role played by Christian ethics, it would be wrong to overlook the practical economic implications and financial benefits of contact with foreign missionaries and church organizations. Members of the non-Chinese community use services provided by local Christian travel agents, cleaners, maids, and drivers; converts throughout Yunnan find employment with Christian charity organizations; and Christian residents of poor rural areas are at times given the opportunity of moving to Kunming for further theological training, being sent to conferences in Hong Kong or elsewhere, or pursuing higher education outside China.

Several converts and activists I met noted that Christian organization may offer aid in reducing the fine for having a child beyond the limits of the state's family-planning regulations (Casey, conversation, October 11, 2012). One missionary voiced concern that offers to recent converts concerning study abroad may be counterproductive to the promotion of the Christian message, by attracting those whose intentions are pragmatic rather than spiritual (Peter, interview, June 13, 2010). These concerns echo similar voices among some Chinese academics who have accused converts to Christianity of being "too utilitarian" (*gongli xing*) by converting for material benefits (Liu Daixia 2008, 111).

The complex nature of the material-economic element of the Christian mission in Yunnan was likewise emphasized by Li, a Han Chinese and enthusiastic Christian with extensive ties to the Christian Miao. Li, who leads groups of foreign Christian visitors to Miao areas, described how the relatively poor Miao receive various types of aid, such as money, clothing, and employment opportunities, noting that jobs can be arranged for those who are interested. Unlike Western missionaries who expressed uneasiness regarding the material gains of conversion, Li did not seem to think such connections were problematic. He did not make any distinction between the Miao's material and spiritual needs. Li mentioned that the Miao's "heart is very pure," implying a conversion motivated by spiritual incentives. At the same time, he added that the material benefit that they receive from foreign Christians is immense (Li, interview, May 26, 2010).

The significance of the elaborate economic ties between local and foreign Christians goes far beyond the purely financial realm. As research of a Chinese Christian community in the US has shown, aid of an altruistic nature signifies membership in a community of benevolence and kindness and a triumph over selfishness (Abel 2006). Aid provided by Christians may be seen as a symbolic defiance of the traditional *guangxi* system, in which gifts are always given in return for other gifts. Approximately half of the converts interviewed reported that their conversion was inspired by the fact that the Christians they had met were "good and honest" (*shanliang*) (Abel 2006, 165).

The following accounts of converts reveal that conversion in contemporary Yunnan is often the result of an encounter with a moral role model who functions outside the norms of traditional reciprocity. At the same time, the aid provided within the Christian community is not translated into a critique of the economic system. On the contrary, members of the community view their ethical code as a way of being, surviving, and thriving within the free-market reality.

Throughout my fieldwork in Yunnan, I met many converts to Christianity from a variety of backgrounds and ethnicities. Some had been born into Christian families and considered themselves Christian by birth, but the overwhelming majority adopted Christianity on their own. Motivations for conversion varied. It was not uncommon to hear of conversions inspired by a healing experience—an ailing family member who was cured as a result of Christian prayer or a declaration of faith in Jesus. However, the most common conversion story I encountered involved a meeting with an inspiring Christian teacher or other person in a position of authority. My experience is corroborated by David Aikman, who has claimed, "almost every urban young Chinese I met in China had come to the faith through a foreign, English-speaking teacher" (2003, 279; see also P. Anderson 2006, 150; Wielander 2013, 6). While Aikman's statement is most probably exaggerated, foreign influence on conversions is significant. Overall, the power of the encounter lay in the feeling, reported by many converts, that the person involved had demonstrated a standard of morality and kindness unparalleled among previously known local teachers or leaders. As the following cases demonstrate, the moral element described by converts as an impetus for conversion is almost invariably accompanied by the altering of certain behaviors: refraining from smoking, drinking, and gambling and cultivation of marital fidelity.

Many of the role models are teachers who are involved in welfare projects, not businesspeople. However, the example set by individual Christians is of particular importance in the free-market era because it stands in stark contrast to the realities of ruthless competition in the post-Maoist era. Thus, by providing an ethical framework applicable to the realities of the free market, missionaries are often perceived by converts as representing a set of values that is superior to the one promoted by traditional leaders and to the chaotic and fiercely competitive market economy. Furthermore, by providing a moral-ethical framework for life in a globalized and economically privatized Yunnan, Christian professionals are fulfilling the goals sought after by the state of establishing a "harmonious society."

Tsering

I met Tsering through Barry, an American ex-missionary who was living in Shangrila at the time. The city is home to a small, mostly Han, Christian community, with a small Tibetan minority. Compared to other parts of Yunnan, in Shangrila ethnicity and religion are sensitive issues and more closely monitored by the authorities. This is probably because, unlike the other minorities in Yunnan, Tibetans are associated with a separatist ideology and political unrest. According to Samuel, a café owner, during the

2008 riots in Lhasa and other Tibetan areas, security forces were posted in his café to protect foreigners, and army forces were massed in a stadium nearby; at the time, a number of minor violent incidents occurred in the countryside around the city, including the destruction of a gas station and the beating of a number of local policemen (interview, August 9, 2010). The sensitivity of issues related to ethnicity and religion holds important implications for local Christians. Foreign Christians are closely monitored, and house churches are kept small. Due to the official categorization of Tibetans as Buddhists, no official Three Self churches have been established. I was advised to be particularly discreet in my research, more so than in other regions of Yunnan.

The relative strictness of local authorities in Shangrila with regard to Christianity and foreigners seems to conflict with one of the main arguments of this work: that the state maintains a moderate approach to Christianity because Christian activity is beneficial to development and in this case to the state's civilizing project. Christian activity among Yunnanese Tibetans reveals a close correspondence between Christian and state narratives with regard to the modernization and modification of Tibetan culture. Limitations on Christian activity may reflect the will of the authorities to appease locals who are sensitive to any attempts made to undermine Tibetan culture. Yet, as a number of scholars have written, tight government control does not necessarily conflict with an overall policy of tolerance (Lu Yaoming 2011, 80; Qin 2014, 23). Thus, while Christianity is closely monitored, it is possible that it is simultaneously being used as an agent to control, civilize, and modernize the Tibetan periphery.

Arranging a meeting with Tibetan converts was not an easy task. According to Barry's wife, Leah, the Tibetan Christians in Shangrila were tied to the foreign missionaries in town in a form of unofficial patronage (interview, August 20, 2010). Each missionary had their "own Tibetans"—converts under their influence and often also employed by them. The system of patronage sometimes led to arguments over specific converts. For example, the conversion of a local ex-monk who accepted Christianity after experiencing a revelation on his way from India to Tibet was considered a great success story and was mentioned to me by different people on several occasions. According to Barry, the ex-monk's importance was such that missionaries in town were arguing over him, each claiming to have had critical influence over his Christian training. Moreover, many members of the small Christian community, including Tsering, were employed by Christian aid organizations run by foreign Christians.

As a result, my attempts to meet Tibetan Christians were often thwarted by their respective patrons.

Tsering was exceptional in that he did not seem to fully accept the authority of his foreign Christian employers on this matter. He was also extremely curious to meet a Jew and had prepared many questions about the Bible and the Hebrew language, which we discussed regularly. His journey toward Christianity had begun ten years earlier, when he was nineteen. His family, particularly his father, were not devout Buddhists, although his father would perform certain rituals for healing purposes. Tsering did not consider the lives of the teachers, lamas, and other figures of authority in his life to be particularly moral, and this troubled him greatly. Some of the lamas he met made it clear that they did not really believe in Buddhism and that their monkhood had financial motivations. Tsering had become interested in life's great questions and in spiritual issues. He first began to search for answers within his own Buddhist tradition, but finding a teacher was not easy, as many of the monks seemed to have limited knowledge of their own religious tradition. He fostered a relationship with one elderly lama ("He was good"), but while most monks spoke about compassion, a concept central to Buddhist philosophy, Tsering did not see its practical implications in their lives, as they were not involved in any kind of charity work.

In many ways, Tsering's failure to reach satisfactory and relevant answers for his questions reflects the crisis of authority plaguing local ethnic religions. Local religions have suffered from state policies in the Maoist era and more recently from the challenges of globalization, resulting in lack of knowledge among older generations and lack of interest among the youth. As a number of Chinese scholars have argued, this process has aided the growth of Christianity (Ma Huacheng 2010; Sun Haoran 2013, 98). According to Thakpa, the founder of the Shangrila Thanka Academy, ignorance and lack of interest regarding Tibetan culture and religion are rampant, particularly among younger generation Tibetan; thus, most Tibetans in the region are not literate in Tibetan (interview, August 18, 2010).

The reservations that Tsering expressed regarding the guidance of the monks were also related to the financial power enjoyed by the strong religious establishment of Tibetan Buddhism. Tsering tended to avoid the subject, but a perspective on the issue was provided by Tom, a local missionary. Tom claimed that important Buddhist lamas become financially well-off by attracting large donations for their villages. Thus, from Tom's perspective, the most difficult places to penetrate with the gospel are villages with important lamas, particularly those who have been trained outside China. Conversion to Christianity is quite rare in such locations, since Christian converts are no longer full members of the community and cannot enjoy the financial wealth generated by their local lama (Tom, interview, August 23, 2010).

After Tsering failed to find relevant answers to his questions on faith and morality, he encountered Barry, an English teacher in his school. According to Barry, Tsering spent over a year asking him numerous questions about religion. Barry had come to Shangrila as a missionary but developed reservations regarding the idea of proselytizing and had broken with the missionary community. He was reluctant to provide answers that could lead Tsering to conversion. Finally, Tsering's persistence led Barry to refer him to other Christians in town. In this way, Tsering met an African Christian doctor who worked across the road from the school he attended. Tsering was impressed that the doctor "helped many people" and seemed to be living "a very simple life." The doctor told Tsering about Christianity and the Bible, stories that Tsering found interesting; yet, at that time, he was reluctant to adopt a new faith system, an act considered by many Tibetans as a betrayal of Tibetan identity. Some years later, when he attended a college in Deqin, he met a number of devout Lisu Christians and finally decided to accept Christianity.

During our conversation, it became clear to me that Tsering's discernment between true and false religiosity was based, first and foremost, on the question of moral conduct. In Tsering's mind, the morality of Christianity is closely related to its transcendent nature and the faith in God. He perceived Christianity and Buddhism as fundamentally different, as Buddhists "believe in man" rather than in a divine being. It is the transcendent divinity that provides Christian morality with its absolute authority, motivating people to move across the globe to provide aid to complete strangers. A similar expression of the validity of Christianity was conveyed to me by Tom, who argued that Christian superiority can be seen in the fact that "you can go online and see who does the most good in the world," referring to the many Christian-run aid and welfare agencies (interview, August 23, 2010).

Indeed, Tsering's concept of morality revolved around Christian activity in the realm of welfare, a topic discussed at length in chapter 4. However, it also included a specific code of behavior. Thus, Tsering observed with a certain amount of disappointment that even among the foreign Christians working in town, who had come to teach and set an example for Tibetans, some lived "immorally" and engaged in drinking and smoking. Associating Christian morals with abstinence from substance abuse is common in China and may be considered a stereotype of Christian behavior. In a private conversation with a preacher in the large church in the Yi town of Sanyinpan, I asked about the major effects Christianity had on the local Yi, and the preacher emphasized that Christians refrain from drinking and smoking (interview, January 12, 2009). While common among Chinese Christians, associating abstinence with correct religious behavior is criticized by foreign evangelical missionaries as a form of "legalism" that reduces Christianity to a set of social regulations and diminishes the element of personal faith and transformation (John, interview, January 1, 2010; Mark, interview, December 8, 2010; Chris, interview, May 25, 2010).

Alu

I met Alu by chance on the street, with her employers, a European–South American couple who work with lepers (illustrating Leah's description of convert-missionary relations). The story Alu told regarding her conversion began in Kunming, where she had studied to be a nurse. At the time, she found work with a Christian organization that worked with physically disabled people, and she was impressed with their devotion and kindness. Despite the staff's efforts to tell Alu about Christianity, she had no interest in conversion at first. "There was nothing wrong with me," said Alu, "so I saw no reason to convert" (conversation, August 22, 2010). However, after experiencing a crisis of unspecified "inner problems" and inspired by an encounter with Christian welfare workers and the moral code they represented, she opted for conversion to Christianity. Christianity became a source of comfort and faith, a religion associated in her mind with generosity and morality. She eventually became an enthusiastic Christian and convinced her father to convert. Alu told me how after her father's conversion, a cousin remarked that her father had "converted too early," the implication being that an acceptance of Christianity entails abstinence from worldly pleasures like cigarettes and alcohol—a moral code that stands in contrast with youthful desire and is therefore appropriate only for old age. Alu was pleased to tell me that her father's reply was that he does not find his new religion difficult and that he thinks he converted too late, referring to the many years in which he was ignorant of Christianity.

The nature of perceived Christian morality in the context of Tibetan Yunnan came to light when Alu's European employer, Lukas, began telling me about the work done with lepers. Lepers in Tibetan society suffer from extreme marginalization and stigmas, according to Lukas. The disease is perceived to be the result of a curse (the term "leper" is used as a swearword). Existence of the disease is often denied, and patients receive no treatment in its early stages. Working with lepers involves dealing with both the physical condition and the social stigma. Christian involvement in work among lepers is a powerful symbol of the willingness to come to the aid of those who are the "untouchables" of society. Alu's willingness to be associated with lepers indicates her choice to remove herself from mainstream Tibetan culture in favor of the higher moral standards she encountered among Christians. When asked about her Tibetan identity, Alu replied, "I am Tibetan. There is nothing to do about it" (*mei banfa*). Her reply implies that while her Tibetan nationality is undeniable, the focal point of her identity is now her Christianity.

Indeed, like many converts throughout Yunnan, both Tsering and Alu had encountered significant resistance to their acceptance of Christianity from their environment and had been routinely accused of adopting a foreign religion and abandoning their ethnic identity (Yang Zhong 2013, 38; Joseph, interview, April 4, 2010; Jason, interview, May 6, 2010). Among Tibetans, the problematic nature of conversion is all the more pronounced since Tibetan Buddhism and its clergy are perceived as the essence of Tibetan ethnic identity, described by Marku Tsering as "a rallying point for cultural revival" (Hillman 2005, 33; Stoltz 2007, 66). Attempts to win converts to Christianity are viewed negatively, as echoed by many of the people I met in Shangrila. Indeed, in a survey regarding feelings toward Christianity, out of eighty-seven people from various ethnic backgrounds, the two Tibetans were the only ones to define Christianity as "an evil cult" (P. Anderson 2006, 279).

While Tsering's parents seem to have accepted his decision, he has often been accused by others of being a traitor to his people, to which he usually replies that Buddhism was also imported from elsewhere. Tsering defines himself as a "follower of Jesus" rather than a "Christian," possibly reflecting an attempt to deemphasize his conversion and its perceived meaning as a rejection of Tibetan identity. More than Tsering, Alu has been ostracized from much of her original environment. She lives and works in Shangrila and refrains from visiting the village of her birth in the Deqin area, where attitudes toward her are openly hostile. According to Alu's foreign employer, Alu's father, who still lives in the village, bravely withstands regular pressure from villagers who consider his conversion an act of treason.

Hostility to Christian missionary work among Tibetans is not a new phenomenon. According to Jeff Fuchs, the last group of Catholic missionaries to work among the Tibetans in Cizong before the Communist takeover were assassinated by locals at the instigation of the lamas sometime around the 1949 revolution (interview, August 12, 2010; on the difficulty experienced by early missionaries in Tibet, see Nam 2009). The story was confirmed by Samuel, a Christian café owner living in Shangrila, who claimed to have met one of the murderers (now a man in his eighties) as well as some of the men who carried the bodies to the city of Shangrila (interview, August 16, 2010). Hostility between Christians and Tibetan Buddhists is mutual, with Christians often describing Tibetan Buddhism as the "darkest" of religions (Brewington 1995, 21; Stoltz 2007, 54). Thus, conversion to Christianity is an act of significant and often complicated social implications, one that cannot be explained by material gains alone.

Christian Life, Work, and Family: Lessons from "The Cross"

Moral authority as an incentive for conversion is also expressed by some converts in their ideas regarding the superiority of Christian family life. Some describe Christianity as "the religion that can reassure harmony in the family" (Hunter and Chan 1993, 8). The aura surrounding Christian married life is expressed in the conversion of Benjamin, Mark's young interpreter. Benjamin met a couple of Canadian Christians who taught English when he was a university student. He found their affectionate relationship so compelling that he became attracted to Christianity. Likewise, the missionary Simon told me that a high-ranking government official decided to accept Christianity after being exposed to Simon's family life. The official and his wife had been making regular visits to Simon's house for the purpose of studying English. Although the official knew that Simon was a believing Christian, no mention of religion was ever made. In fact, Simon was particularly cautious in light of his student's official position. He was taken by complete surprise when the official suddenly informed him of his wish to become Christian, explaining the decision as a reaction to the family life he had witnessed when visiting Simon's house, a quality he associated with Christianity.

This association between Christianity, morality, and family life is clearly visible in the way Chinese Christianity is presented in Christian movies like *The Cross*, a series produced by Yuan Zhiming. Before becoming a Christian, Yuan became well-known for coproducing the controversial documentary series *River Elegy* in the late 1980s. That series presented Chinese history as a narrative of restriction and backwardness and concluded with the image of the great Yellow River, a symbol of China, emptying into the ocean, symbolizing China's long-delayed entrance into a distinctly Western international order (Shue 2002, 213–14; Aikman 2003, 261). The series came under severe criticism and was banned in China. After the 1989 Tiananmen Square protests, Yuan fled to the United States. In 1992, he was baptized to Christianity and later attended a theological seminary. Another of Yuan's coproducers of the series also converted to Christianity, and another seriously considered conversion (Buruma 1999). Yuan and other Christian intellectuals have been identified as a "Sino-foreign Protestant elite." They play an instrumental role in the Christian revival in China (Wielander 2013, 6). Yuan explained the connection between *River Elegy* and his conversion to Christianity: "*River Elegy*'s conclusion was that the solution for China was democracy and human rights. But it was only when I got to the West that I realized that the root of this was Christianity. It was the Bible. It creates something more important than rights given by a constitution or a government. It creates God-given rights—endowed by our Creator" (Johnson 2012).

In 2001, Yuan set out to make *The Cross*, a series dedicated to Christianity in China today. In a subsequent interview, Yuan clearly expressed his intention of using the series to influence decision-makers: "We want to let government leaders see the movie" (Aikman 2003, 265). David Aikman, the interviewer, clearly expresses his enthusiasm regarding the movies. He notes that the series was shown to officials of the State Administration of Religious Affairs throughout the country with the intent of providing background for the perceived threat of Christian expansion. According to one pastor, the presentation of Christian converts, in particular "the stories of repentant criminals, healed marriages, honest businessmen and well-behaved teenagers as a result of conversion to the Christian faith" led some officials to reject the prevalent view that Christianity is a threat to Chinese society (Aikman 2003, 265). Aikman's examples of personal change refer to the major problems of reform-era society in China: crime, the breakup of the family, corruption, and delinquent youth.

The series' episode titled "Spring of Life" begins with a description of the decline of moral values and "hollow moral core" in contemporary China, accompanied by shots of massage parlors and newspaper headlines about corruption.[2] The episode continues with a series of personal stories, all following a similar story line of an individual being caught up in addiction or infidelity, followed by dramatic change and redemption through Christianity. In the first story, a young man who gambled away twenty years of savings describes the way he tried and failed to find comfort in nightclubs and bars. He eventually found the Bible and God, after which he "quit smoking, drinking, marijuana, and popping ecstasy pills." Today, he says, he enjoys just walking with his wife and spending time with his family. The narrative moves from the personal stories of redeemed individuals to the implications for society at large. The individuals featured realize their sinful nature and repent. They experience dramatic personal change, which is projected outward, first to their family and later, through their caring for others and responsible behavior, to their social environment. One recent convert asserted, "If more people believe in God, peace will spread out from family units into the whole of society."

The series puts forward the argument that Christianity is the answer to China's social problems. It draws a straight line between Christianity and morality, economic independence, marital fidelity, and the stability and happiness of the family unit. The imagery and rhetoric used in *The Cross*, particularly when the family unit is concerned, is often highly reminiscent of state rhetoric and propaganda. The conversion stories conclude with shots of harmonious families, composed of two smiling parents with a single child, strongly resembling official posters used to encourage adherence to the One Child Policy. In theory, evangelical Christians are deeply opposed to the Chinese government's policy of encouraging abortions among women who have already given birth to one child. Abortion is extremely common in the PRC, but approximately 80 percent of Chinese Christians consider the practice unacceptable (Yang Zhong 2013, 42). Yet, even on this contentious issue, missionaries work within the confines of the existing state system, providing aid discreetly and refraining from openly encouraging having more babies or challenging state policies.

Answers offered to the social problems of the reform era are based entirely on individuals rather than government involvement. The series praises Christian philanthropy and the cultivation of compassion to prompt the establishment of welfare organizations. It does not call on government involvement, nor does it criticize current lack of government policy to deal with social issues. Indeed, the films do not express any expectations from state authorities regarding the expansion of welfare services or educational programs. Compassion and the inclination to care for others are presented in *The Cross* as a natural outcome of faith and a feeling of personal wholeness. In contrast, lack of compassion is presented as the result of personal selfishness, moral hollowness, and humans' inherent sinful nature. As such, it appears to be entirely beyond the realm of state policy and responsibility. Aside from the implied request to refrain from curtailing the spread of Christianity, the state is virtually absent from the series's narrative.

To summarize, converts of both Han and non-Han background are often drawn to Christianity through an encounter with people whom they perceive as exhibiting exemplary moral standards, kindness, compassion, and socially responsible behavior. The converts I met did not, for the most part, cite the relationship between Protestantism and the free-market system as an incentive for conversion, in contrast to many Chinese scholars addressing the subject and certain segments of the missionary community. Rather, for most converts, the economic system is a given part of reality, the legitimacy of which they do not question. Converts are concerned with functioning within that reality, without being overwhelmed by its temptations, and retaining a moral center. Thus, the effects of conversion are largely related to concepts of economic prudence, such as refraining from substance abuse, a problem of particular magnitude in Yunnan. However, the connection between morality and the cultivation of free-market economy is emphasized by Chinese scholars, as elaborated in the next section.

Agents of Harmony: Chinese Scholarly Perspectives on the Civilizing Effects of Christian Expansion

In recent years, a growing number of Chinese scholars have argued that Christianity is generally compatible with the state's vision of constructing a harmonious society (Shen and Zhu 1998; Li and Ma 2010; Chen 2012). According to Lu Yaoming, Christianity's contribution to Chinese society is rooted in its tradition of free thinking, compatible both with the Confucian tradition and with "socialist market economy" (2011, 76; see also Clark 2005). Lu presents Confucianism and Christianity as two pieces of a single puzzle. Confucianism stresses harmony and morality based on the family and advocates development and self-improvement but lacks a tradition of personal freedom and is potentially oppressive. Christianity stresses personal freedom, an idea that empowers the individual but often leads to the atomization of society and feelings of alienation and lack of meaning (78).

The recent trend of writing on the social function of religion is particularly pronounced when minorities from southwestern China are concerned.

Indeed, while the theoretical advantages of Christianity are considered with regard to China as a whole, when minorities are discussed, the discussion shifts from ideological comparisons of Christian theology, Marxism, and Confucianism to moral standards and social problems plaguing the Chinese periphery. Furthermore, analysis of Christianity in minority areas is intertwined with issues of minority culture, such as family structure, hygiene, and gender, issues that are distinctly evocative of "civilizing project" rhetoric.

One striking example of a positive narrative of Christian presence in Yunnan published by the official Nanjing Theological Seminary notes the importance of preserving local cultures in the face of Christian proselytism, calling it "an urgent task" (You, Wang, and Gong 2004, 114). The article praises Christianity's contribution to the modernization project and concludes that Christianity contributes to "social cohesiveness" and "increased levels of social consolidation among these minorities" (116). Christianity is presented as a positive force for easing tensions between ethnic groups, a prevalent opinion among Han and minority Christians (Wang, interview, December 1, 2009; Mosi, conversation, May 20, 2010).

Another article begins with an overall positive appraisal of Christianity in the Nujiang region, emphasizing Christianity as an element of social stability responsible for "almost eliminating drinking, gambling, fornication and other ugly phenomena" (Li and Mei 2007, 12). In a clear divergence from Maoist-era writing on the subject, the history of Protestant Christianity in Yunnan is described with no reference to the colonial context in which missionaries were active. Thus, missionary activity of the past is described in terms strongly reminiscent of the writing of the missionary scholar Ralph Covell as a means of saving Yunnan's nationalities from poverty and marginalization.

Li and Mei do not separate between the economic, cultural, and social realms. They praise the introduction of modern schools and hospitals, the eradication of addiction, the raising of hygienic standards, the strengthening of respect for elders, the promotion of monogamy, and the elimination of "superstition" such as faith in the spirit world (2007, 14), all regarded by the authors as elements in the modernization process. The authors credit Christianity with creating a Weberian-style Protestant work ethic and a "correct view of labor" (*zhengque de laodong guandian*) that encourages productivity and eradication of former patterns of wastefulness, typified in the traditional practice of spending money on ritual offerings. Thus, Christianity is presented as an ally of the state by providing a moral-ethical code of conduct highly compatible with Confucian mores. At the same time, it encourages the free-market system by emphasizing productivity, personal initiative, and thrift and deploring wastefulness.

A similar perspective is presented in Qin Heping's (2011, 14) work on the Wa minority, praising the decision made by local cadres in the 1980s to "allow freedom of religion." Qin describes the advantages of Christianity: the morality of the Ten Commandments and their effect on the reduction of violence, substance abuse, and aspects of what he perceives to be sexual promiscuity. Christianity is also presented as suitable to "consumer society" (*shangpin shehui*). One church leader is quoted saying that "the Bible teaches us to create wealth with our own hands" (*Shenjing zhong shuoyong women de shuangshou chuangzao caifu*; 21).

Similar assessments of ethno-Christianity appear in He Ming and Zhongli Yue's work on the Miao (2007) in the Fumin region, famous for their church choir, which became a profitable enterprise, successful throughout China. Christianity is presented as providing psychological balance to villagers who can "tell their troubles to Jesus" (110). This serves as an antidote to the Miao's potential discontent with the failures of the welfare system and the economic gap between themselves and the more affluent Han villages of the region. He and Zhong explain the prevalence of house churches as a reflection of the spiritual needs and preferences of believers, largely devoid of public and political implications. They see no difference between official and house churches, in terms of members' patriotism (111).

Other scholars take a more critical view, voicing concerns over the erosion of state authority and the damage to minority culture and ethnic religions (J. Ma 2011; Sun Haoran 2013, 98). The same activities in the realms of welfare and public health praised by the scholars noted earlier are viewed by others as potentially dangerous and undermining of the ultimate authority of the state (Tian and Wang 2000, 79).

One can note a clear parallel between the celebrated achievements of Christians in Yunnan and the values of the Chinese civilizing mission. Thus, in accordance with traditional stereotypes of minority people as dirty (Blum 2001, 77; Harrell 1990, 526), Christian influence is described as being instrumental in improving hygienic practices, a central element of Chinese civilizing rhetoric: "The idea of pollution—dirt and danger—is also extended to minorities. Lack of sanitation is one of the stories Han ethnologists almost always bring up" (Harrell 1996, 13). Harrell quotes a Chinese researcher as saying, "each *minzu* has its own way of *zangfa*" (way of being dirty; Harrell 1996, 13).[3] Likewise, the emphasis on the monogamous family structure is an assertion of the superiority of Han society and the idea that minority family structures such as matriarchy, polygamy, and polyandry are relics of the "primitive" past (Gladney 1994, 101; Schein 1997, 72).

The use of Christianity as a means of dealing with the effects of modernization and globalization is relevant to China as a whole. However, the relationship to free-market ideology is of particular importance in the marginal areas of ethnic Yunnan, both as a means of encouraging enterprise and as a way of dealing with the uncertainties of free-market realities. At the same time, Christianity works as a civilizing force, eliminating "wasteful" local spirit worship, encouraging men to be loyal husbands and responsible fathers, and reshaping minority culture in the image of the Han center.

Samuel's Tight Ship and the Feminization of Tibetans

The final section of this chapter deals with the way missionary activity among Yunnan's Tibetans mimics the state's civilizing mission in both its Confucian and Communist elements. To illustrate this point, I offer an analysis of the attitudes of foreign and Chinese missionaries toward questions of faith, economic behavior, and ethnic identity, beginning with Samuel, a dedicated missionary and successful businessman.

I first heard about Samuel a number of months before moving to Shangrila. My classmate Yan had told me about a trip he made there with a friend to visit the friend's spiritual leader, who ran a restaurant in the city. The teacher, Samuel, was an ethnic Chinese from outside the PRC and a devoted evangelical Christian. Yan spent many hours in conversation with Samuel, an encounter that had clearly made a great impression on him. In particular, he was impressed with the orderly and systematic way Samuel dealt with his all-Tibetan staff of young men and women from the countryside. "He told us he 'runs a tight ship'" said Yan smilingly (interview, October 14, 2009). According to Yan, Samuel considered the staff "his church." Staff members live in homes, divided according to their progress in the training program, which included professional and religious instruction. "Everybody is asked to sacrifice and pay a price," said Yan, explaining that the more experienced staff members are requested to take in younger and newer members and "raise their level."

A number of months later, when I finally met Samuel, I came to understand that the "tight ship" he ran was much more than an organized form of Christian preaching. In fact, it was a vehicle of acculturation intended to transform his rural ethnic staff into what Samuel saw as responsible, morally upright, and cultured citizens, fully capable of functioning independently in the context of reform-era China. It was based on instruction and Samuel's personal example. He went to great lengths to uphold an image of a strict, meticulous, and authoritative model of a Christian businessman.

"Things here are done intentionally," said Samuel in our first conversation (interview, August 9, 2010). Staff members are selected according to recommendations provided by those who already work in the restaurant. Samuel often expressed his pride with the fact that someone can turn from "a shepherd, who throws stones at yaks all day, to a restaurant chef." Although the larger part of the day is dedicated to professional instruction of cooks, waiters, and cleaners, the café has a clear spiritual orientation. Every morning begins with a "quiet time," devoted to prayer, reflection, and reading from the Bible before the café opens. While the staff members usually know little or nothing about Christianity when they come in from the countryside, Samuel asserted, "today, all of our workers are believers." Samuel instructs his staff members to refrain from preaching to customers (my own experience has confirmed that they do not). Nevertheless, he hopes the nature of his café may inspire visitors without the use of words—he would like those who enter to "feel the presence of God."

Samuel makes a point of being a role model of authority to his workers, based on morality and honesty. He stressed that unlike local employers, he will apologize to a worker when it is necessary, does not demand flattery, and shows a personal interest in each of his employees. Samuel's moral strictures are not confined to the staff. He prided himself on paying the highest taxes of any business in town, because he reports all his income without exception. He said that the honesty and transparency of his business activities are impressive not only to his workers but also to the authorities. Samuel tries to convey that he is not greedy by closing the restaurant on Sundays. This has aroused mixed responses, with some locals openly calling him a fool for not working on the busy weekend. However, Samuel believes that most people look on his decision with respect.

Samuel's self-cultivated image is reminiscent of a modern-day *junzi*, the Confucian gentleman-entrepreneur often portrayed in Chinese media as a successful, socially responsible, and inherently ethical businessman (Zhao Yuezhi 2002). In recent years, it has become common to ascribe the success of Asian economies to prudent economic behavior and hard work, behavior heavily influenced by their Confucian heritage. The connection between the market economy and Confucianism has been raised to the status of state ideology by Singapore's ex-president Lee Kuan Yew, whose ideas have had significant influence on PRC Chinese scholars (Jochim 1992, 137–40; Lu Yaoming 2011; Tamney and Chiang 2002, 49). Thus, the process of economic liberalization has been accompanied by an attempt at "defining Chinese business activities as a kind of moral economy based on Confucian ideals" (Bell 2007, 23; see also Ong 1997, 182).

Samuel seems to be the kind of businessman the state approves of: a clear supporter of reform-era liberalization with a strict moral code and a deep sense of community and the public good. Indeed, Samuel is an enthusiastic advocate of the free-market system. His criticism of the Chinese authorities and many NGOs working in Yunnan is directed at what he perceives as an excessive welfare system that does not encourage free enterprise. He is critical of the authorities for throwing money at the Tibetans in the region, making them dependent and economically passive. Thus, when the Deqin airport was constructed to serve the Shangrila region, locals whose houses stood on the airport site were compensated with three and a half million Yuan (approximately half a million US dollars). He believed that most Tibetans did not know what to do with such an outrageously large sum and therefore wasted it. In addition, locals routinely receive large loans from banks on the basis of their houses, a policy that Samuel considers economically irresponsible. In contrast to the welfare provided by local authorities and NGOs, Samuel provides professional training and encourages his staff to be economically independent and enterprising.

Following the idea that becoming economically independent and entrepreneurial goes beyond finance and professional skills and is a process of becoming civilized, Samuel told me the following story. A number of years ago, a sixteen-year-old girl arrived from a remote village, located a number of hours walking distance from the nearest road. Her first night in town was spent in Samuel's home. In the morning, Samuel and his wife saw that the bed the girl had slept in was covered with menstrual blood. He was shocked that her facial expression did not reveal any embarrassment; she just sat on her bed quietly. Samuel perceived the girl's behavior as a both unhygienic and morally degrading. He called some female workers in the restaurant to help clean her up. Despite this unpromising start, Samuel proudly told me that after years of working in the restaurant, the same girl is currently a senior staff member who helps with the training of younger newcomers.

Samuel's reaction to the display of menstrual blood parallels the Chinese perception of menstrual blood as dirty and polluting (Chu 1980, 38) and also the perception of Tibetans as a threat to the patriarchic Confucian order.

Anouska Komlosy discusses menstrual blood and femininity among the Dai of Xishuangbanna (2009, 132) and the double nature of the polluting aspect of menstrual blood: it is understood as unhygienic and as containing dangerous magical power, posing a threat to society on the natural and cosmic levels. In this context, menstrual blood as a pollutant may be seen as a potent symbol of the interaction between Samuel and his Tibetan disciples. The cleaning and concealment of the girl's blood signify the process of taming and civilizing.

The story that Samuel chose to tell is instructive of the contrast he made between the perceived passivity of rural Tibetans and the values of free-market self-sufficiency guiding his restaurant enterprise. The girl's backwardness is expressed in her hygienic practices, an accusation often found among Han people regarding Tibetans and other minorities. The girl's passivity is strongly reminiscent of the representation of minority people in general as passive and archaic compared to Han activity and dynamism (Gladney 1994, 99–103; Schein 1997, 88), marking her as the epitome of backwardness. Finally, the girl in Samuel's story is presented as a child—entirely passive and requiring education and guidance (Harrell 1996, 13–15). The process of acculturation and civilizing, beginning with the procedure of physically cleaning the girl, is conducted by other members of the staff, working as agents of Samuel's local "civilizing project." The project, as described by Samuel, has been a great success: the girl has been transformed from backward and passive to a dynamic member of a modern, Western-style staff, able to train and cultivate others.

These values are closely related to the form of conversion Samuel promotes. "I am not here only as a Christian," said Samuel, "but as a Christian who wants to build something." He is critical of overly enthusiastic missionaries who come to produce converts, preaching loudly and indiscriminately to anyone they meet. He is more interested in what he calls his "apprenticeship"—providing personal and technical training, based on human relationships and intended to create personal change and development. The training process must be accompanied by a gradual progression toward personal change. In Samuel's words, "You can make mistakes here, but we have to see progress."

Samuel's "apprenticeship" is based on the cultivation of human relations and in-depth knowledge of the people he comes in contact with. He believes that "if you do not have a relationship with someone, you have no right to preach to him about conversion." However, what Samuel means by "relationship" does not necessarily imply a sense of intimacy or deep acquaintance.

Rather, it is a relationship of authority. According to his description of the training process, the relationship between himself as an employer and his new workers is sufficient for the introduction of Christian content from the very beginning of the training process.

The benevolent hierarchy expressed in Samuel's style of leadership and authority is largely compatible with recent trends in China of reinstating Confucian values of hierarchy and harmony based on respect of authority within the family and in society at large (Bresciani 2001, 447–48). When asked about Tibetan culture, Samuel expressed admiration of the respect given to parents and elders among the rural Tibetan of the region. According to Samuel, among Tibetans, children are expected to return to their family farms at harvest time and help their parents. Likewise, contradicting a parent in public is unacceptable in Tibetan society. In fact, as Samuel noted admiringly, respect for elders is far more solid in Tibetan Yunnan than in Samuel's own country of origin.

Thus, when Samuel offers praise to local Tibetan culture, it is for its proximity to values also considered important in the Confucian and Christian worldviews. However, when Tibetan culture as a whole is discussed, Samuel's outlook is considerably less favorable. Like other Christians working in Yunnan, he considers Tibetan Buddhism as a form of spiritual oppression. His criticism often took the shape of empathy directed at the monks. Samuel described the difficulty involved in celibacy and told me he knew of one monk who had fallen in love with a woman, was under great pressure to remain in the monastery, and eventually ended up killing himself in a hotel room.

While Samuel's position on Tibetan Buddhism is critical but empathetic, this is not the case among other missionaries I met working in Yunnan, who expressed extreme hostility toward Tibetan Buddhism, often portraying the religion as devil worship and idolatry. Tibet has been described by Christians as the "heart of darkness" (Brewington 1995), and Tibetan religion, particularly the elements derived from the original Bon animism, has been portrayed as "the darkest expression of occultic evil" (Brewington 1995, 21).

The negative opinions expressed by Christians regarding Tibetan Buddhism are unusually severe compared to those voiced by Yunnan's missionaries working elsewhere. They are highly reminiscent of the derogatory terms used by missionaries to describe local religions in China in the nineteenth century (Reinders 2004, 8–11). Christian hostility toward Tibetan Buddhism goes back to the early days of mission work in China and is often expressed as an equation between geographic and spiritual remoteness. Tibet was, and to a large extent still is, considered to be the last frontier of evangelical work, an idea expressed by William Blackstone in 1886: "God seems to be holding back that little place [Tibet] to be the last field entered just before his coming" (Stoltz 2007, 64).

In a similar vein, the well-known missionary scholar Tony Lambert describes a recent visit to Tibet in the following way:

> The taking of life in any form is a great sin. My Tibetan guide, an educated man, told me quite seriously that it was forbidden to kill mosquitoes or disease-bearing vermin such as rats. It is not surprising that early travelers who arrived in Lhasa found a society far from the paradise envisaged by modern New Age dreamers. Disease was rife, and most of the population were serfs working for the nobility or high lamas in very poor conditions. A handful of Tibetan youths sent to Britain to study were unable on their return to introduce any lasting reforms or scientific advances because of entrenched superstition. (2011, 2)

Lambert's writing bears a striking resemblance to the Chinese state narrative regarding Tibet and the Tibetans in a number of ways. Lambert presents pre-Communist Tibet as poverty stricken and controlled by an oppressive aristocracy of Buddhist clergy (for a typical example of the CCP's narrative of Tibet's pre-1949 feudal theocracy, see Information Office of the State Council of the PRC's "White Paper on Tibet's March Towards Modernization," 2001). Lambert likewise echoes the image of Tibetans as lacking in basic hygienic practices (Blum 2001, 77). Finally, he presents Buddhism, with its respect for all living creatures, as a barrier to development and modernization, symbolized by the unwillingness of locals to eliminate disease-bearing insects and animals. Similarly, Buddhism has been called "primitive and harmful" for its objection to the use of pesticide (Luo 1991, 181; McCarthy 2009, 81–82).

In Lambert's description, civilization has not yet taken root in Tibet. Even Westernized, British-trained Tibetans were unable to counter local beliefs, which Lambert calls "superstitions." Lambert concludes that Tibetan beliefs have "hindered scientific, technological and medical progress, which is only now being introduced by the Chinese and often not altogether welcome" (2011, 2). Lambert is equally damning in his description of Tantric Buddhism, claiming that the tradition "is frankly sexual in both practice and imagery. In fact, in the Lama temple in Beijing the Chinese authorities have covered some of the more obscene images from public view" (2011, 2). Once again, the idea of minorities as promiscuous and uncivilized is clearly expressed. Moreover, Lambert presents the Chinese authorities as the civilized defenders of decency, covering up scenes of inappropriate content.

The unique approach toward Tibetan culture may be seen in Christian attitudes toward local history and myth. When other minority groups are involved, Christians often attempt to identify elements of native religion and mythology as corresponding to the story of the Bible. To cite one example, the missionary Tom told me of Yi legends regarding a supreme God and his single son who came down to Earth and later returned to heaven (for a similar description, see Swain 1995, 152). According to Tom, the Yi believe that this supreme deity can bring them to heaven but that upon arrival, they will be forced to labor for him. Therefore, they prefer to worship other gods. However, when asked about parallels between Christianity and Tibetan beliefs, Tom mentioned an affinity between Tibetan ritual and the idolatry of the Bible, including a tendency to sacrifice on mountain tops, as mentioned in the book of Jeremiah, and the financial corruption prevalent in local temples, reminiscent of Jesus's encounter with the money changers in the temple in Jerusalem. In short, whereas Tom presented the Yi as possessing a distorted and distant connection to monotheism, Tibetan culture is perceived as inherently negative, distinctly related to the "others" of the Bible—the Canaanite idolaters.[4]

Negative portrayal of Tibetan Buddhism is particularly strong among Han Christians like Tom's employee Yage. In our conversations, Yage emphasized that Tibetans worship the devil (*mogui*), the lamas are lazy and ignorant, and common Tibetans follow them blindly and irrationally (interview, August 11, 2010). Yage's description of Tibetan Buddhism seemed strongly reflective of Marxist and Maoist rhetoric regarding religion and Tibetan Buddhism in particular. Yage was adamant that Christianity is not a religion, a category he associates with a humanly devised means of oppression and control. Thus, Yage's perspective on Tibetan and Christian religiosity may be seen as a convergence of traditional Chinese, Communist, and Christian ideas of civilization and development. Yage invoked a universal identity based on humanity rather than ethnicity, a vision reminiscent of both Confucian universality and Christian ecumenism.

While Yage expressed the opinion that Tibetans should pray and read the Bible in their own language, he added that in his opinion the preservation of Tibetan culture was meaningless and that the process of gradual

Hanization of minority people was inevitable and positive. He was puzzled by Western foreigners' desire to preserve Tibetan religious culture. Like Tsering, Yage stressed his belief that cultures should be judged solely according to the moral standards they live by. He perceived the behavior of the Tibetan lamas as immoral and unproductive, forming a set of cultural practices that should be overcome rather than preserved.

Yage's view of Tibetan monks may be understood as a double narrative of morality and work ethic. From a Christian point of view, monks are devoted to a dark spirituality and do not worship God but preserve a modern manifestation of ancient idolatry. At the same time, monks are labeled as lazy and unproductive, in contrast to the state narrative of development and modernity. Yage's perception of monks as idle mirrors a common missionary description of Tibetan men in general, described by Tom as "a public menace" with a strong tendency toward gambling, drinking, and violence (interview, August 23, 2010). In Tom's opinion, the ambience of sloth and selfishness among local men is closely related to the prevalence of monkhood among the Tibetans, an institution he views as devotion to a life of idleness. Likewise, many of the Christian workers in Shangrila complained about the tendency of Tibetan men toward domestic violence, womanizing, and other behavior associated with an ideal of machismo. On a follow-up trip conducted in 2016, I heard Tsering voice severe criticism of the prevalence of domestic violence among Tibetans. He added that the division of gender roles was such that his own involvement in caring for his infant daughter is considered "un-Tibetan" (Tsering's wife is Han Chinese; Tsering, interview, August 25, 2016).

The machismo of Tibetan males is equally emphasized by expats outside the Shangrila Christian community. The scholar Jeff Fuchs told me he had only once met a Tibetan convert to Christianity whose conversion he considered to be the result of genuine faith, unrelated to material gain. As evidence of this woman's genuine conversion, he noted that she told her non-Christian boyfriend that he must mend his ways and behave morally. In response, he beat her: "because you don't tell a Tibetan man what to do" (conversation, August 12, 2010).[5]

Another example that Tom offered for what he perceived as the unproductive nature of Tibetans was the practice of fraternal polyandry—one woman marrying two or more brothers. While illegal, it is still practiced in some rural areas. According to Tom, such marriages invariably result in the women bearing the economic burden for both men (interview, August 23, 2010). The opinion that polyandry is evidence of the Tibetans' cultural inferiority is common among non-Tibetan in Yunnan. A Bai shop owner in

Shangrila, originally from Dali, told me that he thought "the cultural level [of the Tibetans] is quite low" (*wenhua shuiping bijiao di*), owing primarily to Tibetan marriage customs. Despite maintaining good neighborly relations, he said he would not allow either of his two children to marry Tibetans (Chan, conversation, August 6, 2010).

This criticism of Tibetan men corresponds with larger trends in evangelical Christianity. Evangelical conversion works through a "mutation of culture: restoration of the family, the rejection of machismo, the adaptation of economic and work disciplines and new priorities" (Martin 1999, 39). While these elements of cultural change are widely relevant in Yunnan, the issue of machismo plays a major role in the Tibetan context. Han and foreign Christians are particularly hostile to Tibetan men. Martin sums up the goal of missionary work in this regard, claiming that with the fulfillment of the conversion process, "the male ceases to be predatory and irresponsible and becomes domesticated" (42).

Similarly, Chinese "internal Orientalism" (Gladney 1994; Komlosy 2009; Schein 1997, 2000) represents most minority people as feminine, docile, impressionable, and ready to be molded. However, minorities like the Hui, Mongols, Uighurs, and Tibetans are often represented as masculine, "exoticized as strong and virile, ... possessing extraordinary physical abilities in sport, work and the ability to consume large amounts of alcohol" (Gladney 1994, 97; see also Hillman and Henfry 2006, 251–60). A recent representation of Mongolian masculinity can be found in the Chinese novel *Wolf Totem* by Jiang Rong. The novel recounts the experiences of young Han students in rural Inner Mongolia in the late 1960s and early 1970s. Throughout the novel, the Mongols are idealized as manly, virile, and generous, in contrast to the pettiness and weakness of the Han (Jiang 2008; see also Tenzin Jinba's analysis of the novel: 2014, 40–46).

Han Chinese attitudes toward Tibetan males are deeply ambivalent. While Tibetan masculinity is often presented as admirable, impressive, and even enviable, it holds a subtext of violence, savagery, and political revolt that must be tamed. Thus, Tibetans are perceived as possessing a masculinity based on a physical and martial ideal (*wu*), one that stands in contrast to the traditional Chinese perception of masculinity based on mental and cultural civil power (*wen*). As such, the Tibetans are both virile and dangerous, thus reaffirming the position of Han Chinese "at the advanced end of a modernization trajectory" (Hillman and Henfry 2006, 268–69).

The Chinese association of Tibetans with virility and physical power is shared by the Tibetans, who often describe themselves as "real men," in contrast with Han Chinese men, thought of by Tibetans to be feminine.

Tibetan manliness (referred to in Tibetan as *phokhyokha*) contains a number of central features: preferring the company of other men, refraining from displaying emotion, and spending money generously. In contrast, the qualities Tibetans associate with the Han are a tendency toward open display of emotion, attachment to family, and frugal economic planning. Interestingly, while the concept of "manhood" contains an element of sexual conquest, it also applies to Buddhist monks who show strength by living according to their vows by abstaining from worldly pleasures (Hillman and Henfry 2006).

Likewise, Tibetans themselves also perceive economic prudence as an un-Tibetan quality and see themselves as disinclined toward hard work. Emily Yeh quotes a Lhasa businessman who complained that "Tibetans sit around all day, don't want to work hard" (2013, 163). Mirroring the missionary criticism of Buddhist clergy, Yeh suggests that Tibetans perceive their religious tradition as offering a work ethic opposed to Weber's spirit of capitalism—the amassing of wealth, hard work, and self-denial (172). Accordingly, many of the Tibetans she encountered argued that Buddhist doctrine runs contrary to the pursuit of profit and the accumulation of wealth and emphasizes the fleeting and temporary essence of life. Tibetan attitudes on the subject may be seen as a form of resistance to Chinese concepts of development: "a limited refusal ... of development's association in China today with market rationality and capitalist relations of production" (175). Chinese-style development and the behavior of the Han stand in contrast with the Tibetan "pride themselves on their ability to have a good time" (173). Likewise, the concern for money, as well as Chinese fussiness about food and comfort, is viewed as as small-mindedness, the opposite of Tibetan generosity and general lack of economic planning (Hillman and Henfry 2006, 264).

These qualities associated with the Han are precisely those applauded by Christians and promoted by the state. As mentioned, emphasis on open displays of love, a commitment to family life, and economic prudence features prominently in *The Cross* and in the ideas presented by Yage and Tom. According to some missionaries, many Chinese perceive Christianity as a "feminine" religion, as it emphasizes emotional expression and a dependence on God, rather than self-reliance (Mona, interview, August 5, 2009).[6] Similarly, the solidity of the family structure, marital fidelity, and prudent economic behavior feature prominently in the rhetoric of development, as seen in the Chinese articles quoted earlier. The contrast between Tibetan concepts of masculinity and the model offered in both Christian and Chinese state rhetoric reveals the convergence of civilizing projects in the effort to change and pacify Tibetan culture.

Thus, Christianity may be conceptualized as a force working toward the feminization and domestication of Tibetans. Some informants have argued that the presence of missionaries in Tibetan regions is part of an intentional policy by the state to weaken Tibetan identity and masculine resistance to the Chinese state. Jeff Fuchs noted that missionaries were permitted to stay in Lhasa during the 2008 riots, when other expats were forced by the authorities to leave (conversation, August 12, 2010). In a discussion of free health care offered by Christian organizations to Tibetan children with heart diseases, it was stated that "in Tibet, Chinese authorities often turn a blind eye toward Christian missionaries who would be stopped elsewhere in the nation." This phenomenon was explained by the campaign's communications director as a drive "to dilute the influence of Tibetan Buddhism. . . . The missionary group has written permission to tell the families of all children it screens and treats that this service is offered in the name of Christ, and to explain the Christian faith to them" (Rodgers 2006). Similar claims have been made regarding tolerance of missionaries in the predominantly Tibetan province of Qinghai (Barnett 1992; Sebag-Montifiore 2013; see also Kaiman 2013). The idea that the state is intentionally using Christian influence against Tibetan Buddhism has also been voiced by the anti-Communist New Tang Dynasty TV network, affiliated with the Falun Gong.[7]

Whether or not a state policy of weakening Tibetan Buddhism through evangelical Christianity actually exists is difficult to ascertain, as there is no direct evidence from the state regarding policy considerations. However, one may rightly assume that the many parallels between the Christian and state civilizing missions have, at the very least, not gone unnoticed by state authorities.

Conclusion: The Capitalist Civilizing Project

In this chapter, I have demonstrated the profound impact that perceptions of Christian morality have had on individual converts and on a number of Chinese scholars who have been calling for active encouragement of Christianity as an aid to the development of Chinese rural and ethnic periphery. Foreign and local Christians actively promote Christianity as a solution for the social problems of China. They do so through films like *The Cross* and through the personal example of missionaries, representing the ideals of charity, honesty, and productivity. In the case of Yunnan's ethnic minorities, perceived Christian morality may be seen as an attempt at "civilizing" them, in a way that is reminiscent of the state's own efforts in that regard.

The ability to promote Christian ethics may be attributed to two central points of convergence between Christianity and state policies. First, Christianity in China is often associated with Max Weber's spirit of capitalism, invoking hard work, economic prudence, entrepreneurship, and social responsibility. As a number of Chinese intellectuals have noted, it is also compatible with the modern-day Confucian vision of constructing a "harmonious society," with its emphasis on the family unit and socially conservative values. The need for social stability and economic responsibility is particularly acute in Yunnan, a province plagued by poverty, drug addiction, and other social ills. The second point of convergence between Christianity and the state in an ethnic context is the affinity between Christian ethics and the Chinese civilizing mission. Thus, in the dominant narratives of China, the supposed prevalence of substance abuse and gambling among minorities is presented as one element in a general condition of backwardness. Christian and state narratives of ethnic conditions reflect a combination of economic poverty, polygamy, superstition, idleness, and low hygienic standards.

The similarity between these two varieties of civilizing rhetoric is particularly notable in the case of the Tibetan minority. In both Chinese and Christian descriptions, Tibetans, particularly Tibetan males, are presented as the binary opposite of Weberian-style Protestantism. They are accused of lack of productivity and holding onto numerous premodern cultural attributes, ranging from excessive alcohol consumption to celibate monkhood and nonmonogamous marriages. Perceptions of Tibetan culture and particularly of Tibetan masculinity portray Tibetans as wild and defiant toward the capitalist spirit and the hierarchy of Confucian harmony. Tibetan virility gains the admiration of some and at the same time contains clear overtones of danger and violence, posing a threat to the current economic system as well as to the integrity of the state. While I did not find direct evidence that Christianity is actively encouraged in the Tibetan regions of Yunnan, there is some evidence that tolerance of missionaries in Tibetan Qinghai and in the Tibetan Autonomous Region is part of an intentional state policy. At the very least, one may wonder if the strong Christian criticism of Tibetan society and the description of pre-Communist Tibet as a feudal theocracy are not designed to curry the favor of state authorities by invoking the constructive role that Christianity may play in the harmonious development of ethnic Yunnan.

Chapter 4

THE WELFARE OPTION

Yunnan's Faith-Based Organizations

> But if Mr. Webb did so much, how much more might a thoroughly trained medical man have accomplished! There is no more effective missionary than a medical missionary, but thus far in the work among the tribes we have not had the help of a medical man. Will not one offer for such a work as this?
>
> —SAMUEL CLARKE, *AMONG THE TRIBES IN SOUTH-WEST CHINA*

Thus far, this book has been focused primarily on the relationship between ethnicity and religion and the convergence and divergence of state, missionary, and minority perspectives on ethnic identity. In this chapter, I examine the issue of missionary Christianity as a reflection of the specific socioeconomic circumstances of present-day Yunnan. As elsewhere in China and the world, rapid privatization, free-market economics, and the opening of borders have created the mixed results of vast wealth, a growing middle class, expanding inequality, and alarming social problems. Indeed, while Yunnan's economy continues to grow, the reform era has also witnessed the emergence of drug addiction, prostitution, and the spread of HIV/AIDS.

As a result of the province's proximity to the opium-producing regions of Southeast Asia and its peripheral position within China, Yunnan has been particularly hard hit by these social ills. The province is home to an estimated number of 150,000 drug users (Zhang Guanbai et al. 2018). Over 80 percent of intravenous drug users are infected with the HIV virus, and Yunnan has the largest concentration of HIV cases in China, with over 100,000 cases by 2012 (Xinhua 2012), making it the "birthplace" of China's HIV/AIDS crisis (Benewick and Donald 2009, 80; UNESCO Bangkok 2006; Yan et al. 2007).

The situation is particularly harsh among ethnic minorities: a disproportionate number of people living below the poverty line in China reside in minority regions, and the economic gap between minorities and Han is on the rise (Gustafson and Li 2003; Heberer 2000, 12; Sullivan 2011; Unger 1997). According to Michael, whose drug rehabilitation center is described later in this chapter, approximately half of the center's patients are of non-Han origin, with a particularly large number of Dai (interview, October 2, 2012). The percentage of minorities among sex workers in Kunming and elsewhere in Yunnan is even higher (Ann, interview, September 30, 2012).

With the dismantling of the Chinese welfare state, social services have been largely replaced by NGOs, many of which are Christian based (Schak 2011, 81–82). Indeed, apart from teaching English, work in the field of welfare is by far the most common occupation among foreign Christian workers in Yunnan. As the examples in this chapter reveal, conversion to Christianity is often a central feature of the rehabilitation or aid process. Furthermore, Christian organizations dealing with welfare vary widely in their legal status. Some are legally registered, but many others are illegal yet tolerated (McCarthy 2007, 6).

In chapter 3, I referred to the compatibility of Christian and Confucian morality in the eyes of some Chinese scholars, a perspective echoed in Yuan Zhimin's movie *The Cross*. However, the missionaries involved in welfare work whom I interviewed present a different perspective. Many of them are highly critical of certain aspects of Chinese culture, usually referred to generally as "Confucianism," a term employed to include social hierarchy, authoritative families, and the issue of "face" (*mian zi*). Accordingly, Christian welfare activity often includes the active promotion of values such as individualism and an emphasis on horizontal rather than vertical and hierarchical relationships. These values are promoted openly and are frequently presented by workers in faith-based organizations as the by-product of or precursor to full conversion. The liberty given to Christian faith-based organizations (FBOs) is all the more puzzling when one remembers that

Christian attacks on Confucianism come at a time when the central government is actively promoting a return to Confucian values, often the very same values being negated by missionaries (Bell 2007; Ong 1997, 182). In light of all this, it would seem that the question of why the government allows and sometimes even encourages FBO activities in Yunnan has not been sufficiently answered.

In this chapter, I argue that despite the apparent conflict between missionary activity and local authorities, the circumstances in reform-era Yunnan, with its combination of rapid development, major social problems, and inadequate social services, have resulted in an unwritten compromise between missionaries and local authorities. Accordingly, the presence of Christian NGOs in Yunnan reflects the acute need for professional, contemporary knowledge in the realms of welfare and aid, such as drug rehabilitation, medical care, dealing with prostitution, and development of various forms of therapy and counseling. The state is unable to provide funding for social services, and the methods for dealing with addiction and prostitution are often outdated and inadequate. The essential role played by Christian NGOs in social welfare is offered here as an explanation for state tolerance of these organizations and of Christianity in general, despite their missionary nature. Accordingly, authorities overlook the Christian element of their welfare activity, while missionaries provide aid without openly challenging the state system.

It is important to note that Christian organizations are not the only religious actors in the world of Chinese philanthropy. State support of religious philanthropy became official in 2012 when a number of central state agencies enthusiastically supported religious charity works and later created "religious charity week" in Wuhan, now an annual event (McCarthy 2017, 72; Wielander 2013). There are also Buddhist foundations, many of them active in many social realms such as founding schools for disabled children and offering disaster relief, often with the open encouragement of state authorities (Laliberté 2011, 114; 2012). However, unlike Christian NGOs, there is no evidence that Buddhist welfare activity includes the dissemination of Buddhist doctrine or that those who are aided through a Buddhist association tend to adopt the Buddhist faith system. While Islamic faith-based organizations are also active in China, promoting Islamic practice and identity, their activity is limited to within the officially recognized Muslim communities (McCarthy 2017, 75).

A number of scholars have addressed the issue of Christian welfare activity provided in peripheral areas (Bays 2003; Chan and Yamamori 2002;

Hamrin 2003; Hirono 2008; Ma Huacheng 2010). Yet, for the most part, writing on the subject has dealt with Christian aid as a phenomenon largely unrelated to the dissemination of the religion of Christianity. FBO activities are an essential part of the central Chinese government's policy of developing the regions, as well as a natural outcome of the privatization of institutions such as hospitals and schools (Hamrin 2003). Gerda Wielander (2011, 119–20) has argued that public sentiment favors Christian organizations and that the entire Harmonious Society policy is inspired by the ideology of Christian aid, marking an unspoken acceptance on the side of the state of Christian values. In contrast, I argue that state tolerance is essentially unrelated to the public sentiment regarding NGOs but is rather a function of the acute needs of local government for Western knowledge, funds, and skilled labor power.

Market Economy and the Rise of NGOs

The multifaceted nature of contemporary Christian aid work in Yunnan is exemplified by Matt, an American activist and café owner. Matt was a social worker by training who worked in the US in the field of child welfare (interview, May 26, 2010). A number of years ago, he began feeling that something was wrong with American social services. Workers in the welfare system were overworked, and the state was doing everything it could, in Matt's view, to avoid paying for people in need of social aid. At the time, he was working in a café / social center funded by a local church and open around the clock. One day a Chinese man walked in, and they began to talk about China. When the issue of Chinese welfare services came up, the Chinese man said, "You know, in China they have nothing." That gave Matt an idea—he would simply move his café-center to China.

For Matt, since the essence of welfare work was openness and good neighborly relations, he was intent on building a relationship of trust with the Chinese. Since arriving in Yunnan, he had been involved in a number of projects. He ran an "English Corner" situated next to a large mosque, where people could come free of charge and practice their English. "They knew I was a Christian, and there was no problem with that," said Matt. He had also been involved in a number of agricultural projects, primarily in the growing of moringa trees. These trees have leaves and pods that are high in protein and are being promoted to alleviate poverty and enhance nutrition in a number of locations worldwide.

At the same time, Matt had a deep interest in the Hui and other Muslim minorities. His café served halal food and provided weekly Arabic lessons, given by an Egyptian Coptic businessman. Matt had studied the Koran and concluded that a closer examination of the book would lead Muslims to realize that it is an incomplete revelation and induce them to search for further knowledge in the Bible and particularly in the New Testament. He said, "All I want to do is make people think." Accordingly, Matt has collected verses from both the Koran and the Hadith that he believes imply the divinity of Jesus.

In many ways, Matt's story epitomizes the issue of Christian welfare in present-day China. Matt's conversation with a Chinese customer in Arizona led him to see China as a land of opportunity for missionaries involved in social activity. The country has considerable social problems and an inadequate welfare system, particularly in poor provinces like Yunnan (Chan and Yamamori 2002, 52; Hamrin 2003; J. Ma 2011, 189). Matt's decision to move to China reflects the feeling among many Christians that despite the illegality of missionary work, when welfare and aid are concerned, China and particularly Yunnan are places where their knowledge, including the English language, social work, and agriculture, is in high demand (Forney 2001).

Yet, while Matt is involved in charity work, he is equally interested in providing "spiritual aid" and spreading the gospel. His interaction with locals is change oriented: it is aimed not only at providing material assistance but also at promoting an inner change among those who use the center's services. Gaining people's confidence and using his knowledge, Matt attempts to "make people think" by arguing that an in-depth examination of their own tradition will reveal the truth of Christianity. Indeed, in the eyes of many Christian NGO workers, the spiritual and physical dimension of welfare are largely inseparable.

The issue of aid is widely featured in missionary literature and is perceived by many missionaries to be a central tenet of Christianity. A classification given by Michael, a Christian whose work in the realm of drug rehabilitation is discussed below, can be of some assistance here. According to him, Christian activists can be divided into the "three *w*'s: words, wonders, and works." The first two refer to preachers and miracle makers, respectively. The discussion here will focus on "works": missionaries whose main activity is in the realm of aid and welfare.

During the first wave of Protestant missionary work in the late nineteenth and early twentieth centuries, missionaries built schools and hospitals and made extensive use of advanced Western technology. As early as 1920, some argued in favor of placing welfare work at the center of the missionary project (Kepler 1966, 16–21). Yet, despite the important work of pre-1949 missionaries in the realms of medicine and education, they were primarily people of "words" dedicated to the preaching of the gospel, both orally and through the dissemination of written material.¹ However, during the decolonization process of the 1960s, and in light of growing public opinion in the West against imperialism, missionaries began to replace the old rhetoric of "civilizing" with the newer one of "development" (Manji and O'Coill 2002, 574). At the same time, American missionaries began turning their energy toward welfare in their own inner cities and slums. Interestingly, the shift toward aid was largely inspired by a biography of the Chinese Pastor Hsi (Xi Sheng Mo), a nineteenth-century convert and missionary who worked with opium addicts in Shaanxi (Austin 2007, 241).

The emphasis on aid work reflects the difference in circumstances between evangelizing pre-1949 and in contemporary times. Today, although some tracts can be found, the possibilities of publicly disseminating printed material to people outside the Christian community are extremely limited. Such direct evangelization would be a breach of the delicate balance of church-state relations and in most cases would not be tolerated by the authorities. With the option of direct public preaching largely gone, works of charity and aid have emerged as one of the major Christian inroads into China today. Moreover, the dissemination of knowledge in the fields of welfare, rehabilitation, and medicine places missionaries in a position of superiority, one that may be employed to convey the superiority of Christianity over local traditions.

As in the past, the supremacy of Western knowledge has not gone uncontested. In one case I encountered, assistance offered by Christian workers to a local organization dealing with early child education had been discontinued on the grounds that they are "not respectful of Chinese tradition" (Maya, conversation, January 6, 2010).² Certainly, official rhetoric is somewhat less enamored with the West and tends to emphasize the value of a Chinese or Asian version of modernity (Ong 1997, 194–96), particularly since Xi Jinping's rise to power in 2012. Nevertheless, the idea that Western technology and knowledge are the key to China's future progress is still a potent one. Equating the West and all its manifestations with modernity is still a major factor of conversion to Christianity (Kalir 2009; F. Yang 2005). It is a disposition that is deeply ingrained in modern Chinese thought, creating what Mayfair Yang has termed "'the post-colonial complex,' in which the imperialists are discarded but their denigrations of the collective self and models of modernity leave a deep imprint on the collective psyche" (M. Yang 2004b, 724).

The current need for Western knowledge reflects the move toward market reforms, a process with vast implications for Chinese society. Free-market economy, widespread privatization, and rapid dismantling of the welfare state have redefined the state's relationship with its citizens. This process is not unique to China; it is part of a global trend of market reform, deregulation, and privatization. The transferring of welfare services into private hands is strongly supported by international economic organizations such as the International Monetary Fund and World Trade Organization. In fact, the process of downgrading government support for welfare and substituting it with the work of nongovernmental organizations is considered a mark of advanced economies and a basic requirement for countries seeking aid from the developed world. The rise of NGOs is often viewed as a mark of an emerging civil society, considered in turn to be one of the major features of democratization (Banks and Hulme 2012; G. Clarke 1998). However, creating a regulatory system for nonprofit organizations may also be perceived as a strategy employed by the state to control the existing reality. This seems to be the case in China, where the authorities have been engaged in creating a legal structure for foreign NGOs in the past decade, culminating in the legislation of the Overseas NGO Domestic Activities Management Law in 2017 (Jia Xijin 2017). At the same time, China has also passed the Charity Law requiring international groups to partner with domestic organizations. This new legislation "shows the extent to which China's leaders have become more wary of civil society" (Lam 2018) and is aimed at tightening state control (Santos 2016).

The rise of NGOs in China is dramatic considering the fact that before 1979, the nongovernmental sphere was virtually nonexistent (Wallace 2005). As of 2007, there were 315,000 registered organizations throughout China and another unknown number, perhaps two to three million, unregistered ones (McCarthy 2007, 3). This trend has been particularly pronounced in Yunnan Province beginning in the 1990s. By 1996, Yunnan had approximately 10,000 registered organizations, more than Shanghai, which had 7,000. The NGOs vary widely in size and function, from small, local, community-based organizations to large international organizations such as the Red Cross and UNICEF (Hirono 2008). A 1995 survey reveals that Yunnan is also home to a large number of unregistered organizations, with only thirteen of one hundred foundations properly registered with the

Bank of China. Nevertheless, the term "nongovernmental organization" is problematic in the Chinese context, even regarding unregistered organizations, as some level of state control is always maintained (Saich 2000, 136).

The situation changed in 2008 when Yunnan was chosen as the location for a pilot program of the Ministry of Civil Affairs to oversee the registration of overseas NGOs, leading to the passing of the Standard Overseas NGO Activities Provisional Regulation of Yunnan (Jia Xijin 2017). A 2015 listing of NGOs provided by the Yunnan's Foreign Affairs Office together with the People's Association for Friendship with Foreign Countries lists only three Christian organizations, which address linguistic and cultural preservation, education in rural areas, and free plastic surgery for deformities such as cleft lip.[3] According to the information on Yunnan's Public Security Bureau Department for NGO Management office website, there are currently twenty-five registered international NGOs working in Yunnan. Twelve of them, including Bless China International, discussed later in this chapter, are Christian oriented. Most of the Christian NGOs are identified as based in Hong Kong or the US.[4]

Organizations adapt various strategies regarding the publicity of their religious affiliations, ranging from the scientific-secular image of the Summer Institute of Linguistics discussed in chapter 5 to the overtly Christian identity of the Medical Services International (MSI) Professional Services, founded by James Hudson Taylor III, the descendant of the legendary father of the China Inland Mission. The MSI website openly declares its dedication to the people of Sichuan, Yunnan, and Chongqing, "where physical and spiritual needs . . . are great and the resources available to meet those needs are scarce."[5]

Today, Chinese media often praise the "people's organizations" (*minjian zuzhi*), giving this expression of a liberal capitalist society an ironically Marxist veneer. In another twist of phrase and recycling of ideological terminology, NGO leaders are sometimes referred to as "model workers" and celebrated as modern-day, reform-era heroes like Lei-Feng. Indeed, the state allocates large sums of money to NGOs for poverty alleviation and other major projects. This support has been explained as an expression of the state's belief in the superiority of NGOs in dealing with social matters, possessing "innovative approaches that government agencies with their ingrained cultures, incentive structures and work style may not be able to provide" and "a more nuanced understanding of local problems" (McCarthy 2007, 6).

The prevalence of NGOs in Yunnan also reflects the massive development programs of the past decade and the drive to modernize and remold the province from a peripheral backwater to the major commercial hub of Southeast Asia (*Economist* 2011). China has been promoting the development of transportation and water management and the enhancement of electrical capacity as well as a drive to standardize bureaucratic procedures throughout the region, with particular emphasis put on the Kunming-Bangkok corridor (McCarthy 2009, 83). In the past decade, Yunnan's gross domestic product (GDP) has tripled, and numerous roads, rail lines, and airports have been built, culminating in the opening of the new Kunming international airport in 2012, the fourth largest airport in China. In January 2013, the tiny Lisu village of Shudi became the last village in the province to be connected to the electric grid, thus completing a seven-year-long project of bringing electricity to every home in Yunnan (Li and Guo 2013). However, as mentioned, rapid development and privatization have come with serious social consequences. Unwilling or unable to continue financing social services, the government has allowed private NGOs to deal with some of the darker aspects and consequences of its economic policy.

Finding a New Father: Drug Rehabilitation

Michael and his wife, Lea, run a café-restaurant in the fashionable center of Kunming's expat community. The café is quite popular among foreign students and well-known for its good and reasonably priced coffee. However, the coffee is only half the story; the seemingly ordinary expat hangout is actually part of a Christian drug-rehabilitation program. All the workers are recovered addicts who have undergone lengthy therapy, usually lasting seven years. The café serves a double purpose: it provides the ex-addicts with employment after an initial phase of therapy (less than the full seven years, conducted in a separate section of the building), and it simultaneously helps finance the rehabilitation center. Neither the rehabilitation program nor its Christian content are visible in the café; the music, art, and magazines available are all secular in nature. The only public indications of the drug rehabilitation program are a few antidrug pamphlets in Chinese, placed inconspicuously in the corner of the room. As such, many foreigners living in the city are completely unaware of the café's other functions. While the program is not flaunted, it is not concealed either. Indeed, my interviews with Michael were conducted in the public space of the café. The café–rehabilitation center is a church-based project, supported and initially partially funded by an association of approximately ten churches in Michael's home country. As of 2012, the funds generated by the café were sufficient to fund the rehabilitation center, while the churches still financed Michael's personal expenses (Michael, interview, October 2, 2012).

Unlike other forms of aid work, dealing with addiction has been part of mission work since the opening of Hudson Taylor's opium asylum in 1859 (Austin 2007, 14). Taylor's example has been an inspiration for Michael, who defines himself as a man of "works" and not of "words" and tries to follow similar objectives in present-day China (interview, October 22, 2009). He feels uneasy with some of the other Christian activity in town, which he views as a superficial and "instant" type of Christianity that he calls "selling tickets to heaven." He contrasts the predominant American style of "a mile wide and an inch deep" with what he is trying to achieve, "an inch wide and a mile deep," referring to his attempt to make meaningful changes in the lives of a limited number of addicts he works with, rather than convert China's millions en masse.

The absence of religious manifestations in the space of the café does not reflect the nature of the rehabilitation program, which is of a distinctly religious character. The program is small, limited to ten to fifteen patients at any given time. Michael refers to the method used as "gospel rehab." Based on an idea called "reparenting," it aims to help addicts by recreating a sense of family relationships. Initially, the therapist functions as a parental figure, but in time, a parent-child relationship is formed between the patient and the "Heavenly Father." In other words, rehabilitation at Michael's center is essentially based on the construction of an in-depth, intimate, and binding connection with God as a father figure.

The religious nature of the rehabilitation process is never hidden, and the image of God as a father figure is discussed from the very first meeting. Mornings at the rehab center always begin with a short prayer, followed by reading from the Bible and a discussion focused on implementing the text in everyday life. The Bible is the only text read, and the emphasis is always concrete and pragmatic. To cite one example from the time I was conducting this research, Michael's wife, Lea, was teaching about the vision of God's chariot in the first chapter of the book of Ezekiel. Her emphasis was on each face of the chariot as a different aspect of an individual's soul: the lion represents the will to rule and control one's destiny; the eagle, the will to soar; the ox, being grounded in reality; and man, the world of human emotion.

In Michael's experience, addicts often tend to be "spiritually sensitive in an above-average way," making the spiritual message included in the therapy sessions widely appealing. In fact, Michael views the addiction itself as an expression of an unfulfilled spiritual need. Thus, conversion is not a prerequisite of the therapy process—it happens naturally. For example, Michael finds that addicts have a hard time with verbal prayer, but they are often attracted to the Pentecostal practice of "speaking in tongues" based on spontaneous nonverbal expressions sometimes defined as "primal language" (Cox 1995, 85–97). Indeed, the emotional and nonverbal religiosity of the program is seen by Michael as an essential part of the conversion process: accordingly, patients experience the prayer meetings and eventually "feel the vibe" and accept Christianity. The process of rehabilitation and subsequent conversion may be seen as the final phases of a long and painful spiritual journey. Often, the process moves beyond the individual convert—as Michael noted, it was not uncommon for families of recovered addicts to follow them into the Christian fold.

Patients at the center come from a variety of family backgrounds. About half are from a nonreligious background, with the other half mostly from strong Buddhist homes, mostly Dai. From Michael's perspective, the Buddhist addicts are the most interesting. They frequently arrive at the rehabilitation center after having tried to rid themselves of their addiction through Buddhist rituals such as visiting temples, offering incense, and wearing amulets, to no avail. After entering the rehabilitation program, many of the devoutly Buddhist addicts experience headaches and physical discomfort at prayer times. Michael understands these feelings as the outcome of a spiritual connection they have with other forces such as local gods and spirits, coming into conflict with the connection being constructed with God. Indeed, this spiritual conflict is sometimes severe enough that addicts leave the rehabilitation center without concluding the process. Those who stay in the program must, at a certain point, cut their connections with the past. This is particularly true for those who wish to be baptized. In such cases, Michael explains to the potential converts that they are not obliged to convert but that if they are interested in concluding the process, it is essential to draw a line between their past and present selves. Michael illustrated this point physically during our conversation, by moving his hand in a cutting gesture above his head.

According to Michael, the issue of the patient's relationship with the past invariably surfaces during the rehabilitation process. Often, after the initial addiction is broken, patients' families try to convince them to return home. Michael discourages this, viewing such a return as having a dangerous potential for regression, as many come from regions where drugs are easily accessible. However, Michael's objection to ex-addicts returning to their family homes is also related to his opinion that the Chinese family as a social institution is based on a hierarchical "power system," which he associates with Confucian thinking that discourages the formation of individual choice. In this regard, Michael makes no distinction between Han and minority families. Seen in this light, "reparenting" is a process intending to replace an old family model based on power and hierarchy with a newer one, based on individual choice. Accordingly, the psychological process of "refathering" can be seen as having a double purpose. On the one hand, constructing a relationship with God, through prayer and other methods, is primarily meant to create an individual will and feeling of self-worth to counter the problem of addiction. At the same time, "refathering" contains a parallel process of disassociation from one's biological family and past. The line drawn between the addict present and past is a process in which the addict is reborn, in the full religious sense of the term.

Indeed, in Michael's view, a wide gulf exists between the therapeutic method used in the center and traditional Confucian concepts of family and hierarchy. In his experience, the most difficult thing for addicts to accept is the idea of reciprocal and open relationships at the core of the "reparenting" therapy method. So, for example, upon entering the home where program participants live, the first thing they ask is whether Michael or his Chinese coworker (an ex-addict) is in charge. The answer is that the home is run jointly, with no boss. Michael described laughingly the fierce objection raised by patients to this challenging of their hierarchical worldview.

It is important to note that Michael does not perceive himself as a promoter of Western culture or ideals. His concern is with rehabilitation, not democracy, civil society, or human rights. Nevertheless, he firmly believes that there are certain elements in Chinese culture that must be combated if rehabilitation is going to succeed. An example Michael gave was the patients' reactions to the phases of therapy. In the West, the most difficult part of rehabilitation is usually the first phase of breaking the physical addiction. In Michael's experience in Yunnan, the opposite is true—physical rehabilitation, with its strict rules and control, is the easier part. It is the second phase, where individual choices must be made and the past must be confronted, that is the most challenging.

The therapeutic model that Michael offers is therefore of a somewhat culturally subversive nature, containing larger implications than the issue of conversion. As such, the problem is not so much the introduction of God in his fatherly, severe, and punishing form but rather the addict's own role as a son or daughter and the emphasis placed on constructing a mutual, familial relationship with the Creator. This gives rise to a previously unknown religious experience, one that revolves around individual relationships, overriding issues of family, authority, and tradition.

Christian involvement in drug-rehabilitation programs is well-known to Chinese authorities. As Wang Aiguo, deputy chief of the Yunnan Religious Affairs Bureau, has noted, "one less drug addict means one more Christian" (McCarthy 2017, 84). And yet, Michael has not encountered significant problems with the authorities and maintains good relations with local officials. Importantly for the center's purposes, he is also on friendly terms with a local doctor who runs a nearby methadone clinic. Although the doctor is a Communist Party member, it seems that he has had contact with Christianity and, according to some rumors, may even define himself as a Christian (although Michael is unsure of the nature or depth of this self-definition). Over the years, the doctor has shown interest in Michael's work, mostly out of curiosity in the psychological method behind "gospel rehab" therapy.

Michael's center is not officially registered. His work takes place in the "gray market" of unofficial but well-known and tolerated religious activity (F. Yang 2006, 97–98). Indeed, according to Michael, registration is not a single process but rather a spectrum of different shades of "officiality"; accordingly, "the more official the registration, the more weight it carries" (interview, January 6, 2010). Thus, lack of registration of a given organization does not necessarily imply illegality, rather implying that actions are confined to the local level and cannot be carried out in other regions of the country.

Official attitudes toward the center are illustrated in the following story: Some time ago, Michael was notified that two officials from Beijing intended to visit the center. Upon arrival, they asked Michael if they could be present in the morning session. Somewhat alarmed, he asked them if they were aware of the fact that the therapy offered is "rather Christian" and added that he had been given permission to use it. The officials replied that it was not a problem and that they wanted to witness it for themselves. To Michael's surprise, when the morning prayer began, the officials bowed their heads respectfully, along with everybody else.

Michael is clear about the uniqueness of Yunnan in this regard. He had spent time in Hong Kong and, as a speaker of Cantonese, had originally planned on working in Guangxi Province. However, he and other Christians involved in rehabilitation had not been able to successfully work there. There is no doubt in Michael's mind that in a place like Beijing, doing this kind of work would be out of the question. In this context, he quoted the Chinese proverb often used to explain Yunnan's relatively relaxed policies: "The mountains are high and the emperor is far away" (*shan gao huangdi yuan*), attesting to the strong and persistent concept of center and periphery in Chinese culture, with Yunnan as eternally peripheral. In Michael's experience, the situation in Yunnan can and does change, with state control tightening and relaxing periodically but always remaining somewhat more relaxed than in the Chinese center.

To understand state tolerance of gospel rehab, one must consider the options available for drug addicts in Yunnan. Due to the province's proximity to the opium-growing areas in the Golden Triangle region, Yunnan is a major highway of drug smuggling, and drugs are easily available. According to a recent report, between 2005 and 2010, local police caught 109,000 smugglers and seized 51.6 tons of drugs (Xinhua 2014). While the problem is most pronounced in the ethnic border areas of Dehong and Xishuangbanna, it is also present in the provincial capital. According to Michael, in the past, old women of the Yi minority sold drugs fairly openly in one of Kunming's major junctions, adding that they were seldom stopped, apparently because they would carry babies on their backs and the police did not know what to do with the children.

The normal treatment for addicts in China is incarceration: a standard sentence of six months for first offenders and two to three years for addicts caught a second time. During the two years of prison time, counseling for drug users is virtually nonexistent:

> Those who have gone through the first level and relapse are sent to compulsory detoxification centers administered by the Public Security Bureau (second level). They spend at least 6 months in the compulsory detoxification centers where they participate in a combination of detoxification treatment, physical exercise, and manual labor. At the third level, drug users who relapse after receiving compulsory detoxification are mandated to 2 to 3 years of re-education through activities in labor camps administered by the Justice Bureau. As drug users are not allowed to leave the compulsory detoxification centers and labor camps, they are considered incarceration sites. (Li et al. 2010, 2)

The report continues by noting that "police often apply military management approaches" (2). It adds that the majority of treated drug users experience a relapse and do not change their behaviors that put them at risk for contracting HIV after they leave incarceration sites. In 2008, a new law was enacted, aimed at providing several choices of detoxification treatment. However, the authors claim that implementation of the law runs against the "zero tolerance for drug users" approach among law-enforcing authorities. Accordingly, lack of cooperation between government departments will make implementation of the law difficult.

Likewise, Michael notes that since the roots of addiction are never addressed in jail, many ex-convicts find their way back to drugs fairly quickly. The only other alternative to incarceration is the methadone clinic, where addicts can buy methadone, a chemical substitute for opium. Consumption of methadone does not reduce addiction; it is no more than an initial means of breaking out of the physical dependence on opiates. Furthermore, it is expensive. Indeed, according to Michael, his rehabilitation program is the only free option available in the city. Accordingly, what seems to be the overriding factor in the rather accommodating stance of local authorities is the scarcity of other rehabilitation options. For various reasons, the authorities have been unable to forcibly eliminate the flourishing drug trade across the Burmese and Lao borders, and drugs continue to flow into Yunnan. Moreover, prisons are not reducing the problem. Michael's center offers a deeper and largely unknown option, one that is both effective and free.

Indeed, Michael notes that state tolerance for welfare activity like his own contains a distinctly economic aspect. Rehabilitation centers and other welfare institutions of this sort clearly save money for the government. In some cases, the authorities have attempted to maximize profit by initially allowing such establishments to run more or less independently, gradually increasing inspection and regulation, making life increasingly difficult, and eventually taking control and ousting the original founders. This is a story Michael has heard several times, regarding large institutions like hospitals funded by Christian organizations. Thus, money is funneled in from external sources, knowledge is received from foreign specialists, and ideological/spiritual influence is limited to a number of years before it can be eliminated (see also Hamrin 2003).

In our conversations, Michael was cautious about making predictions about the future, noting that state policies tend to fluctuate. However, it would seem that for now, the novelty of therapy and rehabilitation for drug addicts is gaining ground in other parts of the province. The scope of the trend became apparent in one of our last conversations in 2012, when Michael informed me that the St. Stephan's Society, a much larger Christian organization from Hong Kong that is engaged in similar work to his own, has been officially invited to work in Yunnan and will be arriving soon with a large staff.[6]

Saving Bodies and Souls: The Medical Mission

Of all varieties of welfare and charity, the medical mission is by far the oldest, dating back to the early Jesuit mission and a major feature of nineteenth-century missionary work (Fung 2004). Medical missionaries played a central role in the affirmation of Western scientific superiority, introducing knowledge previously unknown in China. As a result, many missionaries became "medicine men," and nineteenth-century missionaries with minimal medical knowledge sometimes functioned as healer-doctors, mixing the mystical and the scientific and playing the double role of saving bodies and souls (Austin 2007, 241).

The reappearance of medical missionaries in China is closely related to the disappearance of universal health care in the reform era, a process with serious consequences for many Chinese citizens (*Economist* 2009). Concern over the withdrawal of health coverage led to the rising interest in traditional medicine and qigong during the 1990s, leading eventually to the birth of large quasi-religious qigong movements such as the Falun Gong (Chang 2004, 4; Shue 2002, 222). Today, one of the most visible manifestations of privatization in China can be seen in the realm of medicine. Advertisements for a wide variety of hospitals, each specializing in a different medical field (women, children, eyes, heart, kidney, etc.), appear on buses and billboards everywhere in Kunming. Low-quality, relatively cheap government hospitals coexist alongside pricy and lavishly decorated hospitals, such as the pricy Richland Hospital and the Singaporean-owned Maria Women's Hospital. In the Chinese system, doctor appointments tend to be inexpensive, with money made on medications and special procedures. For many people, being seriously ill can become a crippling financial burden. Even those who have medical insurance are not covered fully, and for the multitudes of farmers and migrant workers, all expenses must be privately covered (Frick 2007). Indeed, during my time in Yunnan, I heard a number of stories of families who lost huge sums of money because of a sick family member with no medical insurance. As one local Chinese teacher once told me, "Chinese people are more afraid of getting sick than of dying" (Qin, conversation, April 4, 2010).

In this context, the International Clinic is an important alternative. Set up about a decade ago under the auspices of Bless China International (BCI; previously known as Project Grace), the clinic was originally intended to serve both the poorest of Kunming's residents and Western expats, mainly missionaries, living and working in the city. Although my concern here is primarily with the service provided to local populations, it is important to remember that providing Western-standard medical care is of great importance for long-term expat residents of Kunming, particularly when families with children are concerned. As such, it is an essential part of the support system for missionaries living in the city.[7]

In addition to running the clinic, BCI is engaged in a variety of welfare projects, ranging from education to the dissemination of agricultural knowledge. The founder of Project Grace, Rob Cheeley, is a medical doctor who initially served as an official adviser to the Yunnan Ministry of Health, later founding Project Grace in 1997. Cheeley's presentation of BCI to local authorities was straightforward: "Openly and honestly stating to our governmental partners (as well as to the people we are assisting) that we are Christians who care for the poor because Christ loves them and with financial resources supplied by Christian foundations and donors has built trust and friendship between ourselves and local officials" (P. Anderson 2006, 192). Indeed, the financial aspects of activity mentioned by Cheeley have not gone unnoticed by the authorities, and BCI has been generally received enthusiastically in Yunnan. It received the China Friendship Award in 2000, the highest award given to non-Chinese individuals or organizations (Hamrin 2003; Xinhua 2007). Following the reception of the award, the organization was described in the *People's Daily* (2000) as one aimed for the purpose of "luring foreign volunteers to work in Yunnan and provide free medical help and educational programs for local disabled persons." The article continues by describing the activists' high level of education and, importantly, the large funds they have at their disposal, amounting to 5.89 million yuan. BCI's distinctly Christian nature is never mentioned. Thus, official endorsement and praise of BCI has come despite the fact that many of its workers are staunch evangelical Christians, highly supportive of, if not personally active in, missionary work. However, the BCI did encounter a certain amount of trouble with the authorities a number of years after its foundation. Following "'unwise religious' activities on the part of some associated with the organization," an investigation was launched by state authorities, and the organization was advised to split into smaller units (P. Anderson 2006, 192). Today the BCI continues to operate many programs in Yunnan. A description of work among disabled people in Yunnan is fairly explicit regarding the organization's religious affiliation: "Our Rehab section has also cared for three dying patients—and in the process we all grew. All three died knowing Christ.... We also saw young people come to know Christ. And some did it even though there was opposition at home" (Boubacar 2004, 101–2).

I met Dr. Horace of the International Clinic, in one of the major foreign café-restaurant hangouts in a neighborhood with a large Western Christian population. The restaurant and adjacent shop were also part of a longstanding Christian welfare project dedicated to working with the physically impaired (Dr. Horace, Interview, June 28, 2010). Dr. Horace and his wife first came to China in the 1990s. They eventually adopted a Chinese girl and made their home in Kunming, where he began practicing medicine in the International Clinic. In addition, Dr. Horace made regular trips to poor minority areas to see patients who had no access to medical services. The interview with Dr. Horace was conducted in the afternoon, in the café veranda, overlooking the street corner with people coming and going. The semipublic location did not seem to trouble Dr. Horace in the least, a testament to his confidence that the clinic is working within the boundaries of the law. Far from hiding his Christian identity, in the course of our conversation, Dr. Horace identified himself as "a believer" and referred to the work done through the clinic as his "ministry."

Dr. Horace began by provided a short overview of the clinic's history: When the clinic was first established, treatment for locals was free, and Westerners were expected to give a donation. In time, the clinic became quite well-known. The city's poor migrants, including many ethnic Bouyei from the Guizhou border, who are among the poorest laborers in Kunming, came to receive treatment regularly. At the time, the clinic was unregistered, but nobody seemed to care. Nevertheless, Dr. Horace and his colleges were always aware of the fact that something could happen and that being shut down "was only a matter of time." As they expected, in 2009, they were shut down as a result of an unfortunate incident. A mother came in with a toddler who suffered from a stomach problem. He was examined and released to be monitored at home. Their home was quite far, so the clinic put them up in a simple hotel—something that is done when the need arises. The child's condition worsened during the night, and he died. Despite the fact that the child's condition was deteriorating, the mother did not take him to the hospital, as she had no means to pay for treatment and the clinic was closed. According to Dr. Horace, who tried not to be overly critical of the local medical establishment, it is the norm that those who arrive at a hospital without the means to pay will not be treated.[8] Early in the morning, the woman ran to the clinic asking frantically to see the doctor who had checked the child the day before. The clinic had not yet been opened, and the guard, not knowing what to do, called the police. Upon arrival, the police started asking questions about registration and eventually shut the clinic down. While nobody was arrested, the medical work was stopped. The clinic remained closed for almost a year, then eventually found a way to reopen legally, under the umbrella of the Yunnan Kidney Hospital. The story of the child's death came to a remarkable end. The clinic doctors kept in touch with the bereaved family, who have, in Dr. Horace's words, "come to faith." Through the Christian community in town, the mother got a job working at the same café where Dr. Horace and I met. Finally, in a strange twist of fate, the first patient in the newly opened clinic was this family's newborn baby.

The clinic works on a three-tier scale of pricing. Western patients pay full price (usually ranging 200–300 RMB for an average treatment; approximately US$30–45). Normative, middle-class Chinese patients pay approximately half that sum. Those who have no means at all, like the poor migrant Bouyei, pay a symbolic 2 RMB registration fee. The decision regarding payment is made by the Chinese staff of nurses, who are skilled at examining their patients' appearance and behavior and discerning their appropriate price bracket. In case the nurses' assessment is insufficient, the registration form includes a space for noting "difficulty in paying the medical bill." Being a nonprofit establishment, all payments are directed toward staff salaries and maintenance. According to the clinic's brochure, charging money for treatment is done "in order to comply with government regulations." The brochure also states that "expatriates referring Chinese friends to the clinic should escort them to the clinic and be prepared to help them pay for medication and treatment."

In addition to providing medical care, doctors go to great lengths to acquire donations when expensive treatment is necessary. Patients needing complicated procedures that cannot be performed in Yunnan may require medical care in Beijing, Hong Kong, or Bangkok. Contacts with medical institutions elsewhere, both within and outside China, are established through the clinic. These contacts are frequently made through the large, informal network of Christian activists working in hospitals throughout the region.

One of the clinic's unique features is the amount of time dedicated to each patient. Doctor appointments in China (and, according to Dr. Horace, in the US as well) tend to be short and to the point. Financial considerations result in appointments that are purely medical and technical in nature, containing little personal contact between doctors and patients. In contrast, Dr. Horace said he frequently spends an hour with a patient in the clinic. My personal experience with the clinic has been similar. An appointment made for my son with another doctor lasted way beyond the allotted time and evolved into a long and casual conversation between us and the pediatrician on nonmedical issues. There seemed to be no rush to finish the appointment, despite the fact that the receptionist had originally informed us that the doctor's time had been completely booked for that day.

Indeed, the International Clinic may be seen as kind of anomaly, a place where market forces are left at bay. Since payment is used only to cover expenses and is largely negotiable and circumstantial, the clinic essentially functions outside of market realities. Therefore, doctors can spend more time with their patients, getting to know them intimately. This noneconomic model is unusual not only in China but in the West as well. Moreover, the clinic is home to a unique form of doctor-patient relationship in the Chinese context. Dr. Horace described how in China, a doctor is often considered and self-represented as the "gate to knowledge, with the knowledge standing behind him." The description is consistent with the authoritative scientism prevalent in China, where the terms "healthy" and "scientific" are often used as labels of legitimacy (Feuchtawang and Wang 1991, 254).

The doctor-patient relationship presented by Dr. Horace may be seen as an attempt to react to a crisis of authority experienced by the medical establishment in China, where violence against doctors is on the rise (Hesketh et al. 2012; Wei et al. 2013). Conflicts in hospitals reflect the problems with privatized medicine, with families often unable to pay their large medical bills. Indeed, according to Tai Lai Yong, a Christian Singaporean doctor working in Yunnan, the Chinese medical system is also plagued by many patient-doctor disputes: "Mutual distrust . . . [is] a big obstacle in providing health care. . . . My colleagues and I agree that there is a need for wise people to come and address the system of handling medical disputes and patient unhappiness. . . . This takes quite a lot of un-learning and learning as traditionally the culture here is not about information sharing, or empowering the patient" (Tai 2009, 49–50).

The dissemination of knowledge administered by doctors like Tai and the staff of the International Clinic is an essential part of what Dr. Horace refers to as his "ministry." Thus, the clinic can be seen as an elaboration on the old medical-missionary theme. Christians working through medical

FBOs today are still at the forefront of medical knowledge, particularly in a peripheral place like Yunnan. However, their ultimate advantage lies not in their scientific know-how but rather in their holistic approach to treatment. While the Chinese medical system emphasizes its authority through scientific knowledge, just as missionary doctors did a century ago, contemporary Christian doctors imply a sense of superiority through their recognition of the human dimensions of medicine, beyond science.

Dr. Horace's behavior as a doctor further demonstrates this point. Despite his identification as a Christian, he is not in the habit of preaching to his patients. His stated mission is the saving of bodies, not souls. Indeed, as a rule, the clinic's doctors do not preach to their patients about Christianity. Dr. Horace shared his feeling that the gap between himself, an educated Westerner, and his poor, minimally educated patients is so great that his patients tend to agree with everything he says. Therefore, preaching would be unethical and ineffective. However, when treating a patient with a particularly difficult illness, he sometimes asks if the patient is interested in praying with him, explaining that he is only a doctor and therefore a facilitator of healing, not its ultimate source. The appeal of such an approach is multifaceted. By presenting himself as "only a doctor," the image of the invincibility of scientific knowledge is broken. By admitting to being fallible and willing to pray together with a patient, Dr. Horace challenges Chinese perceptions of hierarchy and authority, attempting to create a mutual horizontal relationship between himself and his patients.

It would be inaccurate to view the doctor-patient relationship promoted by Christian medical workers as a discarding of hierarchy in favor of complete equality. Rather, the interaction at the clinic may be seen as an attempt to construct an alternative model of hierarchy, one that is based on holistic wisdom of the kind advocated by Dr. Tai instead of on the primacy of science and its representatives. In many ways, the self-projected image of the Christian doctor is similar to that of the Christian English teachers discussed in chapter 3, whose charisma and authority are rooted in their image as morally upright and humane. Admittedly, there is no way to discern what the rate of conversion to Christianity is among the clinic's patients. However, as the preceding story reveals, it would seem that the contact with the extensive network of Christian charity does produce a certain number of converts.

The practical benefits of the clinic are significant, allowing impoverished urban residents and rural migrants to receive treatment from Western-trained doctors in Kunming and elsewhere. Thus, the clinic and its staff represent a community and a support system of crucial importance in the competitive world of the free market. The benefits of the clinic from a state perspective are referred to in a video on the Bless China International website. In addition to describing the clinic as an attempt to help Yunnan's poor and featuring short interviews with foreign doctors, the video shows Chen Jiaomin, the director of the provincial health office, saying, "We want to build Yunnan up as a bridgehead facing southwestern China. If there are more medical institutions like the Kunming International Clinic providing quality care for patients, there will be more Chinese and foreigners who will be willing to come to Kunming."[9] Chen's praise for the clinic had less to do with providing health care for Kunming's underprivileged residents and more to do with attracting foreigners. To an extent, one may argue that the missionaries themselves, forming a large portion of the city's expat community, have become an asset. Thus, the provincial government's interest in the clinic is clearly related to the advancement of its supreme goal: the development and modernization of Yunnan.

Eden Ministry: Addressing the Underworld of Trafficking Women

Eden Ministry is an organization dedicated to the rescue and rehabilitation of sex workers in Kunming. The general format is similar to Michael's drug-rehabilitation program: it includes two safe houses and a shop where the ex-prostitutes produce and sell jewelry, providing finances and giving the women a marketable skill. However, in stark contradiction to Michael's café, Christianity here is in full view, beginning with the use of the word "ministry" and continuing with the opening line in the brochure overview: "Eden Ministry began in 2003 when several of us sensed God's burden for prostitutes as we walked the streets of China's red-light districts."

What is most interesting about Eden is the way it operates in locating prostitutes and incorporating them into the rehabilitation program. Following a spiritual vision experienced by Ann, Eden's founder, Eden workers deal not only with the women involved but also with the entire line of workers in the prostitution industry, including brothel owners and women traffickers. To this end, the foreign women who run Eden go on "prayer walks," praying and walking between the city's brothels. In addition, they meet with pimps and traffickers in an attempt to convince them to release their workers. Those who are able and willing to get away can find room at one of Eden's two shelters, where counseling is also available "to counsel women through their emotional scars and to help them grow spiritually," according to the brochure. Eden also tries to educate prostitutes about the spread of HIV. The Chinese staff members make regular visits to prisons, where they are allowed to bring food to women accused of prostitution and provide them with spiritual guidance. In Ann's view, the prevalence of prostitution reflects that in Chinese society, "there is no moral foundation" (interview, September 30, 2012). Her ambition is to awaken the people involved in the industry to the immorality of their actions. Ann told me of a dinner meeting she had with a trafficker of women from Northern China. She attempted to confront him with the reality of his actions, saying, "I love you, but I hate what you are doing. Why are you ruining these girls' lives?" To her surprise, the trafficker answered that nobody had ever told him that what he is doing is wrong and that he was interested in hearing from her why she thought it was. Ann's attempts at persuasion and moral awakening are occasionally successful—some girls have been released by their owners, and in at least one case, a woman who was running two brothels decided to close them and engage in other business activities after being in contact with Eden workers.

Eden's activities reveal a harsh picture of reform-era China. Prostitution, largely eliminated by the Communists in the 1950s, has made a massive return to the streets of China. Despite occasional police crackdowns, the sex industry in China is thriving, largely due to rampant corruption. According to Human Rights Watch, "The anti-prostitution drives are useless in terms of controlling the industry, but they lead to a spike in abuses" (Branigan 2013). In Yunnan, prostitution often carries an ethnic flavor, with Han men coming to Yunnan to experience the sexual freedom allegedly typical of minority cultures.[10] Likewise, over half the prostitutes whom Eden workers encounter in Kunming come from minority backgrounds. Prostitution is accompanied by a barrage of social problems. Human trafficking is particularly prevalent in Yunnan, with many women being bought or abducted from poor areas and from across the border in Vietnam or Myanmar. According to the Mekong Sub-regional International Labor Organization, approximately one thousand women a year are trafficked in Yunnan, with approximately 80 percent of them abducted from their homes or lured away on false pretexts (ILO/IPEC 2002, 2). Kunming is often the first stop on the route of trafficking women to the rest of China.

Official response to prostitution is usually of two varieties: Most often, it is simply ignored. On occasion, prostitutes are rounded up and sent to a special jail used only for those who are involved in the sex industry, including pimps, brothel owners, and traffickers. According to Ann, the jail is officially referred to as a "rehabilitation center." However, much like the incarceration center for drug addicts mentioned earlier, activity categorized by jail authorities under the title of "rehabilitation" consists almost entirely of forced labor, such as the production of lightbulbs. In addition, women who arrive at the jail have their heads shaven, following the assumption that if they are not physically attractive, they will not be able to engage in prostitution. The situation is further complicated by the fact that the women are often mistreated and harassed by the police. Apart from being jailed, women have the option of attempting to run away from their owners. Indeed, Ann noted that the more resourceful of them do occasionally escape. However, they encounter further hardship upon returning to their homes. Often they must hide their past; otherwise their families will reject them.

Until very recently, before being sentenced, it was common practice to lead "shame parades" in which a long line of women accused of prostitution were marched through the streets of a city, wearing brightly colored shirts. In a 2006 campaign against prostitution in Shenzhen, one hundred women were marched through the streets in bright-orange clothing, while their names were called out over a loudspeaker. In a nationwide campaign in 2010, police in various locations used a variety of public shaming methods as punishment and deterrent for prostitutes, such as parades, kneeling in the street, and sending notices to families.

Significantly, both the 2006 parade and the 2010 campaigns were severely criticized by many Chinese citizens, who claimed that public humiliation is morally wrong. As a result, the government eventually decided to ban shame parades (Watts 2006). The director of the Public Security Bureau has even declared that the word "prostitute" will no longer be used. The women will be referred to more politely as "fallen women" (Zhao Hongyi 2010). The hostile response of the Chinese public and the government's subsequent ban on the parades are a prime example of the inadequacy of the state's methods of addressing social problems (*South China Morning Post* 2013). Unable or unwilling to deal with the magnitude of the problem, local authorities slipped into pre-reform, Cultural Revolution–style methods of public humiliation, based on the belief that shaming could solve the problem of prostitution. Since the idea of public shaming is based on the active participation of the onlookers, the public's role as indignant viewers is crucial. However, in the past thirty years, the Chinese public has become increasingly aware of a human-rights discourse that does not justify public shaming. Thus, the method has backfired: instead of generating emotional and moral outrage at the women, the anger of many people was directed toward the authorities.

In contrast to the shame parades, Eden workers begin their work by asking prostitutes in their workplaces how they got there. For many of the women, this is the first time anyone has shown any interest in hearing their personal story. Thus, the rehabilitation is more than simply providing a safe house or even an alternative profession. It involves a form of counseling allowing the women to deal with their traumatic past. As such, it runs contrary to the prevalent social ambience of concealment and shame encountered by the women, often even within their own families. Moreover, rather than Eden workers denouncing the women they see as immoral or corrupt, they speak of the women as victims, trying to begin a process of both internal and external personal change.

The content of the process offered by Eden is unmistakably Christian in nature, and the acceptance of Christianity is part of the process of rehabilitation. In a DVD describing Eden, Ann says, "We saw girls receiving Jesus, right there on the street. We saw girls receiving prayer, right there on the street." She continues by claiming that Eden has succeeded in "planting a small church," with about twenty girls coming to worship on Sundays. With Ann's words in the background, the girls are shown praying and reading the Bible. Throughout the film, the connection between the aid offered and Christianity is clearly presented, including Christian background music, numerous references to the Bible, and toward the end, a shot of Jesus on the cross.

Like Michael's rehab program, Eden Ministry is not officially registered with the state. Nevertheless, it has existed for several years and has a stated vision of establishing a women's shelter in every major city in China. Indeed, Eden is in the process of attempting to expand outside Yunnan by opening a branch in Shanghai and possibly in Hong Kong, a major destination for trafficking of women from China. Despite the exposure given to unsavory realties of present-day China, Eden activists are permitted to work, and they feel comfortable enough to have a shop in a public area where one can easily obtain written and audio material explaining their activity. In this case, relatively open proselytizing is ignored by the authorities. From Ann's perspective, state tolerance of Eden's activity reflects the fact that Eden deals with the marginalized of society—people who are of no real concern to the authorities. She said, "If we were dealing with university students or children, they would be on us like a ton of bricks."

Adding to Ann's reasoning, I would argue that local authorities simply have no other method of dealing with prostitution and the related issue of rampant HIV. Previous attempts to root out the problem through shame were based on outdated social norms. Thus, the advantages of the approach advocated by Eden far outweigh its direct financial benefit. Like Michael's café and the International Clinic, Eden introduces therapeutic knowledge and a holistic outlook that is highly effective and badly needed. It is unique in that it attempts to address the entire sex industry and create a multifaceted answer for those who are enslaved by the system by providing safe houses, therapy, professional training, and of course a newfound faith.

Conclusion: Replacing the Welfare State

In this chapter, I have described the work of a number of organizations and individuals active in the fields of welfare, therapy, and medicine. Many of them work among the marginal of society—the most obvious victims of privatization and the dismantling of the welfare state. FBO workers provide aid and counseling, framed within a religious ideology: they are all strong believers in helping society's downtrodden, providing aid as a religious duty following the law "love thy neighbor" (Leviticus 19:18). They are often also highly critical of certain elements of Chinese culture and perceive their faith as an antidote to the fundamental problems of Chinese society. In the examples presented here, many of those who came for aid ended up accepting both its physical and its spiritual content.

Examining the state's relative lenience and its willingness to allow FBOs to expand their activity, a number of reasons can be discerned. The first and most basic reason for state tolerance is the direct financial and physical benefits of FBO activity. Simply put, allowing them to take care of certain social problems saves the authorities money. The most obvious example in this regard is the International Clinic, providing care for people who would otherwise be uncared for or perhaps cared for at the authorities' expense. Furthermore, the prevalence of addiction, prostitution, and the related issues of HIV and women trafficking places a heavy financial burden on the state. Despite the fact that the organizations discussed in this chapter are fairly small, it seems that the financial benefits of their activities override the potential danger posed by the high conversion rate among Yunnan's socially marginalized populations.

However, the financial dimension alone cannot explain the nature of Christian aid activity. Tolerance is also related to the importance of knowledge introduced in the realms of therapy, welfare, and rehabilitation, in the context of Yunnan's limited social services. The need for therapeutic and rehabilitative knowledge of this sort is a testament to the leap Chinese society has made into the world system. The jailing of addicts and prostitutes has proved insufficient, and the shame parades have incurred public indignation. Likewise, the privatization of the medical system, coupled with the traditionally authoritative position of doctors, poses a potential for social discord and anger. Indeed, the gap between the puritan moralism and order of the revolutionary past and the openness and chaos of the economically liberal present may be too large for Chinese authorities to bridge alone. Combined with the massive plans of development and the attempt to turn Kunming into the financial capital of Southeast Asia, more advanced social services are increasingly necessary.

In addition, the work done by people like Michael, Dr. Horace, and Ann serves to ease the social tensions created by addiction, poverty, and prostitution. By taking addicts off the street and representing and providing aid to those who cannot afford to pay fines or medical bills, Christian FBO workers are taking the pressure off state authorities. Indeed, the official praise of organizations like Bless China International may be seen in this light. FBOs are more than happy to replace the government in the realm of welfare, thus both allowing and legitimizing the state's encouragement of the privatization process. While Christians often voice their personal criticism of Chinese health policy, education, and welfare services, most Christian workers I spoke to were extremely supportive of privatization and minimal state involvement in social services, both in China and in their home countries.[11]

The introduction of Western knowledge is, in many ways, a modern rendition of an older theme. The scientific, medical, and educational knowledge introduced by pre-1949 missionaries was largely embraced by the CCP and is lauded today by many Chinese scholars as a major contribution to China's modernization project. Current missionaries provide aid and at the same time assert the superiority of their value system through the promotion of therapeutic and holistic approaches to social issues. FBO workers like Michael, Dr. Horace, and Ann attempt to address the roots of addiction; provide their patients with financial, social, and spiritual aid; and deal with all aspects of the sex industry. At the same time, to varying degrees, they facilitate deep personal change, by associating the process of rehabilitation, healing, and change with a specific form of spirituality: the establishment of an intimate relationship with God or the acceptance of Jesus as one's savior.

In the years prior to the pandemic, involvement of FBOs in Yunnan seemed to be on the rise. As Michael told me at our last meeting, a larger Christian organization has been invited to work in Yunnan with addicts. Likewise, Eden Ministry has opened a similar project in Shanghai, and Bless China International personnel are active in a variety of fields throughout Yunnan, in Dehong, Diqing, Kunming, Nujiang, Wenshan, and Xishuangbanna. However, as Michael noted, and as the turbulent history of the International Clinic reveals, the position of these organizations in Yunnan is still precarious.

The connection made in this chapter between the practical needs of the state and the ability of foreign Christians to provide those needs highlights the circumstantial and unstable nature of missionary-state relationship. To a certain extent, state cooperation with Christian initiatives in the realm of welfare is reminiscent of the late Republican era, when, despite a tendency toward anti-Christian policies in the 1920s, the challenges that China faced during the 1930s led the nationalist government to seek the aid and assistance of Christian organizations in various relief efforts (Junio 2017, 346–47). Similarly, Christian involvement in welfare today is a mark of the transitional nature of the reform era in Yunnan, as the province moves toward greater development. Will the authorities be as lenient when Christian aid and knowledge are no longer in need?

Chapter 5

TRANSLATING CULTURE

Missionary Linguists and the Construction of Authenticity

> When the day of Pentecost had come, they were all together in one place. And suddenly from heaven there came a sound like the rush of a violent wind, and it filled the entire house where they were sitting. Divided tongues, as of fire, appeared among them, and a tongue rested on each of them. All of them were filled with the Holy Spirit and began to speak in other languages, as the Spirit gave them ability. Now there were devout Jews from every nation under heaven living in Jerusalem. And at this sound the crowd gathered and was bewildered, because each one heard them speaking in the native language of each. Amazed and astonished, they asked, "Are not all these who are speaking Galileans? And how is it that we hear, each of us, in our own native language?"
>
> —ACTS 2:1-19

Despite the fact that only one-third of Yunnan's population is non-Han, ethnic minorities feature prominently in both official images and popular perceptions of contemporary Yunnan and its rapidly expanding tourist industry. The renewed popularity and commodification of ethnic markers has not gone unnoticed by Christian activists. Much like the state, they emphasize ethnic costume, singing, and dancing as the major markers of ethnicity (Gladney 1994, 95; Harrell 1996, 27; Blum 2001, 83). However, missionaries are active in another cultural field of great importance, that of language preservation and translation.

Language preservation has been intertwined with missionary efforts among minority people since prerevolutionary times, culminating in the invention of a number of writing systems (Huang Xing 1992, 75; Lemoine 1989, 7; Tien 1993, 45–46). A number of scholars have described missionary-linguistic activity, such as the translation of the Bible into local languages, as an "activity of identity building and maintenance as well as a means of liberation for communities" (Maxey 2010, 175). As the story of the Pentecost in this chapter's epigraph indicates, Maxey also invokes the faith that God's will is to have his words spoken in all of humankind's languages.

Indeed, translatability may be seen as the key to Protestant success. The advantage of translation lies not only in the ability to bring the message to the masses; the use of local language is an act of "validating the vernacular culture" (Dunch 2002, 318). Thus, translating Christian texts into ethnic languages suggests recognition of the importance of the local and ethnic in the face of the all-embracing and expanding Han Chinese standard. As the space created by translation is one that is often denied by the state, language preservation may be seen as an act of defiance, countering the process of officially sanctioned assimilation.

Missionary efforts in the field of language today are conducted with the intended goal of affirming local minority cultures and protecting them from assimilation into the Han majority. Accordingly, missionaries celebrate ethnic-language preservation as a mark of cultural survival. Activity in the realm of ethnic preservation serves to attract converts by creating an equation between Christianity and ethnic preservation, positioning the missionaries and the religion they represent as the guardians of ethnic culture and the key to rejuvenation and transcendence. However, viewing contemporary Christian linguistic work as a challenge to the state and to the predominance of Han hegemony is inaccurate. While missionaries do provide an alternative space for ethnic expression, they do so in ways that closely correspond with state interests.

The fostering of ethnic languages is often presented and perceived as a means of aiding minority children to eventually acquire Chinese and integrate into the school system, rather than a goal in and of itself. Through language, missionaries play an important role in a process described by Chih-yu Shih as "assimilation through ethnicity," a goal achieved through the use of "ethnic language as a stepping stone to the eventual adaptation of Mandarin in teaching, with the ultimate goal of assimilation into the mainstream culture" (2002, 166). The promotion of minority languages as a means of learning Chinese has been labeled "Transitional Bilingual Education" (Tsung, Wang, and Zhang 2012, 108) or "crutch philosophy," implying that ethnic language is used as a crutch, later to be discarded (Dwyer 1998, 80; see also Hartch 2006).

A similar process of constructing ethnicity to enhance state dominance is being carried out by Christian missionaries and linguists. Missionary focus on language preservation may be understood as an attempt to redefine and restructure the nature of ethnic culture and identity: by emphasizing the centrality of language as the paramount expression of ethnic identity, missionaries attempt to reorient minority culture around a linguistic core while deemphasizing or discarding other elements of ethnic culture, such as traditional rituals and myths. Linguistic activity is in line with the trend described throughout this book, namely, the convergence of contemporary missionary and state objectives in the realm of ethnicity.

It is worth recalling that in China, the issue of language and particularly writing is intimately connected with the advancement of culture, a connection reflected in the multilayered meaning of the term *wenhua*. *Wenhua* refers to the process of becoming cultured, a process closely associated with literacy and the use of a writing system (Ping 1995; Poa and LaPolla 2007, 341). The term also relates to an array of practices including "studying the classics, practicing poetry, reading and writing, participation in rituals etc." (Iredale et al. 2001, 52): "In a society which reveres the written canon, the existence of an orthography and body of written materials is taken as indicative of some degree of cultural sophistication. Conversely, national minorities without orthographies were and are still considered backward. One frequently hears members of orthographied minority groups (as well as Hans) refer to minorities without orthographies as 'without civilization'" (Dwyer 1998, 72).

Contemporary Christian missionaries and linguists are active in language preservation in many locations across Southwest China. Some focus primarily on the translation of parts of the Bible, hymns, or other Christian material like *The Jesus Film*, while others are involved in the documentation and analysis of ethnic languages, producing dictionaries and thesauruses with no direct relationship to Christian theology or the Bible.[1] Christian linguists often emphasize their work as a central element of mission, intended to fulfill the "Great Commission" by making disciples from all the nations (Luke 24:47; Acts 1:8). Thus, the task of world evangelization includes a vision in which members of every ethnolinguistic group receive a local version of the gospel, stressing the idea that the gospel is not addressed to any given ethnos. As one missionary scholar has written, "Christ expects ethnic people group evangelizers to communicate the gospel in each ethnic group's heart language.... If we want to identify clearly with a people group, we will learn their heart language. The choice of their heart language will let them know we came specifically to address them" (Slack 2011). Indeed, missionaries often view language as the central criterion for defining ethnicity. Paul Hattaway's *Operation China* contains entries for over four hundred ethnic groups, including fourteen subgroups of the Han, corresponding to linguistic divisions. Hattaway's system of ethnic classification illustrates what Harrell has termed "the hegemony of definition" (1996, 7). Accordingly, the guidelines of any classification system are an essential element of a "civilizing project." The hegemony of definition is clearly discernible when language is concerned, with minority languages defined and standardized by the central government and all major historical and linguistic work published in Beijing (Dwyer 1998, 73). Hattaway's linguistically centered view of ethnicity may be seen as a challenge to the state's own classification system, according to which China consist of only fifty-six nationalities/ethnic groups (*minzu*). In contrast, Paul Hattaway's (2000) contains over four hundred ethnolinguistic groups. Yet, while language preservation could conceivably be perceived as a challenge to the state's ethnic policies and classification, contemporary linguistic activity in Yunnan is relatively unhindered and is often conducted with state approval.

To understand missionary language activity, we must turn to the Protestant notion of translatability—the idea that the Bible can and should be translated into every language, an idea described as "the source of success of Christianity across cultures" (Sanneh 2008, 51). Beyond the functional need to make the Bible accessible to all people, translatability is a theological principle referred to by Lamin Sanneh as a "fundamental concession to the vernacular ... based on an understanding of language as a purely practical element of a given culture, holding no intrinsic religious or mystical value and opposing the idea of a central sacred language or a single authoritative translation" (53). As such, translatability is an idea of powerful flexibility, empowering vernacular languages and local cultures and at the same time investing the translator-missionary with the authority to reinterpret and remold cultural history and myth.

Examining missionary approaches to ethnic languages and the concept of translatability reveals the complex balance missionaries must maintain between ethnic preservation and cultural change. Regarding Bible translation work conducted in Mexico, Todd Hartch argues that "vernacular translations of the Bible were only effective evangelistically if their converts remained committed in some measure to their ethnic roots" (Hartch 2006, 129). Thus, as I have shown, missionaries actively reshape and deethnicize minority cultures. At the same time, for missionary work to be effective, it must not discard ethnicity altogether, as doing so would eliminate its own legitimacy as a means for the furthering of ethnic preservation in the face of assimilation. Accordingly, missionaries attempt to advance a double process of change and preservation, simultaneously emphasizing and remolding ethnic identity.

Ethnic Languages in Reform-Era Yunnan

To understand current activity among Yunnan's minorities in the realm of language, one must consider the precarious position of minority languages in the reform era. As in other parts of the world, the use of indigenous languages in China is currently in rapid decline. According to the *Ethnologue*, China has 128 languages "in trouble" and another 32 defined as "dying."[2]

The disappearance of local languages reflects state policies going back to the early twentieth century. In minority regions, the use of local ethnic languages in the education system has been repressed for decades, beginning in the Republican era, when students were penalized for using their native languages in school (Hansen 1999, 49). At the beginning of the Maoist period, ethnic languages were encouraged and even celebrated as part of the Communist policy of constructing ethnic autonomies. However, at the same time, ethnic amalgamation (*ronghe*) was a central policy objective, and the introduction of Chinese in peripheral regions like Yunnan was an essential part of the Communist "civilizing mission" (Harrell 1996). At the height of Maoism, during the Great Leap Forward and the Cultural Revolution, all languages other than Mandarin were considered worthless at best (Shih 2002, 171). In many places, ethnic languages were seen as a mark of local nationalism that must be uprooted. Mandarin was taught as a means of advancing ethnic minorities and promoting national unity and as "a better means of learning Mao Zedong thought" (Hansen 1999, 59).

Since the beginning of the reform era, language policies have been significantly modified. Bilingual education was reintroduced in the 1980s with far-reaching goals. In the 1990s, a backlash occurred, and many of the earlier decisions regarding wide-scale bilingualism were not implemented (Kolas 2003). Nevertheless, since the 1990s, over ten thousand schools in minority regions all over China have offered bilingual classes (McCarthy 2009, 124). In Tibet and Inner Mongolia, it is now possible to study in Tibetan or Mongolian through high school (Dwyer 1998, 70). The same is true of Korean for the Korean minority in Northeast China and a number of minorities in the Southwest (Ross 2005, 26; Shih 2002, 175). However, despite liberalization, Chinese is still heavily promoted, and Putonghua is legally sanctioned and promoted as the national language (Zhou 2003, 36). Moreover, in recent years, Maoist-style language policies have been strongly implemented in Xinjiang (Millward and Peterson 2020) and to a lesser degree in Inner Mongolia (Davidson 2020).

Indeed, focusing on languages other than Chinese comes at a price. While serving China's image of a multinational state, it stands in contrast with the assumption that schools should be vehicles for social mobility (Ross 2005, 26). As Uradyn E. Bulag has noted, focusing on Mongolian has "made students 'dependent' on Chinese society more than ever; it made them largely 'non-productive,' that is, economically, politically, and even socially incompetent citizens in a Chinese dominated society, that, from the 1980s onward was increasingly market oriented" (2003, 753; see also Borchigud 1995). According to the director of the Summer Institute of Linguistics (SIL) in Kunming, whose activity is described later in this chapter, the only possible profession for students who have been educated only in their ethnic language is to become language teachers (Sean, interview, October 10, 2012). Accordingly, even in bilingual schools, ethnic languages are often taught in a very limited scope, with all major subjects taught in Chinese:[3] "In recent decades, large numbers of previously isolated minority people have migrated to areas where they come in close contact with the Han and Chinese language must be spoken. Even minority people living far from Han centers are increasingly exposed to the products of Chinese commercial culture, such as television and films. At the same time, many Han have moved into minority areas, often becoming the majority of the population. Thus, it would appear that these forces of cultural homogenization have done more to diminish ethnic languages than Maoist era assimilationist policies" (Poa and LaPolla 2007, 341).

Missionary Linguists: Protestantism and Translatability

The threat of extinction hanging over many of China's ethnic languages has led to intense linguistic activity in China's Southwest. Much of the activity is conducted by evangelical organizations, exemplifying the deep connection between Protestant missionary work and the concept of translatability.

According to Sanneh, Protestant confidence in the ability to translate the Bible into any given tongue has been a central feature of the resounding success in the evangelization of Africa. Sanneh compares the Christian tenet of "scriptural translation" with the Islamic theology of Arabic as a divine language and the Koran as untranslatable. Islamic theological concepts are closely related to their specific Arabic term. In Islam, religion is more than the texts' perceived message: the means by which that message is conveyed are of crucial importance.[4] Thus, the Islamic mission is a language mission—it includes the dissemination of a holy book and a holy tongue and works to "disfranchise the vernacular" (Sanneh 2008, 212). In contrast, the verses from the book of Acts in this chapter's epigraph reveal the way in which Christianity from its very beginning was defined as a religion of many languages, none of them exclusive or holy (Sanneh 2008, 213–15).

A radical variation on Protestant notions of translatability can be found in Pentecostal theology, a movement named after the event described in the same verses from Acts. According to Philip Jenkins, "Pentecostal beliefs rely on direct spiritual revelations that supplement or even replace biblical authority" (2011, 63). The transcendence of language is manifested in the Pentecostal practice of "speaking in tongues" or "glossolalia": a spontaneous outburst of unintelligible speech, delivered by believers in a trance-like mode, sometimes referred to as "primal language," aimed at "lifting the curse of Babel" (Cox 1995, 87–97). Moreover, removing all barriers of language and translation is an expression of the primacy of experience over language and conventional religion.

Early Protestant missionaries to China viewed the willingness to translate the Bible as a mark of their progressive thinking, as contrasted with the Catholics, who clung to the Latin of the "Dark Ages" (Reinders 2004, 77). Protestants ridiculed mystical notions of a holy language or the use of mantras to attain spiritual goals, viewing them as a mark of backwardness, diametrically opposed to what they perceived as the rational, straightforward, and accessible message of the Bible. In many ways, these attitudes have persisted among missionaries today, who view the formalized and ceremonial use of language or repetitive mantras as empty ritualism. Faith in the translatability of scripture "across time, language and cultural differences" (Smalley 1991, 85) is expressed in the words and actions of many Christian workers in present-day Yunnan, involved with different minority people, speaking a variety of languages.

One indication of evangelical attitudes toward language today can be seen in the preaching style of a sermon delivered in the foreign Fellowship in Kunming in a visit I discuss at length in chapter 6. Throughout the sermon, the preacher made many references to biblical verses. However, after a while, I noticed an inconsistency between the verses as he read them and what was projected on the screen behind him. While the projected verses contained the words "thou," "thee," or "sayeth," the preacher was simplifying and essentializing the text as he spoke, omitting words he viewed as superfluous. The sermon is an example of the particular form of sanctity held by the biblical text. It is related only loosely to the exact wording of the verses and based on the idea that the simple, straightforward message can easily be ascertained from the text. While the message of the text is revered, the text itself, in its many details, seems to hold no intrinsic value, nor does it contain multiple levels of meaning.[5] It is, first and foremost, a vehicle for inspiration and renewed faith.

Another expression of the concept of translatability can be found in a missionary tool aimed at capturing the main axis of the Christian understanding of the Bible, called "Creation to Christ" (often referred to as "C2C"). It was introduced to me by my old classmate Peter, mentioned in the introduction, who used it occasionally in his work among the Yi. Despite being translated differently into many languages worldwide, the text of C2C follows certain general guidelines. It is divided into eight parts and is meant to be recited by heart, beginning with the words "I'd like to tell you a story" (*wo yao gei nimen jing yige gushi*), followed by a description of creation, paradise, sin, and eventually the crucifixion and resurrection of Jesus. It ends with the formula, "Would you also like to, through Jesus, return and sit beside God and be reconciled with him?" (*ni yao bu yao tongguo yesu huidao shangdi shenbian, gen ta hehao?*). If the answer is yes, the listener is offered the chance to pray together with the storyteller (C2C, document in Chinese, received June 14, 2010). The oral version is accompanied with a set of illustrations printed on a single page, which can be folded in a variety of ways. Peter and Rebecca used the C2C occasionally in conversation "when it felt right" but rarely made use of the pictures. Other missionaries in their community used it often and had memorized it in both Chinese and Yi (Peter, interview, June 13, 2010).

In the International Mission Board website dedicated to missionary work in sub-Saharan Africa, a number of interesting guidelines for telling the story are offered:

> Be simple—Use words that the common villager can understand (craft the story) specific to your people group. One . . . has no idea what is meant by graveyard since they bury their dead in their homes. For this reason, when telling the story, we say that the man lived in the place where the dead are buried. Most religious words that we know well, mean nothing to the Africans. Even if your translator can translate them, the villagers will have no idea what is meant. Instead of eternal life, we say live forever. Accept Jesus into your heart = Become a follower of Jesus. Try to learn as much as you can about the worldview of you people.[6]

The website also provides instructions regarding the simplification and shortening of the text, including the use of no more than three new terms per story, minimizing the use of names, and shortening the story to a maximum of eight minutes so that it may be "learned and reproduced."

The most interesting element of the C2C is its constantly dynamic nature, varying from culture to culture. In the Chinese version given to me by Peter as well as the standard English version found online, the story line includes a description of creation, the Garden of Eden, and original sin, followed by the life of Jesus.[7] There is no mention of the Patriarchs, the people of Israel, or the Exodus from Egypt, all of which are present in the African text. A number of websites stress that the text is not to be handed out or even memorized but rather delivered orally in accordance with a given audience. Thus, the C2C may be seen as a master key of translation. By avoiding the text altogether and depending fully on an oral and simplified version of Christian teleology, missionaries like Peter and Rebecca attempt to introduce the story of the Bible into any given cultural context.

A similar form of translation process was described to me by missionaries in Yunnan and elsewhere. Translation is based on an attempt to identify what one missionary has referred to as "keys and bridges": local cultural and religious concepts that bear resemblance to certain elements in the biblical narrative or in Christian theology. Similarly, I was told that one missionary focused on oral renditions of approximately forty Bible stories intended to capture the essence of the Bible (Scotty, interview, July 7, 2010). The stories were translated several times into a given language with the aid of Wycliffe Bible Translations workers and then conveyed orally to locals. Each story was then relayed to an audience of native speakers a number of times, before a final version was decided on. The goal of the translation, storytelling, and retranslation was not to reach ultimate accuracy but rather to pinpoint the cultural norms regarding the terminology, the emotions, and even the identity of the storyteller to find the version with the most appeal to listeners. Thus, the most effective translations are those that are able to shed light on the listeners' own culture by explaining traditional concepts such as deities and myths in a way that corresponds with Christian theology.

In recent years, the idea of Bible translation has come under serious inspection and criticism, part of the broader critique of missionary work as cultural imperialism. In a 1998 issue of *Semeia*, a liberal Christian journal dealing with issues of biblical criticism, Tina Pippin and Randel Bailey attacked the concept of biblical translation, claiming that "the biblical texts we have are all corrupted" and adding that "translation as evangelism functioned ideologically as a tool of colonization. . . . Translation is a violent act where there is a violation of another people's culture" (1996, 3). A similar critique focuses on missionary work in Asia: "[they have] appropriated the power to represent the Oriental, to translate and explain his thoughts and acts not only to Europeans and Americans but also to the Orientals themselves" (Sugirtharajah 1996, 9). Both authors stress the power and authority that the act of translation holds for the translator, as one who is able to define and reform cultural concepts and symbols.

In fact, the image of the missionary linguist and translator as cultural hero is a central feature of the Christian experience in Yunnan. For early Protestant missionaries, translation was a practical tool, driven by the need to make the Christian message easily accessible to the masses. On China's ethnic periphery, translators assumed a broader role, eventually using their linguistic skills not merely for the purpose of translation but also for the task of cultural-linguistic preservation.

For many converts, the introduction of the new, missionary-devised writing systems (Huang Xing 1992, 75) meant becoming literate for the first time, an event of huge significance in the Chinese context (Lemoine 1989, 7). The symbolic importance of the new scripts is evidenced in the way they were publicly displayed. In the early days of missionary involvement

Fig. 1 Samuel Pollard's grave in Shimenkan. Photo: Gideon Elazar.

in Yunnan, Christian minority women could sometimes be seen carrying scriptures in a special sack, symbolizing the double achievement of faith in Christianity and literacy. Thus, "to be able to read and write became one of the worldly motives for being converted" (Tien 1993, 45–46).

During the first years of the PRC, the development of scripts was continued by the state. In the 1950s, fourteen new scripts, all based on the Latin alphabet, were devised for the use of minorities, some of them intended to replace the "old" missionary scripts. Their use was suspended in the late 1950s as part of the Great Leap Forward and the Campaign Against Local Nationalism and only resumed in 1978 (White 1992, 52). However, their success was limited compared to the relatively prevalent missionary-devised scripts (Huang Xing 1992, 83). The Miao, for example, rejected an alternative Latin alphabet offered by the authorities, explaining their refusal as resistance to the state's attempts to deny their achievement in the realm of education and culture, achievements attained through the missionaries (Lemoine 1989, 7).

Thus, the missionary scripts and to a certain degree the script inventors have become key symbols of ethnic identity (Ortner 1973). In my encounters with the Hua Miao in Yunnan, I discovered that the issue of literacy and the image of Samuel Pollard still loom large. To the Christian Miao I met, Pollard and the other Christians who converted the Miao are cultural heroes. As Zhang, the Hua Miao minister in the Wuding area mentioned in chapter 2, told me, "Before they [the missionaries] came, we had no culture [wenhua]. We had nothing." Likewise, in Shimenkan, Pollard's elaborate grave is well tended and serves as a site of pilgrimage for Miao and non-Miao Christian visitors (L. Sun 2007).

From a missionary perspective, the Pollard script is viewed as a great success. Not only have the Miao acquired a powerful identity marker, but the script is also closely associated with Christianity. Indeed, the writing is not part of Miao school curriculum but is taught exclusively in churches. The fact that the Christian Miao are more closely associated with the preservation of the writing system than their non-Christian kin seems to reaffirm the idea that Christianity is an effective means toward cultural preservation. From the language perspective, Miao Christians can pride themselves on being "more Miao" than their non-Christians relatives. A similar situation can be found among the Lisu, whose script was developed jointly by a Lisu from Burma and the English missionary James Fraser in 1915. Since the early 1990s, the script has been recognized and promoted by the Chinese authorities as the official Lisu alphabet. Nevertheless, according to Zhan, the Christian Lisu mentioned in chapter 2, the script is not studied in schools but rather disseminated through local churches (interview, May 5, 2010).

Today, missionary scripts have been widely accepted by the state. According to the director of the Summer Institute of Linguistics in Kunming, a number of years ago, state authorities in cooperation with SIL created a code number for writing the scripts in the Windows computer operating system. To differentiate between the missionary scripts and the Latin-based systems devised by the state, the terms "Old Lisu script" and "Old Miao script" were given to the Fraser and Pollard alphabets, respectively, lending them an aura of authenticity despite the fact that they are only a century old. Yet, official recognition of the missionary scripts does not subtract from the hegemonic position of the Chinese language: "The writing systems created by the missionaries can be used freely because freedom of religion is guaranteed by the constitution of China. However, significant advances in education and participation in society remain closely linked to mastery of Chinese characters and literacy in Chinese" (Huang Xing 1992, 84).

The Summer Institute of Linguistics

Reacting to the decline of ethnic languages described earlier and following the example of Pollard, Fraser, and others, Christian linguists are active today throughout Yunnan Province, with many working for the nonprofit organization the Summer Institute of Linguistics. As of 2002, SIL is one of the world's largest Christian NGOs, with over five thousand linguists working in over fifty nations worldwide (Hartch 2006, xv). It holds a formal consultative status in UNESCO and publishes the much-respected

Ethnologue, which is currently in its eighteenth edition. SIL workers in China are engaged in compiling dictionaries and vocabulary books in a variety of locations, encouraging literacy, and promoting language education. As the organization's activities are for the most part limited to linguistics and language preservation, SIL is legally recognized by the government. Up to 2020 the organization maintained a working relationship with the Guizhou Minorities University and holds a main office in Kunming.

SIL's religious affiliation is of a subtle, almost hidden nature. Its website contains a single passing reference to the fact that the organization is "faith-based" and dedicated to language and culture, with the stated belief that languages and cultures are "part of God's creation."[8] It specifically states that SIL is dedicated to scientific research and does not engage in the translation of scripture or proselytizing. However, SIL's sister organization, the Wycliffe Bible Translators, is an openly evangelical organization dedicated to Bible translations. The connection between the two organizations is not denied but is understated for practical reasons; while the Wycliffe Bible society appeals to churches, SIL can function easily as a secular organization in places like China (Smalley 1991, 78).

In the past, SIL workers have come under much criticism for the double nature of their organization. On the one hand, SIL has been criticized by evangelicals for not devoting enough to the missionary project, focusing entirely on language rather than conversions (Smalley 1991, 78). At the same time, it is accused by others of being a masked missionary organization and portrayed by anthropologists and social activists as an enemy of social change, responsible for the destruction of local cultures and ethnocide, particularly for its activities in Latin America (Hartch 2006, 148; for an example of anti-SIL writings, see Hvalkof and Aaby 1981).

With the rapid progress of Chinese in the reform era and the opening of virtually all parts of Yunnan to foreign visitors, SIL workers are increasingly found working throughout the region. Some projects in Yunnan feature prominently on SIL's website, while others are conducted more discreetly (Sean, interview, October 10, 2012). The SIL East Asia site features many articles regarding a variety of languages and dialects and reports of books published and linguistic research being conducted. Indeed, it would seem that most SIL activities, including the bilingual school project described later in this chapter, are unrelated to missionary work and not aimed at directly producing converts. At the same time, as my description of activity among the Bouyei in this chapter shows, SIL/Wycliffe workers are occasionally involved in the translation of religious texts.

The organization's showcase project is a ten-year program titled the "Zero Barrier Bilingual Education Program." It is conducted in two locations in Yunnan among the Dai and Bai minorities, with a third project among the Dong of Guizhou. The stated goal of the program is to "help students to learn Han Chinese easier by first learning their mother tongue language," but it is also used to "raise students' self-confidence and ethnic pride."[9] The program was officially launched in 2010 in full coordination with the Yunnan Provincial Education Association Minority Education Committee and the Yunnan Provincial Ethnic Affairs Commission Office for Yunnan Minority Languages Committee. By 2018, all responsibility had been transferred to local county authorities (Billard and Billard, n.d.). What follows is an examination of the Bai bilingual school, located in Jianchuan County, in the Dali Bai Autonomous Prefecture. It should be noted that education levels in Yunnan are well below the national average: only 5.96 years of schooling, compared with the national average of 7.27. Moreover, within the province, there is a ten-year development gap between minority and Han communities (Tsung, Wang, and Zhang 2012, 105).

The bilingual school in Jianchuan was not founded by SIL. It was established under the auspices of the Dali local government and at the instigation of local Bai activists as part of a general reform in minority education in the 1990s. The area of Jianchuan, located approximately halfway between Dali and Lijiang, was chosen to host the bilingual project, as the region is over 90 percent Bai, and as much as 60 percent of the population does not speak Chinese (McCarthy 2009, 121). The school was founded with two major goals. To begin with, bilingual education provided between the ages of four and six was intended to assist local Bai children in their integration to the strictly Mandarin state schooling system. Previously, children from Bai-speaking homes found it difficult to participate in classes, and as a result, the dropout rate was quite high. The school devised a system by which children studied in Bai using the state-devised Bai alphabet, thus providing the children with literacy in Bai and simultaneously acquainting them with a pinyin-like writing system, which could later be used for the study of Chinese.[10] At the same time, local Bai educators emphasized the project's importance as an expression of "the right to nationality autonomy" (McCarthy 2009, 126).

Despite initial success, the project ran into trouble within a few years of its establishment. Most importantly, the Dali government refused to continue funding for the school. The reason cited was that the emphasis on Bai education and the use of Bai script had come to be seen as a step backward for the relatively advanced Bai minority: as the overall aim of the authorities is the successful integration of Bai children into the general education system, focusing on Bai was considered by many to be a waste of funds. Interestingly, similar opposition to the project was voiced by some of the Bai themselves. As the advancement of a given group often implies a process of Hanization, many ordinary people seemed to perceive the study of Bai as a mark of inferiority. In addition, some feared that by advocating the study of Bai, they may be labeled "local nationalists," a label implying secessionist aspirations, while others voiced the opinion that it would be wiser to teach the children English (a similar point is mentioned in Bulag 2003). Funding for the project was suspended, later to be temporarily resumed under the pressure of local, mostly older, Bai educators. Nevertheless, by 2007, the project seemed "moribund," according to Susan McCarthy (2009, 127). However, shortly after the publication of McCarthy's work, the bilingual program was revived, this time under the auspices and funding of SIL. The entrance of a foreign NGO with a Christian background into the realm of education, previously maintained within the firm grip of the state, demonstrates the extent of privatization policies in the reform era.

In October 2012, I contacted the SIL office in Kunming and arranged to visit the school in Jianchuan. The school is located some forty minutes' drive from Jianchuan city in the small village of Shilong in the area of Shibao mountain, not far from the town of Shaxi. This region is considered the heartland of Bai culture, and the mountain is the scene of an annual Bai song festival. The director of SIL in Kunming arranged for me to meet Yang, the school director, who offered to drive me from his office in the city to the school in the countryside. According to Yang, my interest in seeing the school was not unusual in the least. In fact, he had taken out numerous delegations of visitors from a variety of countries. In addition to foreign visitors, the school also hosts many government officials, listed on the SIL East Asia website, in a photo book of the schools in Jianchuan and Jinhong.[11]

The school is a preschool project in which children between the ages of four and six prepare for primary school, located in an adjacent building. As Yang explained, studies in the primary school are in Chinese only. However, that year (2012), the school was planning on introducing a number of Bai-language classes into the curriculum of the lower grades, an accomplishment that Yang was quite proud of. For those who wish to continue their studies beyond primary school, the closest middle school is located in Jianchuan, and the high school is in Xiaguan (Dali), approximately a three-hour drive south. Interestingly, while most students in the school live in the surrounding Bai villages, several originate from poor Yi and Lisu communities farther away and reside at the school during the week. Despite their different ethnic identity, the school is a good option for them, and they study the Bai language along with everybody else. The attendance of children from particularly poor areas reflects another of the project's stated goals, to promote education for those who ordinarily cannot afford it.

Upon my arrival, a teacher was assigned to show me around the school. She explained that in the past, local Bai-speaking children understood little of what occurred in class and were afraid of participating in school classes. The bilingual preschool helps them feel more confident and prepared upon entering the first grade. At the same time, my host added that the bilingual project was also aimed at the preservation of Bai culture and language. Accordingly, the school stresses Bai literacy programs both for the children and for their parents, offering special evening classes for adults, teaching them to read the Bai pinyin. Some of the adults who attend are already literate in Chinese; others are not. My host took me around the school, displaying the neatly organized school equipment, including several sets of traditional Bai costumes for children, used on special occasions, followed by a visit to the classrooms. Classes are fairly small, attended by ten to fifteen children each. In one classroom, a young teacher was holding out cards with words in Bai while the children had to shout the words out loud. In another, the teacher taught a series of children songs, alternating between Chinese and Bai. According to my hosts, all the teachers were local Bai women from the village and its surroundings.

Yang and the teacher who escorted me told me that regular visits are made from the SIL main office in Kunming as well as from SIL staff and donors from different locations. Yet, despite the school being the flagship project of SIL East Asia and featuring prominently on its website, I could not find the organization's name anywhere on the school premises. The absence of SIL from public view and the feeling that the school is no different from any other state-run public institution reveal that despite the legality of the project, foreign involvement in education is still kept relatively low-key.

On our way back to town, I asked Yang and the teacher who accompanied us why their school was so unique; if the project was successful and was even being modestly expanded, why were there no other bilingual schools in the region? Yang replied that there was the problem of staff: teachers trained to teach in both Bai and Putonghua were quite hard to find, an issue that has plagued bilingual education since the 1950s and particularly after the absence of bilingual education for over twenty years from 1958 to the early 1980s (Tsung, Wang, and Zhang 2012, 108, 117). While primary school is free, attending the bilingual preschool costs fifty yuan per semester—a small sum for most urban Chinese but a significant amount of money for many residents of rural Yunnan. In addition, the obligatory-education law applies for nine years from the age of six. As a preschool, the project does not come under the law for mandatory education, resulting in the fact that state authorities are not interested in providing funding. Clearly, as McCarthy predicted, had SIL not stepped in, the school would not have survived.

Upon my return to Kunming, I went to meet Sean, the SIL director, to discuss what I had seen in Jianchuan and the organization at large. Sean explained SIL's official presence in Yunnan as a reflection of the relative tolerance of the provincial authorities (interview, October 10, 2012). Indeed, according to Sean, Yunnan is one of the only places in China where an NGO can potentially register legally. Other organizations register in Hong Kong and conduct activity in Yunnan as foreign NGOs (as mentioned, since the enactment of the new foreign NGO law in 2017, this is no longer the case). The tolerance is also manifested in religious policy; Sean noted that in contrast with other places, the attitude toward contacts between foreign Christians and official Three Self Patriotic Movement (TSPM) churches is quite open. The laxity is such that the official churches themselves are, in Sean's experience, bolder and less controlled than elsewhere in China. He would not be surprised, he added, if some of the churches have initiated Bible translations for minority people on their own accord. Sean's personal explanation for government tolerance in Yunnan compared to other peripheral provinces is that the minority people of Yunnan live together reasonably peacefully, making ethnicity less of an explosive issue. In contrast, Sean had previously lived and conducted linguistic work in Gansu Province, where relations among Tibetans, Hui, and Han are quite tense and state regulations are accordingly quite strict.

According to Sean, SIL's religious affiliation is known to the authorities but considered irrelevant. Indeed, no evidence of Christianity can be found on the SIL East Asia website or in the school building and staff. From Sean's perspective, the Christian basis of SIL activity is rooted in the simple concept that for one to receive the gospel, one must be able to read and comprehend it. Furthermore, from a personal point of view, Sean explained that Christians are dedicated to serve in many different ways, with each man or woman offering what they have. Some provide medical aid, some teach English, others work with the poor and the underprivileged. What Sean has to offer is his training and skill as a linguist.

According to Sean, as a rule, SIL work is request based, working only with those who seek its assistance. In addition, it does not initiate Bible translations, focusing rather on language preservation. Like the early twentieth-century missionaries, it also engages in the development of new scripts for minority languages, mostly similar to pinyin. The advantage of using a pinyin system is that children in the Chinese school system have to acquire pinyin anyway, making it an easily transferable writing system. Interestingly, Sean added that in some cases, a Latin-based alphabet is also preferable for its political neutrality. Sean cited one example of a Turkic ethnic group he had worked with in Gansu, where local activists wanted to develop a pan-Turkic script for their language. Sean thought it was a bad idea that would lead to unwanted and unnecessary political complications and therefore worked to promote the use of a simpler, Latinized writing system. Sean's perspective is corroborated by Arienne M. Dwyer, who has noted that in the past, the state even made a failed attempt to encourage Mongolians, Tibetans, and Uyghurs to adopt a Latinized script, considered politically neutral and therefore preferable from a state perspective (1998, 70). Such efforts to avoid using a script with wider regional implications is indicative of the way SIL is careful in avoiding any possible connection between language development and political activism.

Regarding the school in Jianchuan, Sean said the project was successful, but as of 2012, it was not yet economically independent, since local authorities do not provide funding. While SIL works in close coordination with a number of state bodies, official perspectives on bilingual education differ. Sean described close relations with the Ethnic Affairs Committee, where officials firmly believe in bilingual education, and a system of cooperation with the official body responsible for issues relating to ethnic languages, including joint publications of books based on information compiled by SIL workers. At the same time, he defined relations with the Ministry of Education as "complicated." Nevertheless, SIL continues to fund the program with the ultimate goal of convincing people that bilingual education is possible. In fact, the program in Jianchuan is limited in scope; what Sean would really like to see is a system of bilingual education lasting all the way through high school. However, since lack of proper knowledge of Chinese puts students at a disadvantage in employment and higher education, for the time being, they are content with the preschool as a moderate means toward language preservation.[12]

The reality of the bilingual school in Jianchuan is in many ways a reflection of the state of affairs in ethnic Yunnan in the beginning of the twenty-first century. The 1990s witnessed major reforms in the realm of minority education, leading to the establishment of schools like the one in Jianchuan. However, by the early 2000s, interest among local authorities and some ordinary Bai was waning. The rise of the free market and the development of Yunnan meant that parents and officials were more interested in children acquiring proper Chinese and English to survive and prosper in a competitive economy. Furthermore, state withdrawal of funding reflects the decline of the government's fiscal capacity in the 1990s as a result of decentralization and the growing difficulty in providing support for education in poor areas (Iredale et al. 2001, 68). The diminishing of funding for bilingual schools also exemplifies the way market forces are shaping educational policies. With the government's withdrawal from the project, NGOs like SIL have entered the field. SIL projects like the Jianchuan school can be perceived as a form of charity work, providing aid to the underprivileged. Bai children are assisted in their integration into the state education system, and children from poorer regions are given a chance to study and advance.

At the same time, SIL work is also closely related to issues of ethnic identity and state policy. The nature of SIL in Yunnan is strongly reminiscent of the activity carried out in Mexico, where SIL was highly valued by the Mexican state for the aid it provided the government in dealing with "the Indian problem" (Hartch 2006, 53). Literacy in Native American languages was viewed by the state as a potential bridge toward the acquisition of Spanish. Thus, the advancement of literacy through SIL activity enabled the state to educate and "civilize" its indigenous populations. Similarly, the school in Jianchuan provides local Bai children with an easy road to Chinese speech and writing, enabling them to easily integrate into the state educational system. By promoting language as a means for integration, SIL workers help promote the state's objective of "assimilation through ethnicity" (Shih 2002).

In addition to serving the state's ethnic policy, the project of bilingualism, with its stated goal of cultural preservation, can be seen as an attempt to reinforce a certain idea of "Bainess." Tellingly, the school is located in an area of great significance for the Bai, associated with cultural authenticity. Yet, apart from the occasional use of Bai costume, Bai language is the only feature of Bai culture present in the school. By focusing on language in the same way that state narratives of ethnicity focus on song, dance, and costume as the essence of ethnic identity, SIL linguists play an instrumental role in educating the Bai on the nature of ethnicity. This latter feature of Christian linguistic activity is further apparent in the attempt made by the missionary Simon to construct a church for the Bouyei.

The Bouyei Church

In addition to SIL/Wycliffe, several missionaries in Yunnan are engaged in private initiatives in the realm of language. Such was the case of Simon's Bouyei church. Simon's upbringing was not religious—ironically, his family became estranged from Christianity after the death of an aunt who had come to Yunnan in the 1920s to work as a missionary among the Hani of Mojiang. Unmarried and very young, she became ill with cancer and died. Even though Simon's great-aunt died long before he was born, he recalls seeing her last letters, which he described as "just terrible." Despite the fact that Simon has found himself working in the very same Chinese province, he did not ascribe much meaning to the fact that he has ended up in Yunnan and expressed no interest in visiting Mojiang or seeking out his great-aunt's grave.

I relay this piece of personal past, even though it may be of no significance beyond Simon's personal emotional disposition, because it is part of a set pattern, defining the way evangelical missionaries narrate their personal history. It begins with a description of the unhappiness and ignorance of the past, moving to the moment of conversion, and culminating in the calling to become a missionary. Both turning points are frequently supernatural in essence, involving dreams, visions, and miracles. "Personal salvation," "being born again," "coming to Christ"—these phrases are used interchangeably to signify the central narrative of faith. The narrative of personal salvation is fixed on the defining moment of conversion as a new beginning, remolding the way one's personal past is understood. Everything before that point is only significant as prehistory: an era of darkness. Simon's own narrative of preconversion darkness included an early interest in New Age spirituality and the occult, fortune-telling, tarot cards—practices that were, in his words, "very heavy." At the time, he often suffered from terrible nightmares. Beyond the personal story of salvation, the past is a blank or at the very least of little importance. Tradition, family, or national histories have no place in this extremely personal story of salvation. The story of Simon's missionary aunt may or may not have influenced his decision to come to Yunnan. What is important is that Simon presented it as an irrelevancy. The collective past is never more than a footnote to the individual present.

In a subsequent conversation, Simon told me of an experience he had before becoming interested in Christianity. As a young man in his early twenties, he spent a number of months among the Masai in Kenya. He had heard that the Masai live the same way today as they did three thousand years ago, became interested in authentic knowledge of the kind he had felt was lost in the West, and decided to experience life among them firsthand. His experience among the Masai turned out to be a bitter disappointment. He was aesthetically impressed and could still recall the beauty of "a Masai warrior running across the savannah." Yet, he found their knowledge to be shallow and irrelevant and suffered from what he thought was terrible food. In Simon's eyes, the Masai possessed no understanding of the world and no logic: "they still think a plane is a flying cow." They had nothing to give him. Simon's encounter and disappointment with Masai authenticity are interesting in the context of his later conversion to Pentecostal-style Christianity and his work in China and elsewhere. His romantic idea of ancient knowledge held by noble savages collapsed upon encounter with the Masai. They were not, after all, simple yet profound representatives of long-lost knowledge. Outwardly, they were majestic, but for Simon, a deeper look inside their culture proved uninteresting, even somewhat repulsive.

And yet, the search for authenticity was still a major feature of Simon's efforts. From my first meeting with Simon, it became clear to me that cultural preservation was the central theme of his missionary endeavor. Moreover, by using the term "culture," Simon was referring primarily to language as well as song, dance, and costume (interview, October 21, 2010). Simon viewed the linguistic projects conducted by the early missionaries to Yunnan as the highest form of missionary work, an act of redemption and mercy through which minority cultures have been saved. Not only have they been able to triumph in the face of rapid Hanization, but the script also provided social and cultural cohesion and a sense of identity. So, when I told Simon about my interest in Christians, he strongly encouraged me to go see the Lisu in the Nujiang valley. He had been there and was extremely impressed by the Christian communities he encountered. What attracted him most about the Lisu Christians was their use of Lisu language and the prevalence of the script devised by Fraser. Indeed, the Lisu whom Simon met were literate and used Lisu Bibles and large Lisu hymnals ("This thick!" he said excitedly, marking the size of a large book with his fingers).

At the time, Simon was trying to create a church community for the Bouyei, an ethnic group from Guizhou, many of whom have come to Kunming as migrant workers to seek their fortunes in the big city, working as porters and laborers for mostly Han customers.[13] Like other ethnic groups living in urban centers (Poa and LaPolla 2007, 339–40), the Bouyei in Kunming are rapidly losing the use of the Bouyei language. As poor, rural members of a minority group, they are often looked down on as "primitive" (*luohuo*), and identification as Bouyei through the use of language can hardly be considered a social asset. In contrast, acquiring a good command of Chinese is clearly a prerequisite for any social advancement. According to Simon, while middle-aged women and the elderly still speak Bouyei, the younger generation (both male and female) is increasingly turning toward Chinese.

Concerned about cultural decline and the progress of Hanization, Simon firmly believed that Christianity can play a pivotal role in the preservation of Bouyei culture. Accordingly, Simon's goal was to create a church that would help preserve Bouyei language, by using it in services and Bible reading. In Simon's view, the act of translating texts into Bouyei and composing Bouyei hymns was an act of resistance to the tide of assimilation and a "validation of the vernacular culture" (Dunch 2002, 318).

The Bouyei in Kunming occupy the lowest rungs of the social ladder, working as garbage collectors and hauling around heavy loads of used furniture on tricycles. They are, in Simon's words, "a kind of gypsies," many living outside the state system of registration and control. Some of the Bouyei give birth at home and have four or five unregistered children, sometimes bribing their way into schools (Simon, interview, January 21, 2010). It is precisely their antiestablishment, individualistic character that Simon found so attractive. In his mind, they were, in some passive and not entirely conscious way, resisting the state system. The poor and marginalized Bouyei are to Simon what the Sani Yi were to the French missionary Pere Vial—a primal and authentic face of China (Swain 1995, 151–57). Living in relative freedom outside the mainstream of a centralized and authoritarian state, the Bouyei were portrayed by Simon as the antitheses of Han Chinese conformity and cultural shallowness. Much like Vial's descriptions of the Sani, Simon often described the Bouyei he met as naïve and unsophisticated yet somehow also cunning and wise.

As Simon himself did not speak Bouyei, his efforts to establish the church were made through a small number of Bouyei converts who spoke Chinese. Simon was never willing to disclose how many Bouyei converts were in the community; however, the number was clearly quite small. Like many foreign missionaries working in China, he was also keen on staying in the background of his project. His attempt to remain as invisible as possible had both technical and ideological motives. With regard to the authorities, Simon's avoidance of being in the public view was meant to evade legal issues. Unlike for workers of legally sanctioned NGOs like SIL, caution was prudent in Simon's case, as his activity was not officially authorized. Simon's caution regarding direct contacts between foreigners and the Bouyei held important implications for my fieldwork. While Simon was extremely straightforward and forthcoming in describing his work, when I approached him on the issue of meeting some of the Bouyei, he repeatedly refused to allow it.

Security reasons aside, Simon was also concerned with the ideological problem of what he termed "colonization." Well aware of current opinions prevalent in the West relating the missionary past with the evils of imperialism, Simon preferred to minimize his own centrality in the project and leave things in the hands of the Bouyei converts, hoping the movement toward preservation would be experienced as an internal Bouyei cultural resurgence. However, leaving the project entirely in the hands of the converts would not be possible. To begin with, Simon was interested in cultivating a specific kind of religiosity, one that was based on personal experience and faith, rather than rules and tradition. Like other Western missionaries, Simon was quite critical of Christians like the Korean missionaries working in town, who emphasized rules, hierarchy, and prohibitions, things Simon associated with rigid legalism. To create the kind of personal, faith-based Christianity he would have liked to see, local leaders and preachers had to be trained.

The task of working with the Bouyei was not an easy one. Simon claimed that accepting Christianity was difficult for them, as "they are very superstitious." The central issue was the prevalence of ancestor and spirit worship, which are of critical importance to the Bouyei. In Simon's eyes, the need to appease ancestral spirits has created a culture of fear that Simon would have liked them to discard. Indeed, Simon's deep objection to ancestor and spirit worship is similar to state discourse regarding superstition (*mixin*). The negative connection between strong attachment to ancestor worship and the spread of Christianity is noted by Han Junxue in his analysis of conversion patterns among Yunnan's minority peoples (2000, 158). Thus, although Simon worked to contain and limit the replacement of Bouyei with Chinese, his stand against traditional Bouyei religiosity and his views on ethnicity in general were in line with the policies of local authorities, making Simon's work largely beneficial from a state perspective.

The creation of a church community clearly required the Bouyei to abandon certain cultural practices, a process Simon did not expect the Bouyei themselves to initiate. A major problem facing the establishment of a Bouyei church was that according to Simon's own account, he was much more interested in the preservation of the Bouyei language than were the Bouyei themselves, who did not place much value on language preservation. Indeed, Simon's experience had been that they were perfectly content speaking Chinese and had to be regularly pushed and encouraged to engage and assist in the translation of hymns and biblical passages into their native tongue. Maintaining a relationship with lineage and clan is more central to the Bouyei's sense of identity than is the spoken mode of communication in the present. In other words, for the Bouyei whom Simon worked with, it was the "superstitious" ancestor worship that marked the center of cultural identity rather than the language in which that identity was expressed.

The indifference of the Bouyei toward language preservation has been a feature of minority reaction to missionary attempts in the realm of linguistics since the early twentieth century. Samuel Clarke, the missionary to the Hua Miao, records a similar phenomenon in 1915: "Mr. Bolton opened a school in which boys were taught to read Chinese from Christian books and also to write.... It is worthy of remark, however, that the parents of the scholars were much more interested to read and write in Chinese than in their own language" ([1915] 2009, 137). The attitudes of the pre-1949 Miao are consistent with trends among Naxi parents in the area of Lijiang (Hansen 1999, 65) and the Bai in the area of the bilingual school in Jianchuan, many of whom believe that Chinese should be the sole language of instruction in their children's schools. Beyond the limited social leverage provided by an ethnic language, language preservation is sometimes perceived as a mark of inferiority (Bulag 2003; McCarthy 2009, 127). Thus, it remains the role of the missionaries to emphasize language as a source of ethnic pride and uniqueness.

As a result, the Bouyei church project has not been overly successful. Despite Simon's infatuation with the free spirit of the Bouyei, the difficulties in creating a community have led Simon to develop strong criticism of certain elements in Bouyei culture. In his view, their ignorance is such that they are inherently unaware of the nature of their own authenticity and the importance of preserving it. Furthermore, what the Bouyei perceive as culturally important, namely, the practice of spirit and particularly ancestor worship, is, in Simon's view, not an authentic feature of Bouyei culture at all but a corruption of that culture.

Accordingly, Simon believed that to save the Bouyei from Hanization, they must be taught about authenticity and instructed as to where the core of their culture lies. Invoking the image of the missionary as the translator of culture (Sugirtharajah 1998, 9), Simon's translation project was intended to "translate" Bouyei culture for the Bouyei themselves. His goal was to redefine what it means to be Bouyei, by explaining ancestor worship as superfluous and the use of the Bouyei language as essential. By shifting the focus of culture from ritual to language, Bouyei culture would be converted from a position of incompatibility with Christianity to one in which Christianity is seen as a road to ethnic empowerment.

The vision of Bouyei Bibles and hymnals as thick as the ones found among the Lisu is still far off. But the relatively slow pace of progress has not deterred Simon. He and others have established free unofficial schools for Bouyei children. Beyond providing education for the children, the schools serve as a support system for the community, providing help with bureaucratic issues, thus invoking another pattern from the prerevolutionary past, of missionaries acting as mediators between the government and their minority converts, giving them a voice in a very literal sense. While Simon was quite vague about the specifics of representing the Bouyei to the authorities, it would seem that representation is usually not carried out by the missionaries directly. Rather, the network of support is worked through the schools, which are, in turn, funded by donations from Christians.

Toward the end of my time in Yunnan, Simon told me he had begun production of *The Jesus Film* in Bouyei. To produce the film, Simon had arranged for a special team of SIL/Wycliffe translators from the US to arrive in town. As Simon explained, the process of producing the movie usually begins with a translation of one of the Gospels, in this case, the Gospel of Luke, from Chinese to Bouyei, followed by adaptation to film. The problem was, once again, the Bouyei's general lack of interest in the project. Simon admitted that there was a certain lack of logic in a Bouyei-language production of the film, since the language is rapidly losing ground and will probably be limited to the elderly within a generation. In other words, if long-term evangelism is the goal, one would do better to target the younger generation by using Chinese (a Chinese version of the film already exists). But to Simon, the use of Bouyei was a matter of principle, a reflection of the vision that all nations must "come as they are," meaning with their own culture and language, a further expression of the effort to stress the centrality of Bouyei language as a central symbol of Bouyei culture, despite its much-diminished power as a daily means of communication.

When the work on the Bouyei *Jesus Film* began, Simon shared his concern that the differences of style between himself, with his Pentecostal tendencies, and the more conservative SIL/Wycliff crew might become a cause of tension.[14] For linguists like Sean, the Christian rationale behind SIL activity was simply that for one to receive the gospel, one must be able to read and comprehend it. As such, translation should be as accurate as possible. In contrast, much like the oral renditions of biblical stories and the "Creation to Christ" narrative, for Simon, the centrality of the Bible lies not in the accuracy of the text but rather in its symbolic meaning. For example, in reply to the question of whether he sometimes taught the Bouyei himself, Simon replied that he did not feel the need to do so particularly often. In his view, after a relatively short period of introduction to the Bible, "most people have already learned enough" and can continue studying on their own.

In Simon's own words, the language of the Bible is "the foundation of experience"—the basis of knowledge, intended to provoke a religious conversion. In other words, what Simon wants most is not necessarily for the Bouyei to have extensive knowledge of the Bible. Rather, he would like them to be able to sing and pray in their own language, hence the focus on the Lisu hymnal as a practical tool of Christian ethnicity. Accordingly, language becomes a path toward cultural affirmation and simultaneously serves as a way to transcend the text and develop what Simon calls a "language of the heart."

Conclusion: The Language Mission

The linguistic work described in this chapter highlights the delicate balance maintained by missionaries working among Yunnan's ethnic minorities. Contemporary missionaries in Yunnan are faced with the task of preserving and consolidating ethnic identity while simultaneously attempting to radically remold it. Accordingly, both SIL and Simon are dedicated to the idea that efforts should be made to preserve the culture of Yunnan's minority people. At the same time, their definition of ethnicity is primarily determined by linguistics, and the culture to be preserved is invariably centered on a language core. Indeed, as some scholars have argued (Pippin and Bailey

1996; Sugirtharajah 1996), the act of translation itself may be understood as an attempt to reshape culture by reinterpreting traditional concepts in a new light, making use of "bridges and keys" to connect local cultural values to Christian theology. Moving between fields, cultures, and geographies, the missionary translator is able to translate a given culture for an audience of its own members. By doing so, missionaries attempt to re-create an alternative narrative of culture and cultural authenticity.

Christians involved in the field of ethnic languages in contemporary Yunnan are strong advocates of the principle of translatability that has guided Protestant Christianity since the early Reformation. In many ways, the linguists of SIL and others devoted to language preservation are attempting to repeat the successes of the early twentieth century, when language mission based on the invention of scripts played a crucial role in the conversion of many of Yunnan's minority people. Linguistic activity is often presented by missionaries as an attempt to strengthen ethnic languages in the context of the intense process of Sinification in the reform era. However, while language preservation has been conceptualized as a means of countering the state's linguistic hegemony and the power of the Han majority, in this chapter, I have argued that missionary involvement in minority linguistics serves to enhance rather than minimize state power in two major ways.

First, missionary-linguistic activity in Yunnan may be seen as a form of outsourcing by which the state attempts to promote its own position through the actions of others. NGOs like SIL help minority students acquire language skills that will eventually be instrumental in their integration within the Chinese education system. By providing the "crutch" of proficiency in local languages, SIL linguists help promote integration. Furthermore, as Sean testified, SIL workers make a point of avoiding the potentially problematic connection between languages, ethnicity, and politics by such means as promoting Latin-based writing systems rather than encouraging the development of scripts with politically charged connotations.

Second, missionary language workers advocate an ethnicity based on language and attempt to disassociate between traditional culture and ethnic identity. As both the Jianchuan school and Simon's experience reveal, the centrality of language is an idea promoted among minority people who often view their own culture in other terms. This recentering of ethnicity is beneficial for the state, as it often includes a discarding of practices that both the state and the missionaries consider to be primitive and superstitious.

The position assumed by Christian linguists gives rise to the question of state confidence. Is it possible that the Chinese authorities underemphasize the importance of the translator's identity and the power stemming from linguistic work? Although it is impossible to answer this question, it would seem that for the time being, state policy implies that the benefits of Christian linguistic activity and the reshaping of ethnic identity far outweigh the dangers.

Chapter 6

OUT OF SPACE

Christian Deterritorialization and State Space

> We are not interested in erecting any church buildings. We don't believe the world needs another single church building.
>
> —PAUL HATTAWAY, *BACK TO JERUSALEM*

In the previous chapters, I dealt with the implications of evangelical theology on the relationship between ethnic and Christian identities among the non-Han Christians of Southwest China. In this chapter, I examine the convergence of state and missionary civilizing missions, from the perspective of the state's spatial-territorial sovereignty. I argue that the deterritorialized nature of contemporary evangelical Christianity is of key importance in understanding state tolerance toward the missionary endeavor. An analysis of contemporary evangelical attitudes toward sacred space and the physical construction of churches suggests that an unspoken and unofficial arrangement has emerged, according to which the monopoly over spatial production remains entirely in the hands of state authorities, while evangelical Christians willingly confine themselves to the nonspatial realm. The emergence of a working balance between Chinese authorities and the foreign and local evangelical community regarding the use and appropriation of space is of particular importance in the context of ethnic Yunnan, where a number of minorities have been engaged in the reconstruction of prerevolutionary systems of sacred geography, practices that pose a potential threat both to state sovereignty and to the spread of the gospel.

As others have noted, evangelical Christianity is a religion of the transient and rootless, a movement highly compatible with the deterritorialized nature of the global era (Juergensmeyer 2007; Meyer 1999; Poewe 1994, 247–49). Its global and nonterritorial nature make it easily transmittable and highly adaptable, or as Richard Madsen has noted, "it travels widely because it travels light" (2000, 276). Indeed, nineteenth-century Protestant missionaries to China viewed sacred places and language, as well as local rituals and mantras, as a form of deception—a mask of culture that must be torn off, before faith can be revealed (Reinders 2004, 97). The nonterritorial nature of evangelical Christianity is both ideological and pragmatic. While expanding rapidly among migrants and transient workers, Christianity has encountered the greatest barriers to its expansion in communities with a strong ritual territoriality (Covell 1995, 269).

Considering the centrality of globalism and the crossing and diminishing of national and ethnic boundaries described earlier, one may conclude that the nonterritorial nature of evangelical Christianity poses a threat to the state and its spatial sovereignty. Control over the geographic spread of religious activity is a central element in state policy on religion. Religious policy as expressed in Document 19, issued by the Central Committee of the Communist Party in 1982, "restricts religious activities to approved locations, requires that they be conducted by approved clergy and limits their scope to the geographic sphere in which a given member of the clergy is permitted to practice" (Schak 2011, 72).

Some people have argued that globalization, in the form of contact between minorities and the ethnic groups residing beyond the borders of China, serves to weaken the Chinese state. State officials have described the presence of foreign religions in China as a way of "using religion to destroy the unity of the motherland and of its nationalities" (Mackerras 2003, 115–16). Accordingly, globalized and nonterritorial religions like Christianity experience success "precisely because they do not have traditional religious centers. . . . Many new religious movements are seen almost like rouge states, potentially dangerous in part because they are so hard to pin down geographically" (Juergensmeyer 2007, 144).

In contrast, I argue that with regard to Yunnan's minorities, contact with nonterritorial evangelical Christianity serves to weaken the territoriality of local ethnoreligions and in turn to strengthen state control. As the cases described in this chapter illustrate, the ethnic and religious revival of the reform era have led to the reintroduction of local spatial practices and landscapes. As sporadic temple-destruction campaigns demonstrate, the recreation of nonstate spatial systems is a point of contention and struggle, with the state occasionally working to reaffirm its power to organize space at will.

The global and fluid nature of evangelical Christianity is accommodated by the state, because it is marked by an acceptance on the side of missionaries and local Christians of the separation between the material-geographic realm of the state and the moral-spiritual role of religion. As such, it may be seen as an expression of the Protestant adherence to the separation of church and state and a fulfillment of the New Testament instruction to "render unto Caesar the things that are Caesar's, and unto God the things that are God's" (Mathew 22:21). Indeed, the line separating Caesar and God is closely related to spatial production. As long as Christianity makes no claim on the production and representation of space, in the form of church construction and holy sites, it is tolerated. However, when the state feels its spatial production is being challenged, tolerance may end.

I argue that evangelical approaches toward space differ not only from the actions of local indigenous religious agents but also from those of the official state-authorized church, emphasizing the advantages of the distinctly nonterritorial evangelical Christianity from a state perspective. Rather than offering an alternative territoriality based on a single sacred center, evangelicals tend to emphasize pristine spirituality based on faith alone, unrelated and indeed intentionally detached from the physical and spatial aspects of reality. By focusing on the inner and the individual as the major arenas of faith and conversion, missionaries and local evangelicals refrain from challenging the state's monopoly over spatial production and territorial sovereignty. As such, evangelical Christianity serves as a globalizing force, echoing Oliver Roy's description of religion in the global era: "globalization has blurred the connection between a religion, a pristine culture, a specific society and a territory" (2004, 24).

State Space and Ritual Territoriality in Yunnan

The production of space, according to Henri Lefebvre, is the way in which different societies deploy and represent space to serve their ideological, social, and financial needs. According to Lefebvre, modern capitalist states attempt to create standardized, functional, and commoditized space. In particular, Lefebvre coined the phrase "abstract space" as an alternative to "historical space" that arises with the spread of capitalism: "Abstract space functions 'objectively,' as a set of things/signs and their formal relationships: glass and stone concrete and steel, angles and curves, full and empty. Formal and quantitative, it erases distinctions, as much those which derive from nature and (historical) time as those which originate in the body (age, sex, ethnicity)" (1991, 49).

A similar argument has been made by Zygmunt Bauman, who defined the actions of the modern state as the "monopolization of cartographic rights" (1998, 40). According to Bauman, modern cities are planned by modern states to destroy all "historical accidents" by replacing the old chaotic city with one that is uniform and perfect to create "a site never polluted by history" (38).

Unlike the drive of capitalist states to reorganize space mainly through commodification, the socialist version of abstract space production was focused on centralization and control, a process described with regard to China in the following words: "Socialist space was produced through the tightening of administrative lines that extended across the country into local communities, lines that created a hierarchy of administrative spaces and connected far-flung places back to the center in Beijing" (M. Yang 2004b, 722). Thus, prior to the 1949 revolution, the Chinese landscape was home to elaborate systems of "ritual territoriality": "Village communities, kinship groups and deity cult followers gave geographical form to their common identities and community life by performing their collective rituals in local deity temples, ancestor halls and at tombs.... Collective rituals... ritually demarcated the land into a patchwork of community territories that often did not correspond to state administrative boundaries" (723).

The system of ritual territoriality was dismantled under Maoism, including the confiscation and destruction of "markers of familial space such as kitchen gods, family graves, the spirit tablets,... and resident earth gods and goddesses (*tudi gong, tudi nianniang*)" (M. Yang 2004b, 726). The process came to a climax with the radical policies of the Great Leap Forward, when "virtually all space became enfolded within the single space of the state, a space devoted to production, ideological inculcation and surveillance" (726). The elimination of local sacred geography in ethnic Yunnan was accompanied by a process of centralization, with the Han majority placed at the center and ethnic minorities marking the periphery of Chinese society (Feuchtawang and Wang 1991, 254).

OUT OF SPACE

Fig. 2 Tourist map of Yunnan featuring minority people in full costume. Photo: Gideon Elazar.

Prerevolutionary forms of ritual territoriality and attempts to reenchant space have been returning to the Chinese landscape since the 1980s. These changes are often viewed as a form of compensation for past discrimination, as well as a means of promoting the growing tourist industry, facilitating cross-border trade, and advancing China's position in the southeastern region of Asia. The resurgence of old spatial practices is particularly pronounced in Yunnan, where a number of minority groups have begun to reconstruct traditional and religious spatial systems, which are largely independent of the state (Davis 2003, 2006; Mueggler 2001).

To an observer of contemporary China, some indication of the construction of state space and the ethnic periphery can be ascertained through examination of official posters and staged pictures of minority people. Minorities are often portrayed as revolving around a symbol of state power, especially when all fifty-five minorities are considered together. Often the state appears in the background not as a person as in the Maoist era but rather as a building in the image of the Hall of Supreme Harmony in Beijing's Forbidden City. The Hall of Supreme Harmony represents the geographic and symbolic center of power, the very core of the "central kingdom," standing behind the young and jubilant minority people—a distinctly territorial, spatially grounded presence (for a similar description of the symbolic meaning of Beijing in Nuoso Yi education, see Harrell and Ayi 1998, 65). The symbolic image of Beijing corresponds to what Lefebvre classifies as "representations of space," that which is "tied to the relations of production and to the 'order' which those relations impose, and hence to knowledge, to signs, to codes, and to 'frontal' relations" (1991, 33).

In China, space production is closely related to modernization (M. Yang 2004b, 721), the guiding ethos of the Chinese nation-state, framed largely in contrast to the splintered and underdeveloped image of China prior to the Communist revolution (Duara 1995; McCarthy 2009, 23). Thus, the state's legitimate right to reorganize space stems from its image as the leading force toward modernization and development. As mentioned, Chinese modernization was based on the creation of spatial dominance through neutralizing previous systems of ritual spatial production and struggling against cultures with an ethnoreligious spatial basis.

The revival of ethnicity in the reform era included attempts to re-create older forms of space production through temple networks and the honoring of local deities. In Eric Mueggler's work on the Nuoso Yi, he describes the struggles revolving around a traditional social institution called the *ts'ici* system and the ritual landscape surrounding it. The *ts'ici* system was a rotation of political and ritualistic authority among the area's wealthy and important families, responsible for maintaining a limited and controlled relationship with state officials. The system was violently destroyed during the Great Leap Forward, as the state attempted to incorporate the entire space of China into a single state-run system of communes: "the Socialist state efficiently penetrated this community, installing itself within as the center of production and social reproduction" (Mueggler 2001, 9). According to local belief, the violent dismantling of the *ts'ici* system resulted in the creation of wild, hungry ghosts—the spirits of those who died and were not properly buried who torment the lives and memories of local villagers. Mueggler's descriptions of the elaborate exorcisms performed in the reform era and the struggles revolving around the cultivation of certain fields associated with specific rituals and spirits illustrate the way locals are attempting to re-create a form of ritual territoriality and return the state to its position as an "external Other" (2001, 274).

Another example of ethnoterritorial resurgence can be found among the Theravada Buddhist Dai of Xishuangbanna, who have been engaged in the re-creation of a symbolic ethnogeography spreading from Yunnan through northern Thailand and Myanmar, through the rapid dissemination of written and audio materials facilitated by traveling monks. This includes attempts to reintroduce the old Thai script, rather than the reformed, state-sponsored variety. Judging by the tolerance shown toward Dai ethnic revival, Sara Davis underlines the state's drive to teach minority peoples "that they were no longer at the center. The center was now Beijing, and their new job was to mark the borders. Ethnic minorities and 'their primitive, simple' culture mark the edge of the national map, the limits of the known" (2006, 44).

In the global age, the Chinese state must deal with a number of threats to its exclusive position at the top and center of the national hierarchy. Indeed, the challenges to the state's paramount position often flow from the state's own policies. In the case of Yunnan's Dai, the reconstruction of Buddhist temples and the fostering of relations with Buddhist clergy from Thailand and Myanmar are being encouraged by the local government as a way of promoting the growing ethnotourism industry and as part of the greater attempt to develop the Mekong region (McCarthy 2004, 40–48). The development is part of the major drive of recent years to convert Yunnan into the central commercial hub of Southeast Asia, a goal that may be aided by utilizing cross-border relations between Yunnan's Dai and their kin in Myanmar, Laos, and Thailand (C. Lin 2011; Wade 2011; Yeung 2005, 10).

The relationship between Christianity and the state should be viewed as a dialogical process. Chinese modernity is in many ways the product of "colonial discourse whose missionary traditions regarded Chinese popular religion as 'heathen,' 'uncivilized' and 'superstitious'" (M. Yang 2004b, 723). Indeed, the modern reorganization of space in China predates the rise of the CCP to power and is in many ways a feature of Chinese modernity. Thus, the state's drive to enforce its spatial sovereignty can be seen in the temple-destruction campaigns of the Republican era, which in turn can be traced back to Christian influence. A large part of the Guomindang leadership, including Sun Yat-sen and Chiang Kai-shek, were Christians devoted to the idea that modernization must be preceded by the elimination of much of the Chinese religious tradition (Katz 2014). Guomindang policy toward indigenous religion, focusing specifically on local temples, can be explained as a drive to break the power of local space-based identities and establish its own spatial hegemony. Modernist rejection of local faith systems took on an extreme form in the Marxist staunch secularity. Accordingly, the process of space production in the early days of the People's Republic of China was disastrous for Christianity and included the confiscation of church property, the elimination of all independent churches, and a barrage of persecution.

Yet, while all religions suffered during the radical years of the Maoist period, it would seem that in the long run, Protestant Christianity, with its abstract nature and nondependence on material and geographic manifestations, has benefited from the process. As a number of scholars have argued, the prevalence of house churches can be traced back to the vacuum created after the massive destruction of temples and shrines during the Cultural Revolution. Paul Hattaway has argued that the "removal of idolatry"—by which he means the destruction of temples and idols during the Cultural Revolution—has created "a spiritual void in the hearts of millions" (2003, 12; see also Bays 2011, 186; Lim 2013a, 5; Pickard 1999, 11). Similarly, according to Madsen, "With the traditional religious landscape stripped bare, religion became exclusively a private matter. . . . The Christian God was seen as especially connected with the private sphere, because he did not need to be worshipped in elaborate temples" (2013, 25).

Indeed, the unofficial house church movement, strongly supported by foreign missionaries, exemplifies the principled territorial detachment. House churches can be found anywhere in China: in warehouses, schools, and private homes—any in- or outdoor space available for worship (Liu 2011). This may be seen as a largely technical issue, reflecting the legal or financial abilities and constraints of congregants with regard to constructing new church buildings. However, evangelical Christians often voice their disinterest in creating spatial representations like churches: "We are not interested in erecting any church buildings. We don't believe the world needs another single church building" (Hattaway 2003, 108).

Thus, evangelical Christianity holds two central advantages over other traditional religions from the perspective of Chinese state authorities. To begin with, it has come to be associated with modernity and the free market, as discussed in chapter 2. Moreover, the advantage of missionary Christianity lies in its nonterritorial, global, and abstract theology. As the examples in this chapter demonstrate, missionaries offer a religiosity that is both devoid of spatial and geographical attachments and hostile to traditional spiritual territoriality, often associated with the spirit world. As such, they enable the state to retain its monopoly on the way space is constructed and maintained.

As others have shown, Christianity is of particular appeal to those who have been uprooted by the process of modernization. Philip Jenkins describes charismatic Christianity as "a potent theology for a world of migrants and wanderers, those who define their identity in terms not of roots but of routes" (2011, 116). The process of migration and the formation of "roots" identity is particularly significant in the context of reform-era China, the arena of the largest human migration movement in history, possibly numbering up to 340 million people on the move (Kam Wing Chan, 2012, 81). In Yunnan, internal migration and urbanization are progressing rapidly, while being hailed by authorities as an integral part of the modernization process (Groff 2012). Thus, Christianity is widespread among farmers who work as migrant workers in cities, businesspeople on the move, sometimes known as "boss Christians" (Cao 2008), and laborers in foreign countries (Kalir 2009).

The contrast between Christianity and local religious traditions in this regard is evident in Mayfair Yang's description of the struggle over the reestablishment of an ancestral hall in Wenzhou. In an interview held with local officials in the aftermath of a temple-destruction campaign, Yang asked why it was that in China, modernization had to imply the violent destruction of religious sites, while in the West, modernization was achieved without dismantling churches. One official, Mr. Tan, replied, "It is different with Christianity, which respects science, and science is even an outgrowth of Christianity. It's different with our own religion. It's backward and teaches people to believe in superstitions, magic and devils. It tells people that this and that are bad luck. And religion is used by people as a pretext for making money (*pianqian*). It's the bad aspects of religion that we have to attack" (M. Yang 2004b, 745–46).

While spatial struggles play a smaller part of the negotiation between the state and contemporary evangelical Christianity, state space production and Christian activity do sometimes come into open conflict. A state perspective on Christianity and space in Yunnan was expressed by Professor Xin, an expert of Miao studies whom I met at the Qing Miao wedding in Anning discussed in chapter 2. After the celebration was over, Xin, himself a Miao from a non-Christian subgroup in Guizhou, gave me a ride back into town. Our conversation began with Xin's firm expression of the official line regarding the current situation of Christianity: there are no missionaries in Yunnan, as proselytizing is illegal. In fact, Xin stressed the point that even if there were missionaries working in the province, "they could not even go from Kunming to Anning without permission" (conversation, December 23, 2009). By that time, I had been in Yunnan for several months and was rather shocked at his sweeping denial of what was quite clearly a widespread phenomenon.

When Xin and I met again, we spoke at length about his research of prerevolutionary Christian influence among the Miao. Xin's assessment of

Christianity was generally rather positive: he stressed the fact that missionaries had built schools and hospitals, educated women, and created scripts for the previously illiterate minority peoples. Yet he was concerned about "the unity of China." To that aim, it was necessary to make a clear separation between religion (*zongjiao*) and the material-secular world (*shisu*). Religion as a personal choice was acceptable; it only became problematic when it began to meddle within the concrete reality of the world and attempted to influence it. "Then you have religious wars, like in Israel," said Xin laughingly.

As he was speaking, it became clear to me that his flat denial of missionary activity and indeed any unsanctioned church activity was in fact more than a simple repetition of the party line. What he was trying to stress was that Christianity could be contained because the line had not been crossed: in his view, it did not, on any serious scale, try to penetrate the spatial-material realm of Caesar.

What that realm entailed became clear through a rough illustration drawn by Xin to portray the spatial limitations of evangelization. In this figure, circles were arranged around the historical center of Miao Christianity in Shimenkan, given as an example. As Xin noted, activity within a single and well-confined center like Shimenkan was tolerable. The problem arises when missionary work begins to spread: from a single center to other locations and from there to yet more locations and so on. I understood the concentric circles drawn around each parameter as a symbol of state organization of space, with borders intended on containing and defining missionary activity.

Xin was well aware of the presence of Christian NGOs in Yunnan, noting that they must be working with the authorities and accepting limitations on their movement, refraining from challenging the "single space of the state" (M. Yang 2004b, 722). Xin's understanding of religion and state space is an expression of the way the state continues to draw and redraw the borders of separation between normal and heterodox, legal and illegal, according to its own needs. Those who are engaged in work of borderline legality are well aware of the fact that the unspoken rules of today may become irrelevant tomorrow.

An example of the fluid nature of state policy was conveyed to me by Michael, the operator of a Christian rehabilitation center discussed in chapter 4. According to Michael, someone with connections in the bureaucracy of the Kunming municipality had told him that the current tolerance of house churches will end once the massive development of the city has been completed. Upon completion, the city will build four large Three Self

Patriotic Movement (TSPM) churches, one for each of the city's quarters, and proceed to shut down unofficial church gatherings (Michael, interview, January 6, 2010). Despite the stiffening of policy in recent years, this chain of events has not occurred. However, the idea that such a plan exists reveals that the state retains its monopoly on space production, expressed through the division of the city into quarters and followed by the spatial incorporation of all religious activity as it sees fit.

Christian Spaces

Sanjiang

On April 28, 2014, local authorities in Wenzhou demolished the Sanjiang church, which had been described as "the pride of the city's growing Christian population" (I. Johnson 2014). The demolition of the church was part of a larger campaign in which Zhejiang authorities targeted churches with high visibility, including a ten-story megachurch in Ningbo, focusing specifically on the display of large crosses. The official reason given for the campaign attributed the demolition to the violation of zoning restrictions (Cao 2017; Phillips 2014; Reardon 2015, 39).

The destruction of the Sanjiang church came as a surprise to many Christians, particularly because the church belonged to the official, legally sanctioned Three Self Movement. Indeed, the church had earlier been recognized by the local government as a "model project" (Cao 2017, 33). Wenzhou is home to a large and extremely prosperous Christian community that has become a symbol of the Christianity-capitalism connection (Chen and Huang 2004, 183–84; Cao 2008). As avid supporters of the free-market system and the state's economic policies, Christians in this town had been allowed to practice their religion quite freely and enjoyed positive relations with local authorities.

Congregants explained the demolition as a reaction to the size of the church. Sanjiang was eight stories high and covered over one thousand square meters, boasting a fifty-five-meter spire that was a central feature in the city's skyline. Furthermore, the church was located in an area designated to be Wenzhou's central economic district. Thus, Ian Johnson has hypothesized that Wenzhou officials concluded that "this is not the symbol that we want for our new economic zone" (2014). A leaked state document articulated the goal of the campaign in the following way: "The priority is to remove crosses at religious activity sites on both sides of expressways, national highways and provincial highway" (I. Johnson 2014). Indeed, the trouble began for the Sanjiang church when the Zhejiang provincial party secretary Xia Baolong visited the area in 2013 and expressed his concern over the church's physical prominence and the fact that it dominated the skyline" (Junio 2017, 344). Prior to the destruction, congregants of the church staged a two-week campaign including prayer vigils and a large sit-in to try to prevent the destruction (Hui 2014). In addition, major theologians associated with official Protestant seminaries expressed their criticism of the aggressive and uncompromising way authorities handled the issue. According to Fenggang Yang (2018), Christian resistance to the campaign eventually led to its failure: many of the crosses were not removed, and the campaign was quietly halted.

The destruction of the church reveals the way in which the state reacts when its production of space is challenged. While the use of legal terminology such as "zoning issues" may seem to be hollow rhetoric, I suggest that rather than serving as a façade for the authorities' real motives, the use of such regulations is significant. Thus, the physical prominence of Christianity, expressed in large churches and crosses, was apparently perceived by local authorities as an infringement on the state's spatial sovereignty, particularly as it appeared in spaces associated with the modernization project, such as highways and economic districts. In line with the opinions expressed by Professor Xin, the campaign conveys the message that Christians are requested to confine themselves to the spiritual realm and refrain from visibility within the space of state modernity. The precedence of state modernization over religious expression is evidenced in the slogan chosen to promote the campaign, put up in Wenzhou in the aftermath of the demolition: "make space for development" (Makinen 2014).

As Nanlai Cao has argued, "religious buildings or crosses should not be confused with religious belief itself" (2017, 35), implying that the destruction of churches in Zhejiang need not be perceived as a distinctly anti-Christian measure. Indeed, recent years have witnessed a drive by state authorities to assert control of space production through the destruction of a variety of religious sites. These include the removal of domes from mosques (Feng 2021) and the demolition of Buddhist and Daoist statues, including the tallest standing statue of the goddess Guanyin, demolished in Hebei in 2019 (Shen Xinran 2019).

As Michel Chambon has noted, church buildings are often seen as "agents of the Christianisation" (2017, 101), signifying Christian attempts to reshape the Chinese landscape. Indeed, some Christians have been strongly critical of the construction of large church buildings. Referring specifically to the demolition of the Sanjiang church and in keeping with Hattaway's previously quoted statement of hostility toward the building of new churches, Diana Junio has argued that China "needs Christians who do not care so much about having magnificent church buildings but who are willing to dedicate themselves to promoting social good, especially in China's remote and backward areas, as the main measure of achievement" (2017, 357). In contrast with the story of the Sanjiang church, I turn now to a very different model of space production, as expressed in two unofficial churches in Kunming.

The Fellowship

Many months after Mona and her family left for Central America, I decided the time had come to visit her church, usually referred to as the Northern Fellowship (to distinguish it from another foreign Fellowship located in the west of the city). When we first met in class, Mona had invited me to come to the Fellowship to meet Bob, a missionary who had spent time in Israel and was a major figure in the community. To be more accurate, she spoke to Bob about me, and he told her that "if he's interested in Christianity in China, tell him to come to church." I refrained from visiting because I felt that showing up too early in my research would provoke suspicion among congregants. Those who knew me among the Christian community were already aware of the fact that I was conducting research on Christianity and had, to varying degrees, agreed to cooperate. I felt that appearing at their place of worship might make them feel uneasy.

At the Fellowship, the distance between us would become clearly apparent, since my own religious beliefs would prevent me from actively partaking in the service. Indeed, even arriving as a visitor was problematic. Even though Mona had told me that some people come to services for purely social reasons, I was afraid to stand out as an observer rather than a participant. Previously, I felt that the distance between me and my Christian informants was balanced by some major affinities. Here, in their place of worship, affinities would disappear, and only differences would remain.

Nevertheless, I decided that a visit was inevitable. By this time, I had met many members of the community and felt that my presence would be welcomed or at least politely ignored. In addition, a good reason for attendance had appeared. That week I was invited to the Fellowship by my schoolmate Yan, a young European who had recently married a Chinese Christian. This particular Sunday was of personal significance for the young couple; after their marriage, Yan's bride was now officially allowed to attend a non-Chinese church. This would be the first time they were permitted to worship publicly together.

The Fellowships do not serve the entire community of foreign Christians in Kunming. Many of the missionaries I met preferred to worship in their private homes with a small group of friends or alone. For example, William, the owner of a Christian café and NGO, once told me that he holds services and a Sunday study group with friends in his home. The Fellowship nearby, catering to the foreign Christians in the west of the city, is conservative and "too professional" for his taste. He felt the music on Sundays was too polished and devoid of the rough and rudimentary emotion he sought. In contrast, the Northern Fellowship was, in his opinion, "a bit too crazy" (interview, May 10, 2010). For William and many others, attending the Fellowship is a matter of personal choice and style. Even those who do attend, like Simon, explain their appearance by stressing the importance of community. Prayer conducted within the space of the Fellowship was never presented as more meaningful, religiously valid, effective, or holy.

Kunming is also home to the Trinity International Protestant Church, locally known as the Sanyi, an official church that is open to Kunming's foreign Protestants. The large European-style church was built in 1903 and can seat over two thousand people (C. Yu 2014). According to Sean, an American Christian living in town, the church regularly hosts foreign preachers (interview, October 10, 2012). Thus, the choice to worship in the Fellowship, rather than in the more formal, official church (or at home), may be seen as a favoring of a particular style of prayer and community, one that is disassociated from the physical markers of Western Christianity. Indeed, it is somewhat ironic that the Three Self churches, created with the explicit goal of disassociating Christianity from the West, retain "much of the appearance and tone of the old missionary churches" (Bays 2003, 493).[1]

Yan had always been friendly toward me and assisted my research in the past. He had spent several years in Israel, and it was there that he became a born-again Christian. Like Mona, his helpfulness was to a certain extent the result of his interest in Israel and Judaism. It was also the outcome of the fact that he was an avid and enthusiastic missionary. As such, he was critical of Christians in town who preferred to decline my approaches. Rather than keeping me away, Yan believed I should be brought closer. He had tried to introduce me to the local activists of YWAM (Youth With A

Mission), one of the largest international missionary organizations, but his attempts were rejected, as they felt it was too risky. We also discussed the option of me visiting the Fellowship. He asked whether I was permitted to do so, and I reluctantly shared with him that it was in fact somewhat problematic because, from an Orthodox Jewish point of view and according to many rabbinical authorities, Christianity is an idolatrous religion. Yan's response was, at the time, enigmatic to me. He said, "It's actually not really a church—it's a Fellowship" (interview, October 14, 2009). The statement puzzled me. Was this just a matter of terminology, or was there really a difference?

That Sunday morning, I met Yan and his wife at the bus station, and we walked together to a mostly residential area with a scattering of shops and businesses. The Fellowship was located on the third floor of a somewhat run-down building that seemed to be used mostly for commercial purposes. With the wave of rapid development in Kunming, it occurred to me that this relatively old area will probably be demolished within a few years. On the ground floor was a restaurant, and at the entrance stood a security guard whose official job it was to check passports and make sure that the people attending were non-Chinese citizens only. As we entered, the guard seemed clearly uninterested in checking our documents and took no notice of the people walking upstairs. Arriving at the Fellowship, I was gestured toward a table with coffee and tea. When I took my seat in the back row, I looked around to discover that I knew many of the attendants. They were my schoolmates, people I had seen in the neighborhood cafés and restaurants, people I had interviewed and their friends. In the crowd of over one hundred people, my presence did not draw much attention.

The room was not at all reminiscent of official churches I had seen in Yunnan or elsewhere in China—it was remarkably stark and utterly functional. A simple, ground-level pulpit stood in the front with a large screen behind it. Along the walls on three sides of the large rectangular room were rows of benches. To the left, closer to the entrance, four smaller rooms held activities for babies, young kids, and teens. The last room served as a library. The walls were completely bare. The only decorations were multiple national flags hanging from the ceiling, representing the home states of the participant members and emphasizing the international nature of the community.

Such global metaphors, as represented by the national flags, are prominent among foreign Christians in Yunnan. The school serving the community is named the Kunming International Academy, and the prominent Christian aid agency is named Bless China International. The use of the word "international" is not confined to the Christian expat community. Rather, it is commonly used by local Christians to denote the global nature of Christianity. A kindergarten run by Chinese Christians from Henan was named Global Village Kindergarten (*diqiucun youeryuan*), and the rooms within the kindergarten were given names of different countries. Although it was attended by a small number of non-Chinese children, its international nature seemed to be mostly a reflection of an ideological dedication to Christian globalism. Indeed, as I later found out, many of the teachers in the kindergarten subsequently became involved in missionary endeavors outside China.

Similarly, the decentralized and informal character of the Christian community was expressed in the distinctly nonhierarchical and familial terms used to identify members of the community as such. For example, it is quite common for advertisements in the *Kunming SWAP*, an internet newsletter for community members, to point out that someone seeking a job is a "brother" or a "sister," usually referring to Chinese Christians seeking work as housekeepers or providing other services ("Sister with 8 years' experience working with foreigners as *baomu* [caretaker] and on children's projects looking for work"; *KM SWAP*, September 5, 2012). In addition to the clear crossing of previous ethnic and cultural lines of belonging, referring to each other as siblings is yet another way of emphasizing an ideal of global equality. In a Chinese context, this stands in contrast to the traditional Confucian ethic of a society structured in a series of well-defined hierarchies.

The emphasis on the international nature of the missionary community may be seen simply as a reflection of reality: the missionary community does indeed include nationals of many countries. Although heavily North American, the Christian community of Kunming is home to Europeans, South Americans, Africans, and Asians from Hong Kong, Singapore, the Philippines, and Korea. At the same time, the international nature of the Fellowship, the missionary community, and indeed the community of Chinese evangelical Christians contains a distinctly ideological element. Globalism stands at the center of what Oliver Roy has termed "pristine faith" (2004, 28)—religion based on personal faith and standing above all cultural difference. As such, the ability to adapt to any cultural context is often celebrated as evidence of the validity of Christianity. The transethnic and international element of Christianity has been a central feature of the missionary endeavor in Yunnan since the early twentieth century. Thus, early Hua Miao converts are reported to have engaged in prayer for poverty-stricken Han and to have contributed money for the purpose of conducting missionary work in Brazil (Tien 1993, 52). Accordingly, the use of the terms "global" and "international" confirms the way missionaries display confidence in the global nature and appeal of the gospel they spread.

In addition to the Fellowship's international nature, it was an essentially decentralized institution, holding no official leadership. As one congregant explained to me, various people give sermons each Sunday, and administrative issues are decided by a committee. Not only is there no single leader, but on many issues, there is also no official line. The preacher I heard on that particular Sunday implored people to be less fearful of the authorities and more open regarding their work. When I asked Simon what he thought of that perspective, he commented that he saw it as no more than a personal opinion, claiming that "next week someone could say the opposite" (conversation, May 2, 2010). The nonformal atmosphere of the Fellowship was also evident in the clothing of the attendants. To my surprise, I noticed that everybody was dressed casually, lending the place a distinctly relaxed ambience. The casual clothing of attendants, including the guest preacher, who wore shorts and sandals, is a further reflection of the fact that the space of the Fellowship was not considered to be holy.

The services began with a few routine notices: a young member of the community would be giving a piano concert at the Nordica (a cultural center run by Scandinavian Christians), some community members were leaving town, and a guest preacher had come in from Chicago. It was also announced that the Fellowship was moving to another location. A map of the exact location and the way to get there were projected on the wall, and members of the community were asked to volunteer to assist with moving equipment: a stereo system, speakers, and so on. The move was reported shortly and concisely before the service and not referred to again. Looking around at the congregants, I could not detect any particular emotion regarding the news of the Fellowship's upcoming relocation. The casual way the move was mentioned and the general indifference with which the news was received by community members strengthened the feeling that the space of the Fellowship was viewed by worshipers as purely functional. It held no intrinsic religious or emotional value.

The announcements were followed by collective singing and moderately enthusiastic waving of hands in the air. The music consisted of a series of catchy Christian pop songs, led by a young man with a guitar and a heavy Irish accent. After the music, the visiting preacher got up for an hour-long sermon (I was later told that it was unusually long). The words of the songs and biblical verses preselected by the preacher were projected on a screen. The emotionally charged sermon was peppered with stories of the preacher's personal past and redemption: he had been a petty criminal and became a born-again Christian while serving time in prison; today he ministers at a large evangelical church in Chicago. The sermon was more of a motivational talk than an attempt to make a specific argument, apart from calling on congregants to be open and confident about their faith.

I now understood what my friend Yan had meant, months earlier, when we discussed my religious restriction against entering churches. Previously, the decision to refrain from the use of the term "church" was usually explained to me as an effort to distance the community from being associated with traditional Christianity and with the legacy of pre-1949 missionary work. It was also an attempt to distance community members from the older Christian production of space, expressed in large, overbearing, European-style buildings such as the old Trinity church in Kunming's city center. Interestingly, the attempt to avoid the use of Christian terminology has been part of Christian-Chinese history from the days of Matteo Ricci in the seventeenth century. Ricci made a point of calling the institution he opened a "preaching house," a place dedicated to discussion of the classics, rather than a "church," a term with religious connotations (Gernet 1985, 17).[2]

The term "Fellowship" also holds a direct and literal meaning: it is a place of companionship where believers worshiped together. As such, it held no intrinsic value beyond its congregants, encapsulating the evangelical perspective that the space used for prayer does not become embodied with holiness or enchanted. Rather, space occupied for collective worship is simply a place to meet and "have fellowship." By saying it was not really a church but rather a Fellowship, Yan was implying that the space of the Fellowship is no more sacred to those who worship there than it would be to me.

The Language School House Church

The layout of the Fellowship was highly reminiscent of a house church located in a language school that I had visited earlier, run by James, a half-Yi, half-Han Christian and his Han wife, Cathy.[3] James converted to Christianity in 1998, after a friend introduced him to a house church. Later he and his wife belonged to a community run by an Australian missionary (unusually, James used the term "missionary" himself). As a result, James maintains close relationships with many of the foreign Christians in town.

In recent years, his Yi mother has also converted, and his father, a government official and an atheist, was "slowly changing" (James, interview, May 6, 2010). Like Yan, James tended to be quite critical of the official Three Self churches, particularly disliking the intervention of the state in church affairs. According to James, a Three Self pastor who wished to baptize someone must receive official authorization from the government to do so, a procedure he ardently opposed. He baptized whomever he wanted.

In addition to being devoted church leaders, James and Cathy ran a Chinese-language school for foreign students. I was introduced to them by an Israeli student who told me they were interested in meeting me as they were strong supporters of Israel and had a deep interest in Judaism. After having a meal together on the last day of Passover, James invited me to visit their small house church and teach the congregants something about Judaism and the Bible. Like the members of the Fellowship, he did not use the word "church" (*jiaotang*), a term he associates with a large and formal building. He always referred to the prayer gathering simply as a "meeting" (*hui yi*).

Prayer services and Bible-study lessons were held on weekends in the language school, located on the second floor of an ordinary building in the center of town. As house church activity is officially illegal, the double purpose of the school structure was not publicized. Even the student who introduced me to James and Cathy was unaware of the weekend services. Prayer was held in the school lobby—the space between the classrooms where students usually sit, have tea, chat, and smoke during lesson breaks. This small community (eight women and two men participated in the Sunday service that I attended) was in fact one of two groups belonging to the house church. On Saturdays, a larger group of approximately twenty people met for prayer and discussion. The Sunday group was smaller and more intense, dedicated to training people who would eventually lead communities of their own. The congregants were mostly in their twenties or thirties and were fairly recent converts, with their personal Christian history ranging from as long as twelve years to as short as six months.

The prayer itself was fairly short, lasting only about half an hour. The words to Chinese-Christian pop songs were printed on sheets of paper and pasted onto the whitewashed wall, and the congregants sang, accompanied by James, who played the guitar. While singing, the congregants clapped and excitedly waved their hands in the air. Much like the service in the Fellowship, attendants dressed in everyday clothing, and the prayer seemed relaxed, unofficial, and intimate. The casual intimacy of the prayer was echoed in the music, with simple and catchy Christian pop songs, rather than traditional Christian hymns that can sometimes be heard in official churches.[4] Many of the songs referred to God not by "Shangdi," the Protestants' official translation of the biblical name for God, but rather with the familial term "Heavenly Father" (*tianfu*) or with the even more surprising Hebrew word *Aba*, meaning "Father." The dress, music, and speech combined to create an overall feeling of the church as modern, contemporary, and international in style. After the singing, communion was offered, and the members of the community embraced each other. When the service ended, the printed songs were taken off the wall, and we sat down to have a cup of tea before entering the class for the lesson. As we sat on the sofas in the hallways, I felt we were indeed on class break. Apart from the guitar in James's hand, no evidence of the service that had just taken place could be seen.

Both the house church and the International Fellowship are temporary, improvised institutions that could be set up anywhere. The emotional intensity of the prayer and music in both places contrasted sharply with the functional and emotionally neutral nature of the space in which they were conducted. This similarity is not surprising, as both communities are made up primarily of people whose faith is based on a personal transformative experience. Indeed, both Chinese and non-Chinese communities are overwhelmingly made up of converts—people whose religious identity is based on personal choice rather than tradition or ethnicity. The personal, choice-based nature of faith produced a religious expression tightly associated with the individual's inner world of meaning and largely disassociated from the physical space of worship. Thus, both sites can be seen as communities of rootless, landless, and transient believers, occupying a random, functional space.

Both the Fellowship and James's house church/school correspond to Lefebvre's description of a modern "abstract space," the major feature of modern capitalist global spread. In contrast, Mayfair Yang's description of a struggle between locals and officials regarding the construction of a cultural hall simultaneously serving as a sacred shrine to the local goddess Chen Jinggu can be seen as a battle against modern, statist abstraction of space and an attempt to carve out a spatial domain for the divine. The two Christian institutions I have described here embody an opposite vision of space, one that is largely compatible with state modernity. Their spatial projection is practical, functional, and easily interchangeable, leaving the "strategic deployment of space" (M. Yang 2004b, 721) in the hands of the state. The casual attitude toward the relocation of the Fellowship is also instructive: while demolishing places of worship could potentially generate distress and protest among believers, as with the temples in Wenzhou discussed by Yang, no such voices were heard from the Christian community of northern Kunming. The rapid modernization of the city remains a state affair, unrelated to the core issue of faith and redemption.

When the Yunnanese house church and Fellowship are compared to the Sanjiang church in Wenzhou, the importance that the state attributes to space production and representation is evident. In contrast to the Wenzhou Christians' attempt to construct a physical expression of the power of their faith, the house churches of foreign and local Christians of Kunming represent their attempt to distance themselves from spatial representations. They do so by refraining from the use of the term "church," by utilizing any space available, and by emphasizing the centrality of prayer, community, and fellowship rather than physical buildings. In contrast, congregants of Sanjiang attempted to embody the rising power of Christianity in Wenzhou by investing large sums of money to create a prominent church structure and strongly opposed its demolition.

While the churches in Wenzhou were demolished, the globalized and abstract spaces discussed in this chapter have so far been tolerated, despite their association with foreign missionaries and the illegal house church movement. The contrast underlines the advantages of evangelical Christianity from a state perspective, as a religion with a strongly deterritorialized ideology. However, evangelical attitudes toward spatial production and the compatibility with the state go beyond ideology. They are equally a reflection of the drive to remove ritual territoriality as a prerequisite for Christian expansion among China's southwestern minorities.

Unholy Spaces: Spatial and Spiritual Obstacles to Expansion of Christianity

In Elizabeth McAlister's work on the production of space, based on fieldwork in Haiti, she explores the ways in which the Christian cataloging of ethnicities, such as the Joshua Project, is an ethnic and moral mapping of the world, dividing peoples into categories of "reached" and "unreached." The "unreached," who have not been exposed to the gospel, are primarily located in the "dark and unsacred" part of the world known as the "10/40 window"—the area between ten and forty degrees north latitude. The window contains the bulk of non-Christian people on the planet, including most of Asia and the Islamic world, and has been declared by the missionary movement AD2000 as the core area for evangelism (McAlister 2005, 252; on the 10/40 window, see Hattaway 2003, x; AD2000 and Beyond website, http://www.ad2000.org).

Evangelical preachers in Haiti use a common set of methods and language in their attempts to "win for Jesus" territory that was previously ruled by voodoo spirits, by encouraging converts to move away from locally contextualized religiosity and replace it with a transethnic, global Christian identity. By becoming part of a Christian global order, territorial and national sentiments are diminished, making way for an international and transnational identity. By "winning Haiti for Jesus" and vanquishing the local deities, evangelical Christians engage in their own production of space on a global level (McAlister 2005, 253). Indeed, the nature of space is often cited by missionaries to explain success and failure in the mission field. Ralph Covell makes the claim that "the most resistant [to conversion] areas of the world are controlled by demonic beings" (1995, 267), implying that these spiritual beings are territorial in nature. He continues by suggesting that missionaries must become acquainted with these local demons, with their names and attributes, and devise specific prayers and actions to defeat them.

Missionaries in Yunnan make similar claims, particularly with regard to Tibetan Buddhist areas. Simon mentioned a friend who worked as a missionary in the Tibetan areas of Yunnan but had to leave "because it was too heavy" (interview, May 25, 2010). Simon explained the "heaviness" of the region as the result of local deity worship, creating a space of spiritual oppression. The situation was such that his friends' son became mentally unstable. In contrast, Simon mentioned another friend who had been able to persevere in the same region, having a particularly hardy character. To Simon, it was the land itself, no less than the religion of its inhabitants, that posed a problem for the spread of Christianity, being a space of heaviness and ungodliness, a spiritual-geographic zone controlled by demonic beings. Mark made a similar assessment of Tibetan Buddhism and its "dark spirituality." Remarking on a trip made to the Tibetan areas of Sichuan, Mark described to me the tangible nature of the demonic in these areas: "If you didn't believe in demons before, you have them there like a bunch of flies on a pile of garbage" (interview, March 3, 2010). Likewise, a female missionary working among the Jingpo in the south of Yunnan conveyed her experience that many of the new converts in her region ended up "backsliding" into their old lives as nonbelievers. She ascribed the high rates of dropping out of faith to the evil spirits present in the Jingpo villages, claiming that "it's very dark down there" (Cathy, interview, November 18, 2009).

Simon and Mark's approach is reflected in the page dedicated to Yunnan on the Christian website Pray for China.[5] The website encourages Christians to pray on numerous issues, including the spread of Christianity in different locations and among different minorities and help for persecuted Christians, as well as a prayer "that the governor of Yunnan, Xu Rongkai, would recognize the positive contributions being made to China's development by Christians." Of particular relevance here are the prayer points concerned with the demonic influence of religious sites, as in the following examples:

> Pray against the demonic influence of the Daoist Baohua Monastery in Gejiu. Pray for China's Daoists to see that only the Lord Jesus is the Way, the Truth and the Life (John 14:6).
> Pray against the demonic forces of superstition and idolatry at the Yuantong Temple, Kunming's largest Buddhist temple (Eph. 1:21–22).
> Pray against the demonic forces at Yunnan's Mount Jizu, one of the four sacred mountains for Buddhists (2 Kings 18:4).[6]

While Covell, Simon, and Mark all spoke of the dark and unholy areas, they made no reference to the space of opposite quality or to regions marked as holy and clean. In light of the foregoing analysis, I suggest that the lack of symmetry between holy and unholy spaces in missionary rhetoric can be explained as a negation of the connection between spirituality and space. Thus, while McAlister describes Christian activity in Haiti as space production, it could more accurately be referred to as the deconstruction of space. The emphasis of missionary activity is on breaking the spiritual-physical bond and replacing it not with a similar, physically based construct but rather with a nonterritorial religiosity unrelated to, and transcendent from, the physical world. Accordingly, spaces can be either under the domination of demonic beings or neutral. Indeed, from an evangelical perspective, the confluence of space and spirituality contains spiritual danger of becoming an idolatrous attachment to specific locations and an unwillingness "to display the mobility required in a true servant of God, prepared to move were the Spirit listeth" (Coleman 2009, 34).

In 2012, two years after leaving Yunnan, I returned to follow up on my fieldwork and met Simon again. One afternoon we took a walk together down a dirt road leading to the Dianchi Lake. As we were walking past a small Buddhist shrine, Simon expressed his dissatisfaction at seeing the idolatry. "It's terrible, everything here is based on fear" (conversation, October 11, 2012). He then began telling me about a trip he had recently made to a Guizhou village, to which some of his Bouyei converts have returned. Throughout his time there, he felt overwhelmed by the ambience of "heaviness, fear, and oppression." Simon was not referring to state oppression; rather, his feeling was caused by a perceived prevalence of spirit worship and the constant need to correctly appease local deities.

Life in the villages was challenging for the returning converts. As Simon noted, the anonymity and multiethnic nature of the big city made personal choices, particularly in the realm of faith, much easier. While, for the most part, the Christians of the village were allowed to live their lives as they wish, in some circumstances, Christians came under great social pressure. The biggest problems arise when a community member dies and a burial is required. Naturally, Christians prefer to conduct a Christian burial or at the very least one that does not involve the worship and honoring of local spirits. However, for the other villagers, a burial ceremony that does not take local deities into account is unacceptable, and the performance of such a ceremony would be harmful for the entire community.

Spirits among the animist peoples of Southwest China are often perceived as territorial in nature; like the earth gods (*tudi gong*) and kitchen gods (*zaojun*) of Chinese tradition, they belong to particular valleys, mountains, and fields or even to specific parts of the house. The territorial nature of the earth spirit Agamisimo is described by Mueggler: "from its anchorage on the hill above Chemo, Agamisimo's presence saturated the territory of Zhizuo to its boundaries" (2001, 112). Accordingly, in Zhizuo, local cadres were unable to convince Yi residents to cultivate two small ancestral plots considered to be associated with a specific spirit, as cultivating them outside the boundaries of ritual was considered to be the source of numerous disasters. Similarly, the Guizhou Bouyei felt strongly that spirits and deities that are not appeased would inevitably take their vengeance on the village, perceived as a single body intimately related to specific local spirits.[7] According to Simon, the villagers will not waver on this point—not only must the ceremony be conducted properly, the attendance of the family is mandatory. When a Christian dies, they will often stage a sit-in, occupying the house of the deceased until a proper burial is conducted. The best local Christians can do is to attend the traditional funeral ceremony and try to be as passive as possible (for a similar story regarding Christians among the Hani, see You, Wang, and Gong 2004, 117). Accordingly, the reemergence of ethnic spiritual territoriality poses a challenge both to the state's organization of space and to the spread of the gospel.

Conclusion: Global Spaces

The global era is often spoken of as a time of great opportunity for China. However, it is also a time of unique dangers for the PRC (and indeed for all nation-states). Old methods of control are no longer effective, while new and renewed local identities and the revival of old forms of ritual territoriality pose a danger to state sovereignty as they work to undermine the image of the single unified state space. As the case of the Sanjiang church reveals, the state does not hesitate to act when its spatial production is challenged. Thus, Christianity can be conceived of as part of the problem—a transnational identity unrelated to the state, its territory and nation. In this work, I suggest a contrary view: that the process of territorial detachment offered by evangelical Christianity is in tune with the state's own interests in the realm of religion and ethnicity.

In the case of Yunnan, Christian nonterritoriality is of specific importance, as it coincides with the local state's attempt to encourage decontextualized ethnic identities and to weaken the connection between ethnoreligious identities and specific locations. However, it would seem that the sensitivity of ethnic relations is such that the harsh policies practiced in Wenzhou are considered unsuitable for Yunnan. While ethnicity in Yunnan is much less volatile than in Tibet or Xinjiang, the power of ethnic identity politics in Yunnan should not be overlooked, especially as many of the groups have a history of struggle with the Han and their state. In the aftermath of the 1989 Tiananmen Square crackdown, an article appeared in an important journal in the Zhuang Autonomous Guangxi Province, calling for the Zhuang "to wake up and take charge of the leadership in Guangxi" (Kaup 2000, 2). Accordingly, the potential for encouraging the creation of entities or spatial division beyond the reach of the state must be addressed. This is done by celebrating ethnicity as the marginal outline, thus emphasizing the power nesting at the center, represented by posters and pictures of the Hall of Supreme Harmony in Beijing or the national flag. It can also be achieved with the aid of a globalizing, deethnicizing force such as evangelical Christianity.

The confluence of Christian and state agendas is also a reflection of the fact that ritual territoriality is both practically and ideologically problematic for Christian expansion. On a practical level, minorities that are closely attached to local spirits and deities have been much harder to convert. On an ideological level, the investment of space or bodies with holiness is in and of itself a challenge to the spiritual, global, and abstract nature of the evangelical message of salvation. Thus, missionaries often voice opinions reminiscent of those expressed by state cadres, attacking religious attachment to space among minorities as superstitious and backward and advocating a nonspatial ethnic identity centered on a spiritual and international core.

The question remains whether the position of Christianity can be maintained after the state has employed religion as a means to contain and neutralize ethnicity. While academics like Xin are confident in the ability of the state to maintain a line of separation, others are alarmed by the pace of growth and the potential for foreign involvement in China's internal affairs (Ma Huacheng 2010). Indeed, skeptics may find some of the Christian literature alarming in this regard, such as David Aikman's claim that Christians can be trusted to be forgiving and magnanimous toward China's former leadership once the country becomes entirely Christian (2003, 303). Christian activists are well aware of the delicate balance between themselves and the authorities and the need to refrain from antistate rhetoric. Thus, mission workers like Simon speak of the ability to act in Yunnan, noting that "you have to know not to cross the line" (interview, October 11, 2012).

For the time being, it would seem that an operating modus vivendi has emerged between the contemporary agents of these two civilizing projects, an unwritten agreement regarding the borders of action and the nature of ethnicity and space. Despite the important impact that local authorities and foreign Christians have on the formation of contemporary ethnic identity, it would be incorrect to view ethnic Christians as passive singers and dancers in colorful clothes, whose identity is entirely constructed by other players. Between the internal Orientalism of the state and Christian internationalism, minority Christians find ways to express their ethnic identity and its relationship with Christianity in substantial ways, an issue explored in chapter 7.

Chapter 7

DRAWING THE BORDERS OF ETHNO-CHRISTIANITY

The Nationalities Village

In previous chapters, I addressed Christianity in Yunnan primarily from the perspective of the foreign missionaries living in the province and their work among ethnic minorities. This chapter expounds on the issue of state tolerance of Christianity and the interaction between ethnic Christians and local authorities through an analysis of an official publicly funded and organized "Nationalities Village"—a living museum dedicated to Yunnan's twenty-six ethnic groups, situated at the southern end of the city of Kunming. The analysis offered here follows Charlene Makley's work on the Tibetan section within another "Nationalities Park" in Beijing. Makley argues that rather than viewing the park simply as a commodification of ethnic culture or as state propaganda, ethnic displays must be seen as "an ever-evolving attempt, in the face of the actual unruliness of real people, to structure and render pleasurable citizens' and visitors' participation in the core categories, hierarchies, and thus values of the ascendant PRC" (2010, 129). Accordingly, ethnic parks are instrumental in establishing the supremacy of the category of ethnicity (*minzu*) over that of religion (*zongjiao*).

In the case of the Nationalities Village in Yunnan, religion (Christianity) and ethnicity are carefully negotiated within the framework of the park's various spaces. The spatial layout of the Miao compound within the village, particularly the structure of the compound's church, reveals the way in which the state is able to maintain control over ethnicity and religion, while allowing Christians from ethnic minorities to express their religious beliefs with relative freedom. This is done through a differentiation of spaces and narratives. In the general space of the Nationalities Village, Christianity is absent, and ancient religious traditions are emphasized. In an interim space within the area dedicated to the Miao, the Christian presence in Yunnan is partially acknowledged. In the internal space of the Miao Village church, Christianity is openly expressed and even promoted. At the same time, recognition and tolerance are displayed in a way and within a context that does not challenge the state's primacy or its authority in creating and maintaining categories of ethnicity and religion.

My argument here is twofold. First, Christianity is represented in the village despite its being a relatively new religion in Yunnan, simply because it is present among ethnic minorities to a degree that cannot be overlooked. Such a position is in line with the argument made by Kim-kwong Chan regarding post-Maoist policy on religion in general, shifting from a "religion as enemy" to a "religion as competitor" paradigm (2004, 67; see also DuBois and Zhen 2014; Homer 2010; Madsen 2010). As the former director of the State Religious Affairs Bureau Ye Xiaowen has written, the current leadership of China views religion as a permanent, empiric reality. Former premier Jiang Zemin noted that it may even outlast social classes and nation-states. As such, there is no contradiction between tolerance of religious practice and the active promotion of dialectic materialism (Ye 2005, 447–48).

Second, following recent trends in ethnic policy (Baranovitch 2010; Leibold 2010, 2013), I argue that state accommodation of Christian religio-ethnicity (Lim 2013b, 110) within the Nationalities Village reflects the state's ability to alternate between overlapping and at times conflicting narratives, with varying emphases on ethnic difference and national unity. Thus, when the modern-archaic dichotomy can no longer be applied, the state reverts to "Confucian Ecumenism" (Leibold 2010, 2): a melting pot ideal of harmony and Chinese-centered national identity.

Many scholars of ethnicity in China have written on the Chinese category of *minzu* and its inherent emphasis on the backwardness of ethnicity, a perspective often referred to as "internal Orientalism." Minorities are portrayed as passive, feminine, irrational, and primitive—an image diametrically opposed to the masculinity, rationality, and dynamic nature of the ruling Han majority (Bin 2009, 743; Borchert 2005; Diamond 1995, 99–106; Gladney 1994, 92; 2004; Harrell 1996; Heberer 2000, 8; Komlosy 2009; Litzinger 2000; Schein 1997, 69; Solinger 1977). As Louisa Schein points out, minorities are "never quite fitting the pace and standards of the nation, but always somehow signifying its limits, its margins, its feminized other" (2000, 11).

Viewing the representation of ethnicity through the prism of the modern-Han/archaic-minority dichotomy is highly relevant to certain sections within the Nationalities Village. However, I feel it is insufficient in explaining the representation of Christianity among ethnic minorities, and there is a need for an alternative paradigm. In the Miao church, Christianity is presented as neither archaic nor exotic but rather modern and dynamic. Furthermore, rather than reflecting the ideology of social evolution led by the Han, artifacts within the church offer an alternative, Christian narrative of the Chinese past and the road toward modernity, one that diverges significantly from the official CCP teleology of development. Thus, the Nationalities Village Miao compound combines the prevalent emphasis on "internal Orientalism" with a narrative of unity that obscures ethnic difference and is centered around a Han monoculture. Christian narratives of the past and future expressed in the church's interior refer primarily to Han history and tradition, rather than that of the Miao or other ethnic minorities, asserting the paramount position of Chinese Han culture as a guiding principle and common ground for all ethnic groups. The framing of ethnic religiosity within the context of the history of Christianity in China at large serves the state in its effort to emphasize a single national culture, including but subsuming minority cultures and binding all ethnic nationalities under the banner of unity and harmony.

The Tourism of Living Fossils

Ethnicity is seen everywhere in Yunnan. Billboards with young, colorfully dressed, smiling girls and young women from minority groups adorn the walls of Kunming's central train station. The uniforms of the airport staff are minority costumes. A mix of Dai batiks, Naxi textiles, Bai silver jewelry, and other ethnic-style paraphernalia can be found in shops throughout the province. Performances of minority singing and dancing are heavily promoted, corresponding to official rhetoric and popular views of minority people as those "who are good at singing and dancing" (*nengge-shanwu*) and dress in colorful clothes (Blum 2001, 83; Davis 2006; Gladney 1994, 95; Goodman 2009, 75).

Yunnan is so closely associated with ethnicity that its manifestations can even be found in places where there are actually very few minority people. To give one example of the emblematic presence of ethnicity, in an event held in my son's kindergarten to celebrate "Children's Day" (June 1,

2010), parents were invited to join in a celebration held on the grounds of the Kunming Expo compound. I was surprised that the kindergarten teachers came dressed in ethnic-minority costumes, despite the fact that virtually all of them were Han from Henan Province. The Children's Day program was centered on a sequence of ethnic-minority dances. There seemed to be no direct link between the kindergarten's Children's Day activities at the Expo grounds and the display of minority cultures. In Yunnan, ethnicity was presented simply as a form of recreation, a symbol of Yunnan's local allure; in Beijing, presentations of ethnicity are quite different and less superficial.

This superficial presentation of minority culture is also true in the mostly Han city of Kunming and in cities in minority regions that cater to large number of tourists, such as the Bai town of Dali, Naxi Lijiang, Tibetan Shangrila, and the predominantly Dai prefecture of Xishuangbanna, where tour guides, shop workers, and waiters all dress in stylized ethnic uniforms. The prevalence of ethnic costume is a "paramount emblem of ethnic difference" (Blum 2001, 83). Indeed, the feeling one gets when visiting an ethnic locality or reading a local guide book is that costume and songs are not merely a manifestation of ethnicity but its very core.

According to Susan Blum's survey of Kunming's Han population, while certain negative perceptions of specific minority peoples are not uncommon (most notably regarding the Tibetan and Hui), when minorities are discussed as a whole, the most common perceptions refer not only to singing and dancing but also to traits such as honesty and a general feeling of uninhibited and free-spirited nature (Blum 2001, 85) Above all, minorities are often displayed and perceived as fun-loving, in contrast to the reserved and serious Han (Gladney 1994, 113). The massive promotion of Yunnan's colorful and exotic minorities is a central feature of the ethnotourism business. In recent years, the Chinese government has been investing heavily in domestic tourism to encourage middle-class Chinese to spend money and create revenue for the relatively poor provinces of Southwest China. To that aim, the government has instituted a weeklong holiday around International Labor Day (May 1), with the express goal of promoting tourism (Borchert 2005, 92; Davis 2003, 179; Ghimire and Zhou 2001). At the same time, the provincial government has set out to remake the peripheral province as the major destination of domestic tourism.

Serving primarily as an advertisement for the province, public representations of ethnic identity focus almost exclusively on external manifestations, with relatively little attention devoted to minority belief systems. In Yunnan and elsewhere in China (M. Yang 2004a), tourism to religious sites is mostly focused on elaborate architecture or colorful festivals. Thus, the state is only interested in "those minority religious activities that have viewable components" (Borchert 2005, 94; see also Varutti 2010, 76). The state often sponsors the use and preservation of temples and shrines that have the potential of becoming tourist attractions (Davis 2003; Hillman 2005; McCarthy 2009). Ethnic representation is designed to avoid challenging state policies and the modernization project, mostly emphasizing festivals, dance, and costumes (Harrell 1996, 27). This has been the case since the beginning of the reform era: "the CCP has expressed little interest in what religious people actually believe, only that they not challenge the hegemony of the state" (Bays 2011, 188).

This is not to say that minority religion is not promoted to a certain extent. Indeed, minorities are often associated with religiosity, which is presented as a core element of their alleged backwardness and inherent irrationality, as well as a source of interest and allure. Thus, some local religions, most notably Tibetan Buddhism, have been attracting considerable attention from middle-class urban Chinese intellectuals since the 1990s (Smyer Yu 2012). Several high-profile Chinese celebrities have donated large sums of money to Lamaist temples in Tibet.

One typical example of the way religiosity is used to promote tourism can be found in a brochure introducing the Tropic of Cancer Symbol Garden in Mojiang, devoted to the Hani culture of the region, in which a series of sculptures and reliefs are described. One, titled *Quafoo and Sun*, is dedicated to Hani origin myths. The English caption beneath the picture reads, "It shows that ancient people had a foolish mind [the Chinese text reads, "luohuo yumei," literally translated as "backward and ignorant"] about understanding the sun, but the story is deeply meaningful and worshiped by the Hani people" (Mojiang Tourism Bureau, pamphlet, 2007). Thus, Hani beliefs are respectfully portrayed as "meaningful" to the Hani, invoking interest in Hani culture and at the same time reinforcing their archaic and primitive image. The internal Orientalism inherent in the representation of Hani tradition is often indicative of the relationship between ethnicity, religion, and tourism in China. Thus, the tourist industry revolving around ethnic religious sites in places like Yunnan provides Han tourists who view archaic-looking religious ceremonies "the opportunity to feel modern" (Borchert 2005, 99; see also Gladney 2004, 53).

To a large extent, the archaic image of ethnic minorities is part of official policy on ethnicity. The ethnic classification project carried out in the 1950s followed Soviet precedent by officially classifying ethnic groups generally corresponding to the criteria set out by Stalin.[1] Every one of China's fifty-five minority people has been categorized as belonging to a specific rung in the ladder of development according to Marxist and Morgonian theory (Bin 2009; Gladney 1994, 100; Harrell 1996, 5; Tapp 2002, 67). In the early years of the PRC, policies such as agrarian reform were implemented differently among minorities according to their ascribed developmental phase (Harrell 1990, 532). During the radical years of the Cultural Revolution, an attempt was made to disregard the differences between ethnic groups and apply equal policies to the entire populace of the PRC. In the reform era, particular policies directed toward minorities have once again emerged. These include policies of affirmative action in the realms of family planning and higher education (Heberer 2000, 7; Sautman 1998, 1999).

As part of the archaic-modern dichotomy, the strong religiosity of minority people is often placed in contrast with the essentially secular and modern nature of the Han and the state. Accordingly, Luo Zhufeng asserts, "In our country there has never been a time when religion could influence the political situation" (1991, 35). Similarly, Ye Xiaowen states, "Throughout Chinese history, there was never a theocratic regime and all Chinese religions were accustomed to putting the country's interest first" (2005, 441). Indeed, believers in any religion are not permitted to join the Communist Party unless they belong to an ethnic minority (Kim-kwong Chan 2005, 90).[2] Furthermore, minorities are officially allowed to embrace religions other than the religions that are recognized by the state (Buddhism, Daoism, Islam, Catholicism, and Protestant Christianity) as long as these are part of their national heritage.

In light of recent ethnic violence in Xinjiang and Tibet, China under Xi Jinping seems to be moving away from Soviet-style ethnic policies based on ethnic essentialism and division and turning toward a "melting pot" policy, gradually deemphasizing ethnicity and otherness and stressing a sense of national transethnic identity. The change in ethnic policy, advocated by a number of Chinese academics, may be seen as a gradual return to the older Confucian ideal of the "great unity" (*datong*), a system of ethnic acculturation and fusion into a monoculture, emphasizing unity over diversity (Leibold 2013, 4–5). The current trend has resulted in recent calls from academia, the military, and even from within the government to move away from ethnic difference, possibly removing the *minzu* category from identity cards, strengthening the instruction of Putonghua, and promoting a single national identity (Leibold 2013, 41).

From a somewhat different angle, an analysis of minority representation in Chinese history textbooks suggests that the emphasis on "othering" ethnic minorities may be understood as a feature of state policy in the formative years of the CCP, a means of constructing a solid Han identity. However, Nimrod Baranovitch argues that "now that the core of the new Chinese nation state has been consolidated, it was possible to move on to the next stage of the nation building project, to shift the emphasis to incorporating the periphery" (2010, 111). In the textbooks, the ideal of a multiethnic state is promoted through an emphasis on minority history as an inseparable element of the Chinese historical narrative. Current changes in ethnic policy do not amount to a break from previous policies; they are gradual and small-scale. Ethnic classification and essentialism still loom large in China as a whole and in the social reality of Yunnan. Nevertheless, the drive toward a national monoculture can be read in the nuanced subtext of the Miao church interior, a subtext that stands out only when examined within the context of the entire compound. Furthermore, rather than indicating a unidirectional shift in ethnic policy, the state is able to move in and out of its own constructed paradigms, alternating between multiple narratives of ethnic identity, present within the spatial layout described in the following section.

A Field Trip to the Yunnan Nationalities Village

Situated on the northern shore of the Dianchi Lake, beneath Kunming's western hills, the Yunnan Nationalities Village is divided into twenty-five units referred to as "villages" (*cun*), each representing a single ethnic minority. It is promoted as a living museum, displaying the entire array of Yunnan's ethnic makeup and a place where tourists who lack the time or the will to travel to remote and rugged minority areas can experience a condensed experience of minority culture without leaving the provincial capital. Similar parks dedicated to the ethnic minorities of China exist in a number of locations throughout China, including Shenzhen and Beijing (Gladney 2004).

As a showcase museum portraying an officially constructed image of minorities, Nationalities Villages cater mostly to the domestic tourist market (Gladney 2004, 45). Indeed, English-language reviews of the Nationalities Village tend to be critical: "a generally artificial setting characterizes the Minority Nationalities Park in Kunming. Visitors get a very sanitized version of minority life here, the elephant show being the highlight of the tour" (Goodman 2009, 212). Likewise, many of the comments regarding the village that appear on the popular website Tripadvisor have titles such as "plastic Disneyland," "Instant China," and "a thinly disguised outpost for cheap souvenirs."[3] It is therefore not surprising that there are few non-Chinese visitors to the site: on my full-day visit to the village, I saw none.

Each village in the park houses a number of minority people from ethnic regions brought in to live on the premises and perform songs, dances, or religious rituals for tourists. Compounds also include replicas of minority architecture, arts and crafts, and ceremonial and religious structures. In addition to shows by specific minority performers, the village stages larger shows featuring a colorful collection of many minority dancers and singers, often indiscernible from each other.

All of the villages' inhabitants I saw were young, mostly in their twenties, lending the park a distinctly youthful yet somewhat unnatural feeling. A disproportionate number of the young minority people on the premises were women (Dru Gladney reports a similar phenomenon in the park in Beijing: 2004, 42), thus enhancing the feminized image of minorities. The overall youthfulness of the village on my visit had a single exception in the form of an older woman of the Dulong (Derung) minority. The reason for her presence was obvious: her face was covered with traditional tattoos. The sign at the Dulong Village asserts that the practice of tattooing Dulong girls "began to disappear" in the 1950s. In fact, tattooing ceased at that time as a result of pressure from Communist authorities, who condemned the custom as primitive and oppressive (Mazard 2014).

Signs and displays throughout the village make reference to the minorities' archaic beliefs, ancient roots, and the practice of matriarchy. Emphasis is placed on the informal marriage traditions and loose social institutions, which are understood to be emblems of lower rungs on the social evolutionary ladder. Faith in spirits, totems, and nature gods all feature prominently, consolidating the ethnic minorities in their position as "living fossils of social history" (this phrase has been used by several researchers; see, for example, Bin 2009, 752; Gladney 1994, 99; Harrell 1996, 16). As Steven Harrell has noted, this metaphor is one of three recurrent themes in official depictions of ethnic groups, along with their depiction as feminine and as childlike (innocent and requiring education). Thus, "peripheral people are ancient, unchanged, not so far along the same scale as the people of the civilizing center" (Harrell 1996, 15).

While backwardness is emphasized in some cases, other minorities are praised for moving rapidly toward modernity. The sign describing Yunnan's small community of Manchu (Man) contains no information on costumes or culture. Instead, it praises the Manchu for their academic achievements particularly in the realm of education, citing the number of Manchu holding higher degrees and administrative positions. The message seems clear: progress of a given minority is closely related to its ability to effectively integrate into the modern state system. Far from being lamented, Manchu assimilation into the Han majority is presented as a mark of development and a celebrated success. Inside the village, I found a single young Manchu woman from Baoshan wearing a headdress. When asked about Manchu language and customs, she acknowledged that the Manchu are currently virtually indistinguishable from the Han majority (conversation, April 21, 2010).

A number of the compounds contain central displays dedicated to religious practice. The Dai Village includes a small Theravada Buddhist temple attended by a young monk. Likewise, the Tibetan Village includes a temple where several monks instruct visitors on how to bow, light incense, and circle the temple in the correct direction and give out traditional white scarves. There is also a small Hui mosque, attended by a single Hui man, and a fairly empty Daoist shrine set up in the Yao compound. Walking through the village, I wondered what mention, if any, would be made of Christianity.

The relationship between Christianity and ethnicity seems easier to ignore and more complicated to express. Ethnic groups that have become predominantly Christian contain many nonbelievers as well. For example, while the majority of Hua Miao are Christian, other Miao are not. The same is true of the Lisu: those living in the Nujiang valley in the western part of the province are overwhelmingly Christian, with Fugong county being the most Christianized area in China (Kim-kwong Chan 2009, 56), while others, such as the Lisu of Dehong on the Burmese border, maintain their traditional religion. Accordingly, many Lisu regard Christianity as their "ethnic religious identity" (Kim-kwong Chan 2005, 96); however, according to the Overseas Missionary Fellowship, only approximately half of the Lisu of Yunnan are Christians.[4]

Christianity came to Yunnan as the result of growing Western influence in the last decades of the Imperial era. Many official accounts of minority cultures make little or no mention of Christianity (for a typical example, see Jia Zhongyi 2006; Zhang and Zeng 1993; Christianity is equally absent from official Chinese websites describing the country's minorities).[5] While minorities are considered to be religious, apart from the Dai, Hui, and Tibetan minorities, the religious traditions emphasized in official rhetoric are polytheism and animism, often defined as "primitive religions." As mentioned, the primitive image of ethnicity serves a double purpose. It solidifies the position of minority people as inherently backward and the Han as the driving force toward progress. At the same time, it creates the feeling of authenticity, an essential element of the ethnotourism business (Notar 2006; Xie 2001). Christianity does not quite fit this perspective of ethnicity: being recent, it lacks authenticity; being associated with Western modernity, it seems to contradict the backward and static nature attributed to minorities. Similarly, Dru Gladney notes the absence of Muslim minorities from the Beijing Nationalities Village, a fact he attributes to their lack of compatibility with the modern-archaic dichotomy of ethnicity (2004, 44).

Beyond ideological considerations, one must recall that the Nationalities Village is a profit-making tourist site. As such, emphasis is placed on the most attractive, exotic, and colorful aspects of ethnic life. The great attractions of the village are the performances, such as the elephant show and the various dancing performances and renditions of folk festivals using elaborate costumes. In comparison to Dai and Tibetan rituals, Christianity is not particularly colorful. It is not associated with specific costumes and has no elaborate festivals to speak of. It is also completely devoid of the mildly erotic nature of some ethnic practices, such as the Dai water-splashing festival, Mosuo marriage arrangements,[6] and Zhuang wife snatching (Gladney 1994, 103–11; 2004, 42; Harrell 1996, 10–12; Horth 2004; Jia Zhongyi 2006, 56). Indeed, most Christian areas in Yunnan have not been developed as tourist destinations. From the perspective of promoting tourism, Christianized ethnic groups are clearly lacking exotic allure.

This conclusion regarding the problematic position of Christianity as an ethnicity gains further support from the Nationalities Village website. While separate pages exist for all nationalities featured in the village, much emphasis is placed on a select few, most prominent among them being the Dai, with their famous water festival and eroticized dancing. Neither the Miao nor the other predominantly Christian groups are featured, except for the Jingpo, whose claim to fame on the website is their colorful Munazongge festival. The Jingpo's animist faith, sun god, and spirit worship are referred to extensively. In contrast, a single passing reference that "today there are also believers in Christianity" has recently been omitted.[7]

Accordingly, I assumed that the existence of Christianity among Yunnan's minorities would simply be ignored. Indeed, I found no mention of Christian influence in the Lisu, Lahu, or Jingpo compounds. The sign at the entrance to the Lisu Village states, "The Lisu people worship a primitive religion in which 'everything of earth has a soul' and the Lisu people are keen on contestant skills as well as singing and dancing arts." I found a single mention of Christianity on a sign titled "folk religions" (*minjian zongjiao*) inside the Bouyei Village. The sign describes Bouyei polytheism and animism at length and concludes with the statement, "In modern history, as Catholicism was introduced to Yunnan some Buyi people converted to this religion."[8] I was surprised at the mention of Catholic Christianity in the case of the Bouyei, since the number of Catholic Bouyei is not particularly high. According to missionaries cited by the Joshua Project, their number does not exceed five thousand people, amounting to less than 1 percent of the Bouyei population.[9]

And yet, the Nationalities Village does contain a church, located within the Miao Village. What follows is an analysis of the spatial layout of the Miao compound, which is divided into three arenas representing alternate realms of religious expression and state policy. Moving from the outside inward, these are the outer gate of the village, the liminal area between the village gate and the church, including the church wall, and the church interior.

The First Arena: Outside the Miao Village

The sign posted at the entrance to the Miao compound confirmed my suspicion that Christianity's role in minority culture may be absent from the village. The standard presentation of the Miao on the sign located just outside the village parameter contains a single sentence regarding religion: "Offspring of an ancient frequently migrating ethnic group, the Miao people worship their ancestors."

The sign at the gate largely corresponds to the official image of ethnicity. Thus, ethnicity follows a set of essential, objective, and scientific criteria, allowing no expression of developments such as the recent adoption of a foreign religion. The sign makes no mention of Christianity or its role in the Miao community. Corresponding to the modern-archaic dichotomy, the Miao are defined primarily as "an ancient migratory people" living in Yunnan's mountainous regions far from the Han-occupied lowlands. In accordance with the most common depiction of ethnic groups, what marks the Miao is their migratory history, along with their handicraft and festivals.

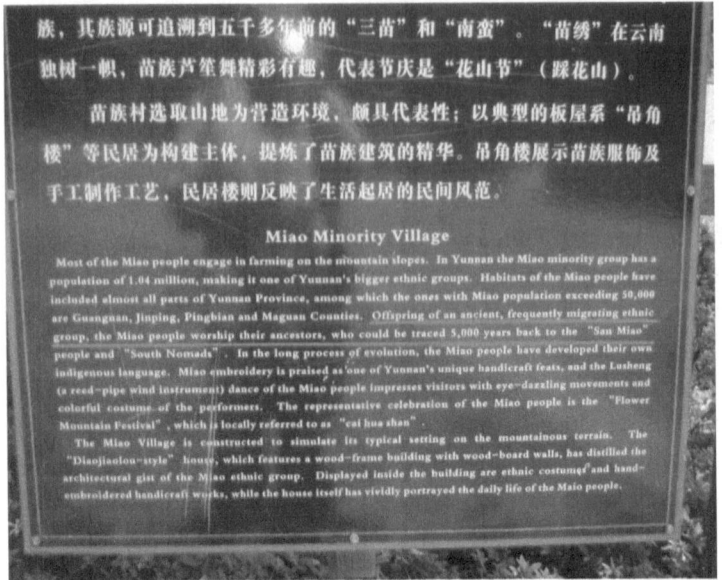

Fig. 3 Miao Village sign. Photo: Gideon Elazar.

As part of the Nationalities Village, the sign at the entrance to the Miao Village may be seen as an assertion that ethnicity is constructed and represented within the space and under the clear guidance of the state (for a similar claim regarding Tibetan representation in the Beijing Nationalities Village, see Makley 2010, 129). Visitors reading the sign outside the compound have yet to enter the area labeled "Miao." They are in the public space of the village, where the official borders of religion, ethnicity, and space are determined by the authorities according to the ethnic classification project (*minzu shibie*) conducted in the 1950s (Bin 2009; Mullaney 2004, 2010; Tapp 2002). The state classification system includes a fixed historical narrative, a geographic zone, and a set of norms and practices. In the words of Henri Lefebvre, "The modern state promotes and imposes itself as a stable center defining (national) societies and spaces . . . as both the end and the means of history" (1991, 23).

Despite the rhetoric of development, the marking of minorities as "living fossils" is inherent to their status as separate ethnicities. Thus, while ethnicity is fluid, the category of *minzu* is essentially fixed and unchanging (Bin 2009, 744; Harrell 1990, 518). Accordingly, while the Miao of Yunnan have been sedentary for over a century, according to the sign at the entrance, they are forever migratory. Likewise, while reform-era China has witnessed a substantial number of rural Miao seeking work in big cities, in the official view, the Miao will always be residents of remote mountain areas. As such, it is hardly surprising that due to the relatively recent penetration of Christian influence from the outside world into Yunnan, the sign at the gate makes no mention of Christianity in Miao society and does not even disclose the existence of the church inside the village.

The Second Arena: In the Village, at the Church Door

The reality presented inside the village compound is quite different from the one articulated at the gate. Upon entering the gate, one immediately notices that the large building dominating the entire village is a church. The second space, stretching from the outer gate to the church gate, can be defined as a liminal middle ground (Thomassen 2009). To the visitor now standing within the village, the imposing building of the church, with its large cross on the roof, is clearly visible, and the centrality of Christianity in Miao life is recognized.

As figure 4 shows, the church stands on a raised platform, making it the highest point in the Miao compound. Unlike the modern-looking chapels I saw in Wuding, with their shiny white-tile fronts and red crosses, the church in the village was built in a style clearly designed to emulate traditional rural architecture, with an earth-colored wooden front and a roof crowned with a large wooden cross. The Miao compound contains other displays, including a small museum exhibit to the left, but the church is the largest and most dominant building.

Walking up the stairs to the church door, visitors encounter a sign at the entrance with the following explanation in English: "Catholicism and Christianity propagated in Yunnan's minority inhabited areas over a century ago and have sizable numbers of disciples among the Miao, Yi, Nu, Lisu and Lahu minority people. To objectively portray this religious folk culture a Christian church is built in the Miao Village."[10] The wording of the sign struck me as awkward and apologetic. The assertion that the church was intended to "objectively" portray religious folk culture seemed to reflect uneasiness, marking the existence of the church as not entirely natural and noting that without the church, the representation of certain groups would lack credibility. In contrast, no such sign existed at the door of the temple on the Tibetan compound or the Hui mosque, despite the fact that both Buddhism and Islam are of foreign origin. Furthermore, the sign on the

Fig. 4 Miao Village church. Photo: Gideon Elazar.

church wall reveals the problematic position of Christianity when ethnic categorization is concerned. While Islam, Theravada Buddhism, and Lamaism are deeply connected to specific ethnic minorities, Christianity defies clearly marked ethnic boundaries, cutting across categories and classifications. Indeed, the choice to place the church in the Miao Village rather than in other villages, such as the Lisu or Jingpo, seemed fairly random and was never explained.

The sign at the entrance of the church is clearly compensating for the lack of any reference to Christianity on the larger sign at the entrance to the Miao Village. Thus, the church sign expresses a concession to reality—an acknowledgment that despite Christianity's incompatibility with official rhetoric, it could not be entirely ignored. An explanation of the contrast between inner and outer spaces, signifying the gap between official rhetoric and the reality of ethnic society in contemporary Yunnan, was needed. Thus, respect is given to the reality of Miao everyday life and the influence of Christianity among other minority peoples. At the same time, Christianity is categorized as a recent, foreign-inspired religion, with the implied connotation of its being an inauthentic addition to Yunnan's landscape.

As such, the sign on the church wall marks the state's attempt to walk the thin line between recognition, containment, and control (Kim-kwong Chan 2004). Following an assertion of the state's sovereignty and its ultimate right to define the nature of ethnicity at the entrance to the village compound, the sign beside the church door indicates that concessions can be made within the space of the village. In line with reform-era moderation, this expression of religious identity is recognized as part of religious folk culture that cannot be ignored but cannot be fully incorporated and therefore must be given an alternative space of its own within the confines of the system.

Interestingly, at the time of this research, the Nationalities Village website was equally inconsistent about the existence of the Miao Village church. Thus, the website made certain passing references to Christianity's presence in Yunnan, avoiding a presentation of the church itself. The Chinese website mentioned polytheism as the Miao's primary faith, adding a one-line reference to the fact that "there are also some who believe in Protestant and Catholic Christianity" (*ye you xinyang jidujiao, tianzhujiao*) and making no reference to the existence of the church within the village. However, in the English version of the page describing the Miao, an additional text, titled "The Church," was displayed, describing the basic tenets of Christianity and followed by an added explanation: "It has been over a century since Catholic Church and Protestantism were spread to minority areas of Yunnan by missionaries, having produced a sizable number of followers among such groups as the Miao, the Yi, the Nu, the Lisu and the Lahu. This church in the Miao Village is a reflection of the reality."[11] Since then, the website has been standardized and changed. Reflecting the current changes in state policy, no mention of Christianity can be found anywhere in the Nationalities Village website.

The penetration of Christian missionaries into Yunnan in the late nineteenth century is mentioned online (but not on the church door) as a neutral historical phenomenon, one that evokes neither praise nor criticism. The connection often made in the past between missionary work and imperialism, Western aggression, and the opium trade is completely absent. The lack of a critical evaluation of missionary work reflects a general trend within the Nationalities Village, which entirely avoids any politically sensitive information or historical facts that may dampen the overall ambience of ethnic harmony, past, present, and future. Thus, another sign placed on the exterior of an adjacent structure emphasizes the recurrent theme of the Miao's migratory nature and refers to tribal wars taking place in antiquity and "frequent local conflicts." Yet at no point is the Miao's main antagonist, the Han Chinese state, specifically mentioned; neither is any other ethnic group. In other words, not only is the story of ethnic strife relegated to the distant past, but the identity of actors in the conflict is also obscured.

Similarly, the depiction of missionary involvement represents a middle ground between state and minority narratives. At the gate, Christianity is simply not mentioned. In the area between the village entrance and the church interior, Christianity is recognized, but the missionary past and its appearance in the colonial context are either mentioned in passing and without judgment (on the website) or ignored (on the church wall). The liminal area approaching the church can therefore be seen as a space of neutrality, a middle ground between conflicting narratives where controversial and problematic elements of the past are subsumed by the overall search for harmony.

At the same time, the liminal space is part of a constructed hierarchy in which the state declares its decision and its implied ability to "objectively portray" the everyday life of the Miao. The idea of state objectivity is expressed through state representation, both in the realm of ethnicity and in the realm of religion. The formulation of the fifty-six *minzu* is the result of the state's "scientific and objective" ethnic classification project (Bin 2009, 753). Likewise, in the realm of religion, the state retains the right to draw the line between normative and orthodox religion and divergent, heterodox superstition (A. Yu 2005, 145). Thus, the church wall's declaration of objectivity can be seen as both a concession to the reality of ethnic life and a reaffirmation of ultimate state primacy and authority.

The Third Arena: The Church Interior

The lack of official recognition at the gate and the apologetic acknowledgment at the church door did not prepare me for what I discovered upon entering the interior space of the church. The first prominent feature of the church, immediately evident upon entrance, was a large television screen showing a middle-aged preacher excitedly talking and singing in Chinese to a large congregation. The preacher and his congregation were dressed in Western-style clothing—the men in suits and ties and the women in modern dresses. The Miao caretaker of the church who welcomed me explained that this is a DVD of a Chinese televangelist living and working in the United States. At the time of my visit, in the early afternoon, there were only two people in the church, both residents of the Miao Village, but the sound of the singing and enthusiastic preaching coming from the big screen generated a feeling of energy and dynamism.

In many ways, the Miao Village church reflects the vitality of Christianity in contemporary Yunnan and China. A handwritten prayer timetable (including a few instructions on behavior) lists the prayers and singing that take place on a daily basis. This reveals the fact that the church is not a museum but rather an active and functional house of prayer, serving the needs of the village residents. In contrast, the small mosque in the

Hui village, maintained by a young Hui who lives alone on the premises, expressly forbids the entrance of non-Muslims.

The large flat-screen TV with the Chinese preacher expresses a narrative far removed from the one presented outside the church and in the Nationalities Village in general. Not only is the TV itself a symbol of modernity, but the choice of the DVD in also noteworthy. One might expect to encounter a DVD of Miao or other minority church music. Indeed, the Hua Miao have created a corpus of Christian hymns, sung in Miao-style choirs. These have become quite famous throughout China and a source of pride and profit for the Hua Miao (Guo 2010; He and Zhongli 2007, 110). A DVD featuring Miao choir songs was proudly shown to me by some of the Christian Hua Miao in Wuding. Most often the hymns are performed by a choir of Miao girls, dressed in traditional garb.[12] Yet, rather than a choir of young Miao singers and dancers, the DVD in the Miao church was of a Han Chinese preacher, preaching in Chinese and wearing a modern Western-style suit.

The placement of the screen directly in front of the entrance door means that all visitors encounter it immediately upon entering the church. This creates a visual challenge to state rhetoric of the minorities as primitive, archaic, and stagnant, whereas in contrast, the enthusiastic televangelist and his congregation are dynamic, energetic, and modern. Furthermore, the choice of featuring an American-based Han Chinese rather than a member of an ethnic minority reflects the international nature of Christianity, transcending the narrow confines of the official ethnic categorization. Indeed, the open display of Christian internationalism seems to contradict the basic principle of Chinese Protestantism since the 1949 revolution: the importance of maintaining a national, patriotic, and self-sufficient church, unrelated to foreign elements (Bays 2003, 493; Hunter and Chan 1993, 23–24; Kindopp 2004, 123–25).

Along the church walls are displays of ethnic-style batik art portraying scenes from the New Testament and Chinese characters of the words "faith" (*xin*), "love" (*ai*), and "hope" (*wang*) (see figure 5). This form of Christian art is quite common and can be found in a number of Christian book and souvenir shops in Kunming. The origin of the batiks is unclear; it is not indicated whether they are produced by a specific minority group. Throughout my time in Yunnan, I asked a number of people who sold the batiks where they came from. Other than pointing out that they came from the "minorities" (*shaoshu minzu*), no one I spoke to could pin down their specific origin and style. As far as I could tell, the batiks, with their

Fig. 5 Christian batiks for sale. Photo: Gideon Elazar.

unrefined, archaic-style artwork, seemed to imply a connection to ethnicity at large.

Also on display at the table by the entrance were a number of pictures and signs. Under the table's plastic covering was a single picture of the English missionary Samuel Pollard, who worked among the Miao in the first decades of the twentieth century, with the caption "English Missionary Pollard." As mentioned in chapter 2, Pollard was largely responsible for the mass conversion of the Hua Miao, the invention of the Pollard script, and the building of the Miao cultural center in the village of Shimenkan in neighboring Guizhou.

Finding a picture of Pollard in a Miao church is not surprising, as he is often mentioned by Miao Christians as a greatly respected and revered figure (interviews with Miao clergymen in Wuding, November 30–December 1, 2009). In the words of the missiologist Ralph Covell, "To the Miao, Pollard represented the justice of God in an unjust society" (2010, 725). However, the Nationalities Village is an official museum, a showcase of Yunnan's ethnic peoples, and the Miao compound is not a real village but rather a tourist site. Pollard was a foreign missionary working in China before the revolution, and the placement of his picture in the church is a reminder of the missionary past and Christianity's relationship to Western colonialism. Furthermore, putting Pollard on display seemed to emphasize Christianity's foreign origin.

The photograph of Pollard was balanced by a series of small cards with Chinese characters, placed right beside his image. The characters are believed by Chinese Christians to contain evidence of biblical stories and concepts, proving that the Chinese of the ancient past worshiped a single supreme deity and held knowledge of the biblical creation story. Seeing my interest in the cards, the Miao host who escorted me on my walk around the church pulled out a pack and gave me one of each, telling me that he personally believed that monotheism was well-known in China six to seven thousand years ago (conversation, April 24, 2010).

The back of each card offers an analysis of the character in Chinese and English. A number of cards contain characters including the element representing a sheep or lamb (*yang*), the lamb being a common symbol for Jesus. These include the character used for "righteousness" (*yi*) and the word for "auspicious" (*xiang*). So, for example, the card with the character "auspicious" contains an explanation of the use of the symbol for "lamb" in the word by stating, "the most auspicious day was when Jesus Christ was born." The other characters were explained on the cards in correspondence with the biblical narrative. The character for "create" (*zao*) contains the elements representing mud, mouth, breath, and walking. All elements put together invoke the biblical story of man's creation as it appears in the book of Genesis: the formation of man by God from the earth, followed by God blowing breath into his mouth, bringing him to life, and setting him to walk in the Garden of Eden (Genesis 2:7–8). Likewise, the character for "boat" (*chuang*) contains the element "eight," for the eight human passengers in Noah's ark (Noah and his wife and their three sons and wives).

This interpretation of the characters is a central element in the hypothesis that the Chinese have an ancient monotheistic past that has been forgotten (Brandner 2011, 223). In addition to the analysis of characters, Christians have argued that an ancient form of Chinese monotheism is evidenced in the ancient Chinese practice of worshiping Shangdi, a single supreme deity, who was later worshiped exclusively by the emperor in the Temple of Heaven in Beijing (Chan and Fu 2009, 111–50; Tong and Petzholt 2002, 9). Indeed, the name Shangdi was chosen by early Protestant missionaries as the appropriate translation of the term "God," thus connecting the Christian message to the ancient Chinese past. The hidden nature of ancient Chinese monotheism is discussed at length in *The Discovery of Genesis: How the Truths of Genesis Were Found Hidden in the Chinese Language* (Kang and Nelson 1979; see also Kui and Hovee 1999). Christian analysis of characters has been termed a form of glyphomancy: an attempt to prove "that Christianity is a public manifestation of the same cosmological view esoterically enshrined in Chinese characters by the sages of antiquity" (Jordan 1993, 287).

In fact, the idea of a monotheistic origin for Chinese culture is as old as the first contact between China and the West. Matteo Ricci viewed the sages of China with reverence and believed that the country had been religiously corrupted by Buddhist influence (Gernet 1985, 23). The seventeenth-century Catholic convert Li Tsu Po was the first of many to claim that the Chinese originally worshiped a single God called Shangdi or sometimes Tian (Cohen 1961, 170). Echoes of a monotheistic version of Chinese history were likewise articulated by leaders of the Taiping Rebellion, who claimed that monotheism was once universal but exists today only in "the barbaric land of the west" (Spence 1996, 173). The idea of a Chinese monotheistic past has featured prominently in missionary work in Yunnan since prerevolutionary times. Degradation theory is the idea that an originally monotheistic culture was later corrupted by idolatry. It can be seen in the works of Paul Vial, missionary to the Sani, who noted a number of parallels pointed out to him by converts between Yi mythology and the Bible (Swain 1995, 152).

The display of the character cards in the church implies that Christianity is not a foreign import but rather an original Chinese tradition (Jordan 1993, 289). In the context of the Miao church, the assertion that monotheism has roots in the earliest stages of Chinese civilization challenges the history presented on the church wall and the claim the Christianity's influence in Yunnan is only a century old. Thus, the character cards present an alternative historical narrative, one in which Christianity may be viewed as a return to the sources of Chinese civilization.

Far from being a purely historical issue, Christianity's foreignness and the continuous attempts at indigenization still loom large in the life of both Han and non-Han converts (Doyle 2014). Many of the people I interviewed throughout my fieldwork were, at some point, confronted with the accusation that they had adopted a non-Chinese religion (interviews with Joseph, April 6, 2010; James, May 6, 2010; Tsering, August 21, 2010). As Yang Zhong has stated, "For a Chinese to become a Christian requires a certain degree of cultural transformation." Yang quotes a common saying: "one more Christian—one less Chinese" (2013, 38). A similar sentiment is expressed in the preface to a book on China's monotheistic past: "My Christian spiritual journey of the past three decades has been a joyous one, but always in the far reaches of my consciousness was an irritant, like a pebble in my shoe: the feeling that I had turned my back on my culture by adopting a foreign faith" (Chan and Fu 2009, 10–11). Indeed, one may assume that visitors to the Miao church perceive Christianity as an essentially foreign religion, a perception the church clearly attempts to challenge.

This hypothesis related to China and the Bible contradicts the implication presented by the photograph of Pollard's distinctly European face, reminding viewers of Christianity's foreignness. It brings to mind the idea of the sign at the church door, in which Christianity is presented as a historical side note, unrelated to the original ethnic identity of the Miao or any other group. The characters, on the other hand, offer the alternative idea that Christianity is in fact a fulfillment of an ancient tradition: a return to the source of Chinese culture, a culture corrupted by emperors and other religions, particularly Buddhism and Daoism.

The creation and promotion of an alternative, monotheistic narrative of Chinese history is a politically sensitive issue, making the presence of the cards in the church all the more surprising. In a conversation I had with Simon, he mentioned a recent convert he had trusted enough to provide him with "forbidden movies." What movies, I was curious to know, were sensitive enough to be categorized as forbidden? Simon's reply was that the series of movies was titled *Shen zhou*, an ancient name for China understood by Christians to mean "God's land" (Chan and Fu 2009, 223). The series is a comprehensive display of the argument referred to earlier regarding China's monotheistic past and its later acceptance of idolatry.[13]

Beyond the apparent challenge to official narratives of history offered by the character cards, what is puzzling about the display is that unlike the Pollard photograph, the cards bear no specific relationship to the Miao or other minorities. Neither Vial's observations regarding early monotheism among the Yi (Swain 1995, 163) nor the proposed narratives of monotheistic myths found among the Miao and other groups (Northrup 1997; S. Clarke [1915] 2009, 58–70) are mentioned in the church. Like the Han Chinese televangelist, the story of the characters seems to be one of Chinese culture and does not relate to ethnicity at all.

The dominance of Han history and culture in the church is increasingly evident in the display of a set of large pictures providing a historical timeline of Christian history, beginning with the creation and moving on through the exodus from Egypt and up to the crucifixion and resurrection. The display then turns to the history of Christianity in China, marking the arrival of Mateo Ricci in the late sixteenth century, the first translation of the Bible into Chinese in 1823, and the publication of the standardized Union Version in 1919. Once again, the historical timeline presented on the church walls is that of Christianity in China and the Chinese Bible. No mention is made of the translation of the Bible into Miao or any other ethnic language. Likewise, the events depicted on the church wall bear no specific relation to the history of Christianity in Yunnan, as the conversion of the Lisu, Miao, and other ethnic groups in the late nineteenth and early twentieth centuries is not noted.

The timeline on the walls culminates with the second coming of Jesus, the creation of a new heaven and earth, and the one-thousand-year reign, all under the title "Year ???" The reference to the second coming is particularly remarkable since the Christian idea of the "end of days" is considered to be extremely problematic in China. According to official rhetoric and regulation, the topic of the second coming is one that preachers in churches are expected to avoid as a form of faith that "interferes with the people's dedication to production" (Spiegel 2004, 47; see also Peale 2005, 76). Like other elements of Chinese official discourse, the ban on sermons regarding the second coming of Christ is not always applied (Schak 2011, 76).

Indeed, Daniel Bays (2009, 7) views the prohibition as a common myth regarding officially sanctioned Christianity in China, mostly disseminated among evangelical church groups in the West, who advocate house churches in their efforts to delegitimize the official Three Self Patriotic Movement (TSPM) churches. Nevertheless, the issue of the end of days does seem to remain somewhat sensitive in nature. China has a long tradition of millenarian and salvationist sects, traditionally considered by authorities to be heterodox and socially destabilizing in nature (Bays 2011, 19; A. Yu 2005, 85). Like Simon's experience regarding forbidden movies, the difficulties of the issue were conveyed to me by Mark in a conversation regarding illegal Christian literature. When I asked what would define a given book as problematic, Mark answered that the most problematic books are those relating the idea that God is the true sovereign, implying that the Chinese government is not. In particular, books discussing the future power of a divine ruler destined to replace current governments are considered politically sensitive and will usually not be sold openly in Christian bookshops (Mark, interview January 5, 2010).

The second coming theme is also considered problematic in that it indicates striving for a new and better creation and suggests that the present reality is lacking. Furthermore, it is perceived as a challenge to the idea that progress and development are the task of the party-state, implying that an exterior, divine force is essential for the completion of the task. In fact, the idea that the attainment of salvation is in the hands of the state rather than the church was one of the founding principles of the official TSPM church and an expression of the break between local churches and Western Christian organization in the 1950s (Kindopp 2004, 125).

Thus, much like the character cards, the historical timeline on the walls marks a divergence from official teleology. The representation of these alternative narratives—the idea of a monotheistic past and the theology of the end of days—marks the Miao church as a space where ideas running contrary to state discourse are expressed freely. Here too, the narratives presented are predominantly framed within Han history, rather than minority history. Thus, while other parts of the village emphasize difference and otherness, the church seems to be working in the opposite direction—diminishing ethnic borders and attempting to bridge the gap between the ethnic observed and the Han observer. While state discourse is seemingly absent from the church interior, it can be found in the way Christianity in the church is deethnicized and replaced with an emphasis on the centrality of Han culture and a celebration of unity and harmony.

Moving on through the church, I encountered a small table to the right of the podium with stacks of Bibles in a variety of minority languages. The caretaker explained that the church serves the needs of all Christians living in the village, from a variety of ethnic backgrounds. The Bibles in minority languages are more for show than for actual use; since it is a multiethnic church, services are always held in Chinese. On the same table, a number of small pamphlets are available for the general public. The pamphlets are titled, "Who Is the True God?" and "Jesus the Savior." A third pamphlet offers blessings for the Chinese New Year and a discussion of the true nature of "good fortune/blessing" (*fu*). The three tracts are published by an organization named Cheng Grace, promoting the sermons of Pastor Samuel Ching, who appears to be centered in Hong Kong. The organization's website provides Christian texts, books, and sermons for Chinese living in China and Hong Kong as well as in the US and Europe.[14]

The printed material is perhaps the most unusual aspect of the church and a clear testament to state tolerance. While the material may be presented as containing general information about Christianity for the interested visitor, it is hard to ignore its missionary nature. The title of the first two tracts, with the phrases "true God" and "savior," leave no room for doubt that the material on display is meant to convince people of the truth of Christianity. Indeed, the "true God" track attacks the worship of idols as false and harmful. The section titled "worshiping idols does not bring tranquility" (*bai ouxiang meiyou pingan*) links idol worship to crippling fear of spirits, ghosts, and bad feng shui, contrasted with the inner peace induced by faith in Jesus. The tract ends with a short prayer and declaration of faith. Likewise, the "Jesus is Savior" pamphlet asserts that all other religions are manmade, while Christianity is divinely inspired and the only way to personal salvation. The pamphlet dedicated to the true nature of "good fortune" aims at convincing readers that fortune is not financial but rather spiritual and can be found by embracing Christianity. For those who are interested in knowing more about Christianity, each pamphlet contains a reference to the organization's website and email, where more material on Christianity can be obtained.

Although the pamphlets do not contain any overt criticism of the state, they clearly promote an exclusive religiosity that stands in contrast with the principle of historical materialism. The fact that the pamphlets are available as handouts means that visitors to the church not only are observers of Christianity but are given the opportunity to become full participants. Here too, the information displayed is unrelated to the Miao, making specific reference to the Han cultural concept and practices revolving around the "good fortune" character.

To summarize, despite being located in an official state museum, some of the displays available in the church not only differ from the official line as it is presented outside the church but also clearly pose an alternative narrative of Christianity in China. These include

- a Chinese American evangelist preaching the gospel on the widescreen;
- a clear reference to the end of times and the second coming;
- a photograph of the foreign missionary Samuel Pollard;
- missionary material available for the general public; and
- cards depicting Chinese characters as containing evidence of a monotheistic past and ancient knowledge of the stories of the Bible.

The Miao Village may be seen as a reflection of a negotiated balance between the state and ethnic Christianity. Accordingly, the state continues to define space and set the standards for objectivity and normality, while minority Christians are free to express their religious identity and even to challenge official narratives of the past, within the confines of their own religious space. Following the logic of this argument, one may conclude that after the state has asserted its paramount position through the drawing of borders between the varying discourses, it has conceded to virtually withdraw from the inner space of ethnic life.

Fig. 6 Sign reading "No person who has not received permission is allowed to get on the pulpit. Please respect ethnic religion." Photo: Gideon Elazar.

One artifact in the church stands out as the single most direct expression of the authority beyond the walls. It is a sign on the preaching pulpit forbidding unauthorized preaching and asking preachers to show respect toward "ethnic religion," implying religions other than Christianity (see figure 6). The sign marks the permitted limits of religious expression, reducing regulation to the bare minimum and at the same time legitimizing all content that does not result in a disruption of ethnic relations. Interestingly, the statements made in the pamphlet "Who Is the Real God?" regarding idolatry seem not to have invoked sanction.

This sign, located at the center of the church, is the only reminder to visitors of the fact that the Miao church exists within a larger context and of the role of the authorities in maintaining harmony and peace within China's complex ethnic mosaic. The sign reflects the principle of ethnic harmony and unity, a theme emphasized throughout the Nationalities Village. Forbidding preachers in the church to attack other religions relates to one of the state's central goals, that of maintaining and promoting the "unity of nationalities" (*minzu tuanjie*). Accordingly, ethnic tensions and state policies of the Maoist era are never mentioned. The connection between Christianity and colonialism is similarly absent. At the same time, song and dance shows performed regularly in "Harmony Square" at the center of the Nationalities Village feature a mixture of ethnic groups, clearly emphasizing their harmonious relations. The "unity of nationalities" is evocative of the old Confucian value of harmony, a value implying a hierarchy ordered under the paternal guidance of the Chinese state (Leibold 2013, 4–5; Ye 2005, 450). The Miao compound may therefore be seen as an idealized form of state neo-Confucianism, providing a space for Christians to express their ethnicity through Christianity while at the same time establishing the primacy of Han culture as the guiding principle of ethnic relations and state sovereignty.

The promotion of state-sponsored harmony is not confined to the limitation on argumentative or demeaning preaching regarding ethnic religions. Nor is it relegated to the two outer spaces of the Miao compound. Rather, it is present within the confines of the church in the form of Han-centered content, reflecting the pivotal nature of Han culture. Indeed, the only direct expression of ethnicity in the church is the appearance of the ethnic-style batiks of vague origin and the stack of Bibles in minority languages. The sole connection to the Miao themselves is the picture of Samuel Pollard, the English missionary to the Hua Miao and inventor of the Miao script.

To a certain extent, the dominance of Chinese language and culture can be seen as a practical consideration. Since the church serves a number of ethnic groups, the use of Chinese in church services is a natural choice. Furthermore, as the vast majority of tourists arriving in the village are Han, references to key concepts in their own culture are understandable. Nevertheless, the Hanness of Christianity within the church goes beyond practical and linguistic considerations. The references to the translation of the Bible into Chinese, Chinese cultural concepts, and the Chinese past all point to an underlying logic within the idea of ethnic unity: that ethnicity and ethnoreligious expression take place within the realm of the dominant Han culture and that Han centrality and ethnic harmony are synonymous (Leibold 2013, 47). Thus, while ethnoreligious identity is tolerated and allowed a remarkable degree of freedom, it exists within the larger context of Chinese culture and Chinese identity. Considering the spatial layout of the church, the different spaces of the village express varying narratives of religion and ethnicity. As such, Han history and culture can be likened to the physical ground or the space uniting all spaces where ethnicity is defined and limited.

The contrast between the church and the rest of the Miao Village became evident to me once again after I exited the church and moved back out into the other parts of the village. In a small building adjacent to the church, other religious traditions observed by the non-Christian Miao subgroups are presented, in a mostly empty structure containing a dusty reproduction of a Miao totem and a few old artifacts apparently used for divination. The difference between the two buildings is striking—while the church conveys a strong message of Christianity as a vital, modern, and dynamic religion, the representation of Miao animism is lifeless. Returning to the paradigm of internal Orientalism, the display of non-Christian religious paraphernalia gives the distinct impression of looking into the distant past of archaic otherness, a reality far removed from the life of the average visitor to the village. In contrast, the church emphasizes Christianity as a religion active in the Chinese cultural sphere, attempting to create a feeling of cultural kinship.

Conclusion: Defining Ethnoreligious Boundaries

Writing on the decision made by the Chinese government in a conference on religion summoned by Jiang Zemin in 2001, Kim-kwong Chan described contemporary state policy on religion as containing five principles: recognition, containment, guidance, nationalism, and suppression (2004, 66). These five modes of action reflect reform-era acknowledgment of religion as a permanent feature of the Chinese social landscape. The Nationalities Village church displays three of Chan's tactics. The church's existence in the Miao Village despite its absence from the sign on the village gate is an expression of the state's recognition of Christianity's prevalence among minority groups. The spatial layout of the Miao compound reflects a policy of containment, allowing religious expression within certain geographic boundaries. Recognition and containment are expressed through the open display of Christianity and alternative narratives of the past and future within the church walls. These displays generate an overall feeling of confidence in the ability of the state to maintain its dominant role in shaping and representing ethnic identity. Finally, the nature of the church interior reflects a degree of subtle nationalism and an attempt to promote a national monoculture—a Chinese common ground uniting all nationalities.

Whether the state's confidence in its ability to control ethnicity is well founded or misplaced is beyond the scope of this research. Either way, the Miao compound within the Nationalities Village clearly reflects the belief that the realities of ethnoreligious identity and the existence of a vibrant Christian community can be tolerated within certain well-defined spaces.

Thus, within the confines of the Miao church, a foreign-based televangelist can be viewed, a photograph of an early twentieth-century missionary is on display, and missionary material can be freely obtained, without undermining state authority.

The multilayered representation of ethnic Christianity sheds light on the larger issue of state tolerance of missionary activity in Yunnan. Officially, foreign missionary work is strictly prohibited in China. In fact, while asserting the government commitment to religious freedom, Ye Xiaowen stated that the state "recognizes that WTO accession may trigger a new wave of foreign religious influence and it has every intention to resist such influence and will make every effort to do so" (Kim-kwong Chan 2005, 90). And yet, many foreign Christian missionaries continue to live and work in Yunnan. As Yunnan is already home to many Christians, its designation as a region of relative, if not official, tolerance is in keeping with the basics of state religious policy. Moreover, the Miao Village church reinforces the argument that tolerance of missionary work and the dissemination of Christianity in Yunnan may be seen as an outcome of the Christian approach to ethnicity. Thus, while the church apparently celebrates the vitality of Christianity among ethnic groups, a closer look at the church interior reveals that the blurring of differences between ethnic groups inevitably results in the strengthening of the hegemonic Chinese culture promoted by the state.

CONCLUSION

The Future of State Tolerance of Religion in China

Peter and Rebecca

In the spring of 2010, I was finally able to spend a number of days with my former classmates Peter and Rebecca. At the time, they were living in a Yi area in Sichuan, working for a Pentecostal organization (on the Yi of Sichuan, see Dong 2003).[1] They had created a small local Christian community, which met regularly for prayer and learning. Much as I had remembered Peter, his style was open and familiar. As a man of "words, not works," he was not engaged in any particular welfare activity, although he and Rebecca did fund the studies of about fifteen local students from poor families who were enrolled in a technical college. In addition to Peter continuing his Chinese studies and leading his community's weekly prayer and study, much of his time was dedicated to simply speaking to people he met in town. According to Peter, the city in which they were operating only had about eighty foreigners, all but two of whom were Christian. Peter's foreignness clearly attracted attention, and he was more than willing to play along. As we walked together through the streets of the city, he would constantly stop and chat with people and was happy to have his picture taken or to exchange email addresses with anybody he encountered. He told me that in general, he did not discuss issues of faith with people he met for the first time. Instead, he would try to cultivate a relationship that would eventually lead to the subject. The children living in Peter and Rebecca's building would come occasionally to their apartment to play or to watch a DVD of animated biblical stories. As Peter said, "Some of these kids will be in the kingdom of God, I assure you" (conversation, June 13, 2010).

My visit took place during the Dragon Boat Festival, and the city was full of Yi villagers who came in for the day. Peter was an attraction for many of them and was even interviewed for a local TV station. I found myself surprised once again: despite the fact that he ran an unregistered church community, he seemed confident that his presence would not draw unwanted attention. Peter told me that when he arrived, he was warned by other missionaries to avoid a certain Southern Baptist couple who were considered too outspoken, so as not to endanger his own work. He decided not to take the advice, and in fact, they became good friends. Peter said he felt that if people were going to be deported for preaching the gospel, he was willing to be among them.

I spent a number of days with Peter and Rebecca, discussing their work and witnessing their prayer meetings. During this time, I was able to recognize a number of the themes I have discussed in this book. First, their community was multiethnic, including Yi and Han congregants. All members were recent converts, and their Christianity was based on individual experience rather than on ethnic identity or family history. Peter and Rebecca, who are European, led their community together with a Taiwanese missionary, giving the community a distinctly international style, which was clearly an attraction for some of the people present. Indeed, my own presence as an Israeli Jew created some excitement in that regard.

The international spirit of Christianity was emphasized. For example, at the beginning of the community gathering I attended, a DVD was shown of a concert filmed in 2008 at the Beijing International Fellowship, where an American, Bruce Springsteen–sounding, Christian rock singer appeared in front of a crowd of over a thousand people.[2] In addition to being in English and featuring foreign Christians in China, the concert video distinctly focused on the multiracial composure of the audience, further strengthening the transnational nature of Christianity that was being transmitted to the viewers.

Peter and Rebecca's attitude toward ethnicity exemplifies the effort to maintain the delicate balance between preservation and remolding that I have discussed throughout this book. Quoting a teacher whom they had studied with in their home country, Rebecca defined their work as "planting churches," a term they understood as taking "seeds" from their own cultural context and planting them in local "soil" rather than transplanting a fully formed "building" (conversation, June 12, 2010).

This church-planting process included helping local Yi converts find God within their own traditional culture. Thus, while Peter and Rebecca were highly critical of local animism and spirit worship, as well as other elements of Yi life, such as traditional educational methods and hygienic practices, they routinely suggested to converts interpretations and ways of acting that would enable them to participate in ethnic festivals and funerals. Moreover, as a symbol of their affirmation of Yi culture, they made a point of acquiring a basic knowledge of the local dialect and employing it as frequently as possible.

Finally, Peter and Rebecca were acutely aware of the limits of state tolerance of their activity. At the time of my visit, Peter and his Taiwanese partner were debating whether the community had grown too large to be ignored by the authorities and discussing the possibility of splitting it in two. To express his acknowledgment of state authority and maintain good relations with local officials, Peter was careful to register every guest he and his wife hosted with the Public Security Bureau office and to report every time they departed and reentered town. Much like the missionaries presented in chapter 6, he was entirely uninterested in the construction of church buildings for either his or any other Christian community. He was adamant that he viewed the construction of Western-style church buildings by early missionaries as a theological mistake.

Furthermore, the teachings provided by Rebecca and Peter at the prayer meetings contained simple messages of morality and social stability, mostly on the theme of being good husbands and wives, dedicated to harmonious family life. Thus, while it is impossible to discern what local officials actually know about Peter and Rebecca's activities, we may assume that some aspects of their work may be viewed favorably by local authorities. Peter and Rebecca's activity reflects a multifaceted relationship between Christians and the state. Throughout this book, I have argued that the specific circumstances created in reform-era Southwest China have given rise to a series of convergences between local governmental authorities, the ambitions of missionaries, and the interests of members of minority ethnic groups. I have attempted to portray the interactions between these players as a multifaceted relationship, touching on issues of ethnic identity, language, space, and welfare.

Ethnic Identity

In this book, I have shown that the balance between enhancing and minimizing ethnicity is key to understanding the role of Christianity in Yunnan. As Hudson Taylor, the nineteenth-century founder of the China Inland Mission, claimed, the advantage of Christianity lies in its ability "to be all things to all men" (Jenkins 2011, 36). Thus, evangelical Christians have been able to work in Yunnan in ways that are attractive to Han and non-Han converts and at the same time are beneficial, or at least unobtrusive, to state authorities. Relationships fostered between Christian aid workers, teachers and linguists from outside the PRC, and local minority converts create a growing sense of connectivity between rural ethnic minorities in China and the global Christian community. Indeed, it is common for converts today to celebrate this connectivity, as it was established by pre-1949 missionaries. For example, ethnic Christians whose ancestors converted in the late nineteenth and early twentieth centuries now recall Pollard or Fraser as cultural heroes whose efforts brought symbolic prestige in the form of a writing system for their native languages, while at the same time providing material progress and modernization.

However, today's missionaries hold a complex and somewhat ambivalent attitude toward ethnicity and culture. On the one hand, they are deeply involved in ethnic preservation, particularly in the realm of language, which is sometimes presented as a means to counter the rapid process of Hanization. At the same time, linguistic work in contemporary Yunnan is often geared toward cultural integration and acquisition of Chinese, rather than encouraging disassociation from the larger entity of China. Moreover, the emphasis placed on language as the central symbol of ethnic identity deemphasizes other features of traditional ethnic life, such as worship of ancestors and spirits.

Missionaries define ethnicity in terms similar to those employed by the state, focusing on costume, song, dance, and language. As my discussion of missionary activity among the Bouyei and Tibetan minorities illustrates, missionaries view other aspects of minority culture, particularly those pertaining to religion and myth, as inauthentic and spiritually harmful. The negative view of traditional local religious practices, including spirit worship and animal sacrifices, is generally in line with the state's efforts to modernize and "civilize" ethnic minorities. Moreover, contemporary evangelical missionaries work to diminish ethnic identity by criticizing the "nominalism" and strongly ethnic and traditional character of Christianity among minority Christians who converted in the pre-1949 era, instead advocating a personal spiritual experience as the true foundation of faith. Finally, as a number of Han and minority Christians have argued, the transethnic nature of many Christian communities works to promote interethnic relations and the state's vision of social harmony.

The Appeal of Christian Internationalism and Modernity

From the perspective of minority converts, Christianity offers an opportunity to transcend the narrow confines of ethnicity and embrace an international Christian identity. Often, identification with a global Christian community holds concrete implications including access to better medical care, employment prospects, and aid in times of crisis. It also offers an alternative to the state narrative of ethnicity and the dichotomy of Han modernity versus minority backwardness. The ability to represent Christian globality as a form of modernity was particularly apparent in the Miao church within the Nationalities Village, discussed in chapter 7.

Christian modernity and globalism come in different forms. For some, such as Ma from Shimenkan, Christianity is associated with the triumphs of the past and the efforts of early missionaries to modernize a remote region. For others, like the Da Hua Miao of Wuding, Christianity has a dual nature, implying both a strong connection with coreligionists around the globe and a symbol of cultural and ethnic survival. Recent converts like Tsering and Alu, who are Tibetans, and Zhan, who is Lisu, identify with the global missionary vanguard, placing less emphasis on their particular ethnicity. In all cases, Christianity seems to offer a workable balance, both retaining and transcending ethnic identity, to varying degrees.

Free-Market Morality and the Spirit of Capitalism

Economic reforms have brought about huge changes in China. Among them, the focus on profit and wealth in the post-Maoist era has led to a deep crisis of meaning. As illustrated in chapter 3, missionaries tend to have strongly positive attitudes toward the economic liberalization of the reform era. Accordingly, both foreign and Chinese Christians actively promote a moral code of conduct to deal with the social and spiritual challenges of the free-market system, while glorifying its central features including entrepreneurship, economic initiative, and the accumulation of wealth. Through the personal example of Christian teachers, businesspeople, and aid workers, converts are taught to be loyal, prudent, law abiding, and economically independent.

In the case of ethnic Yunnan, the free-market values promoted by missionaries often include the "civilizing" elements that are lauded by some Chinese scholars, as mentioned in chapter 3. Thus, the Christianization of minorities is frequently perceived by academics, officials, and indeed the converts themselves as a move toward economic self-sufficiency, exemplified in the discarding of "wasteful" sacrifices and a strict prohibition on substance abuse. Christian missionaries also promote monogamous families and the raising of hygienic standards—all central features of the Chinese state's "civilizing project."

Christian Welfare

In addition to the shared goals mentioned in the preceding section, foreign missionaries contribute to the state's efforts in dealing with Yunnan's most marginalized populations: drug addicts, sex workers, and poor migrants to the cities, many of whom belong to minority ethnic groups. Foreign Christian aid workers provide knowledge, methods, and funds for many projects working with these populations. As discussed in chapter 4, Christian faith-based organizations are instrumental in supplementing the province's outdated methods of dealing with social problems. Since many of the aid organizations are not legally registered, their activists are careful not to challenge or publicly criticize the basic assumptions of state policy and therefore work within the system.

Maintaining the Boundary Between "God and Caesar"

Coexistence between Christianity and the Chinese state is dependent on missionaries' acute awareness of the limits of their activity. This carefully maintained balance is particularly evident in the spatial practices of evangelical Christians. The Chinese state retains a monopoly on the right to define and divide space according to its own interests. Attempts to challenge that monopoly may entail the use of force, as in the case of the demolition of the Sanjiang church in Wenzhou (discussed in chapter 6). Therefore, in general, local and foreign Christians refrain from challenging state definitions of space and make use of makeshift, improvised, and temporary locations for worship. This approach is both practical and ideological. Beyond the issue of avoiding unnecessary conflict, many missionaries feel that their mission is dependent on the removal of traditional systems of ritual territoriality that have been resurfacing among a number of minority groups during the reform era. Again, the containment, control, and weakening of ritual and sacred geography is an interest they share with the state.

Christianity and the Chinese State: An Uneasy Coexistence

When examining the unfolding relationship between Christianity and the Chinese state in the reform era, most foreign and local Christians I spoke to were quite optimistic, viewing the state as increasingly tolerant of their activity. Some even claimed that the only barrier to full cooperation and recognition was the government's fear of local pseudo-Christian groups such as the "Eastern Lightning" (Dongfang Shandian) and "Disciples" (Mentuhui) (Jeff, interview, April 4, 2010).[3]

Indeed, for the time being, it seems that the benefits of the missionary presence in Yunnan outweigh the problems. Christian activity is increasing, at least in the realm of welfare. New and larger organizations have entered the province, such as a Hong Kong–based drug-rehabilitation organization and the expansion of Eden Ministry's activities in combating the trafficking of women to cities outside Yunnan. While plans to revitalize the Chinese welfare and medical systems are under way, their effective implementation seems far off. Furthermore, many of Yunnan's endemic problems, such as the drug trade throughout Southeast Asia, remain unchallenged, leaving plenty of room for the work of foreign NGOs. The same can argued regarding the activity of organizations such as the Summer Institute of Languages. With the rapid diminishment of many of China's ethnic languages, Christian linguists will probably continue to be engaged in preservation work among Yunnan's minority people.

Nevertheless, it is worth wondering what would happen to missionary activity if the foreign Christians' contribution to the development of this peripheral region becomes unnecessary. The rumor that Michael (director of a drug-rehabilitation center) repeated to me regarding a crackdown on house churches once modernization of the city of Kunming is complete (see chapter 4) indicates a fear that coexistence between missionaries and local authorities is circumstantial and may not last. Thus, to the extent that tolerance of missionary activity is related to the rapid development of Yunnan, it is plausible that once modernization is achieved, policies may be altered. To a large degree, this has already begun to happen under the rule of Xi Jinping and the Sinicization of religion campaign.

Clearly, the pattern of state-church relations is in constant flux. The periodic shifts of attitudes, from tolerance to strict regulation and even persecution, are dependent on the ambiguity of regulations on religious conduct, which allow the state to act or refrain from acting according to its needs. Recently, the Chinese government has released a set of amendments to its religious policy guidelines (People's Republic of China, State Council 2017). These include a call for localization of foreign religions, resistance to Western cultural influences, stricter rules on religious education, and more government supervision, including a plan for the Sinicization (*zhongguo hua*) of Christianity and Islam (Cao 2017). The increasing emphasis on Sinicization is strongly reminiscent of the early years of the CCP and the establishment of official "patriotic" religious bodies like the Three Self Movement. Indeed, party official Zhang Chunxian described the objective of the plan as an attempt to block the infiltration of "hostile forces" from outside the region, noting that believers "must first be the nation's citizens" (V. Yu 2015). Thus, it would seem that Xi Jinping has made the decision to repair the religious excesses of the reform era, including prominent church buildings, Middle Eastern–style mosques, and large, recently constructed statues (Madsen 2021). So far, Sinicization seems to imply a series of mostly symbolic actions through which state authority is asserted, such as the reinforcement of state control over space through the removal of crosses and other prominent Christian symbols and demanding that house churches register officially (Bowie and Gitter 2018; Y. Wang 2018). According to recent reports, state involvement in religious affairs has led to an initiative to produce a new translation of the Bible that creates a stronger affinity with socialist ideas (Briggs 2019). Moreover, the state has significantly tightened its control of online Christian websites (A. Wang 2021). Increased control has been followed by a return to the rhetoric of the past, stressing the connection between Christianity and Western colonialism (Gan 2019). As I have argued throughout this book, rhetoric and reality are not necessarily compatible. While crackdowns on house churches and occasional arrests do occur, most of the activity is directed toward blacklisted groups (Hu 2021). Nevertheless, with the shift in religious policy and the closing of China as a result of the COVID-19 pandemic, a return to the levels of tolerance described in this book in the near future seems unlikely.

While such efforts clearly indicate a tightening of state control, they also imply a parallel process of indigenization through which Christianity is recognized as an inseparable feature of the Chinese social landscape, while the state maintains its traditional methods of religious integration and control. The shift in religious policy seems to reflect China's growing confidence in the international sphere. In 2018, China signed an agreement with the Vatican regarding the status of the Catholic Church in China, which had been split into official and nonofficial churches for several decades. While the details of the deal are unclear, it seems that it will allow Chinese authorities to maintain their control over the appointment of bishops, while the Vatican retains a right of veto (Bourne 2018). China's massive crackdown in Xinjiang, including severe anti-Muslim policies, has raised only faint reactions from most Muslim countries, which are reluctant to anger China and to endanger its massive investments in the region.

State tolerance of evangelical Christianity in the reform era is clearly related to the perception of Christianity as a modernizing and civilizing force, bringing Western habits, thinking, and knowledge to the Chinese periphery. Indeed, the idea that Christianity has aided the country's development and continues to do so is strongly promoted by both missionaries and converts. Scholars dealing with the resurgence of Christianity have described Christianity as the "fittest" religion for the present era, the basis for progress and national strength, and the hope of China (Xi Lian 2010, 38). As such, the current state of state-church coexistence may be understood as a reflection of what Mayfair Yang has termed the "post-colonial complex" (2004b, 724): an underlying faith in the superiority of Western culture over local traditions. With China's rise to power, the postcolonial complex and faith in the superiority of the West are gradually making way for a new sense of cultural confidence.

This increased confidence is expressed in the promotion of "Asian values," a version of Asian modernity presented as an alternative to Western values. Thus, Confucianism is being promoted as an ethical code for the reform era, an "ideological regulation" to combat "money worship" (Ong 1997, 179). The core elements of these neo-Confucian Asian values are similar to those associated with Christianity and the Protestant work ethic, stressing economic success, diligence, frugality, fidelity, and the accumulation of wealth. The similarity is so strong that advocates of these values are, in fact, promoters of Western modernism "appropriated and dressed up in timeless oriental guise" (Ong 1997, 189). Nevertheless, associating China's success in the reform era to the Confucian heritage, rather than an emulation of the West, may gradually lead to the disassociation of modernity and Christianity. While it is unclear to what extent the state will continue to pursue this form of revived Confucianism, such a process may mark Christianity as a competitor to the state-sanctioned vision of a moral order.

Indeed, one may ask whether neo-Confucian thought of the kind being promoted by the PRC today can really be reconciled with evangelical Christianity. Some people have argued that the two are naturally compatible (L. Liu 2011). Likewise, Fenggang Yang, in his assessment of China's social landscape in the year 2020, suggested that Christian liberalism and Confucian revivalism may join hands on the basis of a common moral agenda (2007, 51–52). However, Yang also notes that a group of Chinese intellectuals whom he labels "Confucian fundamentalists" have criticized the widespread influence of Western culture in China and social phenomena such as the fashionable trend to celebrate Christmas. Accordingly, Confucian revivalists may become increasingly anti-Christian, emulating the sentiments of the Boxer Uprising.

Christians are also faced with a growing wave of interest in local traditions, particularly in Tibetan Buddhism, which has experienced dramatic growth rates among well-educated Chinese youth since the 1990s (Smyer Yu 2012; Tuttle 2005, 223): "Everyone is talking about Tibetan Buddhism now. Pop stars are talking about it. My friends are talking about it. . . . It is cool" (Lin Meilian 2014). There have been rumors that Buddhism has attracted the attention of a number of members of China's political elite, including Xi Jinping's wife, Peng Liyuan (Sudworth 2015).

Indeed, potential for Christian-state discord can be found in evangelical ideology. Foreign missionaries, as well as some local converts mentioned in this work, maintain critical views of certain aspects of life in China, often saying that China has lost its moral center. Throughout my fieldwork, I heard numerous remarks regarding the formal, legalistic, and hierarchical aspects of Chinese social structures and educational methods. While my informants tended to voice their criticism with caution, foreign Christians clearly view certain aspects of the state system, particularly in the realm of social services, with suspicion. This is true of the medical establishment, the jails that are defined as rehabilitation centers, and the vast, state-sanctioned prevalence of abortions. Missionaries like Mark, Simon, and Michael spoke openly about what they perceived to be the inherent problems of Chinese culture and the need to stimulate deep change among both Han and non-Han converts, particularly with regard to interpersonal, gender, and familial relationships. Significantly, the perceived negative aspects of Chinese culture are often placed by missionaries under the general category "Confucianism." The association of Confucianism with the Chinese concept of "face" and with a religiosity focused on rituals and regulations is often cited by missionaries in their criticism of local Christians.

With the rising interest in various forms of Chinese tradition, including Confucianism, Buddhism, and local religions, I suggest that attitudes toward the Chinese past may become increasingly relevant to the changing trends in religious policy. Thus, the missionaries' tendency to define Confucianism as a value system to be combated may eventually negatively impact state attitudes toward Christianity. In this context, it is worth noting the widespread dissemination of an alternative monotheistic/Christian narrative of Chinese history, as mentioned in chapter 7, being promoted by a number of Chinese and non-Chinese Christians (Kim-kwong Chan 2009; Kui and Hovee 1999; Tong and Petzholt 2002), an idea that has become quite popular among Chinese Christians and was conveyed to me several times by foreign, Chinese, and minority Christians.

In many ways, the monotheistic history of China is in line with the missionary method of finding "keys and bridges" in any religious tradition to "uncover" the vestiges of a long-lost biblical narrative. Indeed, the idea that the ancient Chinese worshiped the supreme deity Shangdi or Tian (Heaven) was first promoted by the Jesuit missionary Mateo Ricci, who set out "to convince the Chinese that they had misunderstood their own traditions" (Gernet 1985, 28). As mentioned earlier, missionaries like Matt are attempting to use similar methods among Muslim minorities. The radical implications of the monotheistic historical narrative lie in the claim that, rather than being a foreign religion, Christianity represents a return to the origins of Chinese civilization and the fulfillment of an ancient and authentic Chinese tradition. Furthermore, the rewriting of Chinese history in monotheistic terms implies that the religions commonly associated with traditional China, in particular Daoism and Buddhism, reflect a process of cultural corruption and decay. The corruption of culture is symbolized by the Chinese adoption of the emblem of the dragon, identified by Christian writers with the Devil (Kim-kwong Chan 2009, 260–91; Dunn 2008).

The idea of Christianity as an authentic part of Chinese tradition was expressed in a film of a group of house church leaders who made a forty-day jeep voyage from Xian to Jerusalem in 2008. The film's narrator states, "The journey from Xian to Zion is not merely a response to a thousand years of history but also a redemption of culture and faith. It is a restoration of our journey to the West, a tradition that has been twisted for two millennia."[4] The mention of the classic Chinese book *Journey to the West* clearly implies that the importation of Buddhism to China was a historical blunder. This was explained to me by my classmate Mona, who told me that she believed that those who went west to pursue spiritual knowledge were in fact attempting to reach Jerusalem but accidentally reached India and the centers of Buddhist learning, to China's great and lasting detriment.

The claim that monotheism is indigenous to China is often used by Chinese Christians to counter the accusations made by families and friends that they have turned their backs on their heritage by adopting a foreign faith. Moreover, the indigenization of Christianity serves to legitimize the missionary project, presenting it as a restoration rather than an altering of culture. The idea of a long-lost, righteous, God-centered culture is evocative of the deeply ingrained Confucian concept that the present is a corruption of an idyllic past. As such, its popularity reveals the importance that the idea of cultural authenticity still plays in the life of many contemporary Chinese.

Final Thoughts on Christian Missions in China, Past, Present, and Future

Finally, it is worth reflecting on the history of Christian missionary activity in China. Throughout history, encounters between missionary Christianity and the Chinese state enjoyed an initial period of grace but tended to end with confrontation. The Jesuit missions of the sixteenth and seventeenth centuries attracted significant attention from the Chinese intellectual elite and the imperial court. This was mostly due to their ability to display superiority through scientific knowledge including geography, mathematics, and engineering. Moreover, Ricci and other Jesuits made a point of expressing their profound respect for the ancient sages Confucius and Mencius and attempted to become part of the Confucian literati class of the time. Eventually, however, the favorable feelings toward the Jesuits began to sour. Jesuit attitudes toward Chinese culture and history played a critical role in this process. While the Jesuits were willing to view ancestor worship as a legitimate, secular practice, they could not deny that like all non-Christians, the sages and emperors of China were condemned to Hell for eternity (Gernet 1985, 167).

Likewise, despite the many achievements of the missionary movement in the realm of modernization, in the late nineteenth and early twentieth centuries, it was viewed by large segments of Chinese society with hostility, culminating in the expulsion of foreign missionaries in the early 1950s. In both cases, the long-term endurance of Christianity in China, despite such hostility, was closely related to the issue of indigenization. Will contemporary Christians be successful in their attempts to convince the Chinese state and populace that their faith is no more foreign than Buddhism? For the time being, it seems that in Yunnan, Christianity has taken root to the extent that it may be seen as an inseparable element of the province's social landscape. However, with the rising confidence in the greatness of China's past and present and the turn toward tightened control of all religions under Xi Jinping, the position occupied by Christianity and Christians in the Chinese world remains unclear and will clearly require further research.

Notes

Introduction

1. Ma's translated article was posted on the site of OMF, directed by Tony Lambert. The OMF is the current name for the China Inland Mission, the most important Protestant mission movement in China, founded by Hudson Taylor in 1865. Lambert presents the article as "a valuable glimpse of what the government is really thinking about Christianity" (2011, 1).

2. These sites include Open Doors, https://globalchristianrelief.org; Voice of the Martyrs, http://www.persecution.com; and Bitter Winter, https://bitterwinter.org.

Chapter 1

1. Although Vial was Catholic, I find his writing on the issues of modernization and ethnic culture largely compatible with Protestant missionary ideology.

2. The Miao/Hmong subgroup living on the Yunnan-Guizhou border is referred to by the Chinese as the "Da Hua Miao" (Big Flowery Miao). They self-identify as the "A-Hmao" and number 443,000 people. They are linguistically distinct from the much smaller Small Hua Miao of Guizhou, sometimes called the "Blue Hmong," who refer to themselves as "Gha-Mu." Both groups were converted by missionaries in the early twentieth century, and currently approximately 80 percent are Christian. Joshua Project, "A-Hmao in China," accessed July 1, 2015, http://joshuaproject.net/people_groups/18388/CH; Joshua Project, "Gha-Mu in China," accessed July 1, 2015, http://joshuaproject.net/people_groups/11877/CH.

3. The Sani Yi belong to the southeastern subgroup of the larger Yi (or Lolo) ethnic group and number approximately 135,000 people, concentrated in the vicinity of the Stone Forest of Shilin.

4. In recent years, Mongolian singing, Tibetan opera, Li textile techniques, the Grand Song of the Dong minority, the dragon boat festival, acupuncture, worship of the goddess Mazu, and numerous other minority and Han traditions have all been recognized by UNESCO as "intangible cultural heritage" worthy of preservation. United Nations Educational, Scientific, and Cultural Organization (UNESCO), "Intangible Cultural Heritage," accessed December 1, 2014, http://www.unesco.org/culture/ich/index.php?lg=en&pg=00001.

Chapter 2

1. Some theologians have criticized Niebuhr for defining culture too broadly, making it include virtually all human activity. The criticism highlights the problematic of the Christ-culture dichotomy. For a short review of criticisms, see Guenther 2005.

2. Joshua Project, "Definitions," accessed November 25, 2014, http://joshuaproject.net/help/definitions#Evangelical.

3. Joshua Project, "Lisu in China," accessed November 25, 2014, http://joshuaproject.net/people-profile.php?peo3=13076&rog3=CH.

4. Like all missionaries I met, Mona used the term "Christian" to imply evangelicals.

5. During my fieldwork in Yunnan, I was told by a non-Christian linguist working among the Dulong of northwestern Yunnan that the Dulong were currently in the process of adopting Christianity. Although he could not provide numbers, he indicated that conversion was taking place on a massive scale. Importantly, the missionary work was being conducted not by foreigners but rather by Lisu missionaries from the Nu River valley (Ros, interview, May 24, 2010). My information on the subject is unfortunately limited to this single report.

6. This Miao subgroup lives throughout upland Southeast Asia. Although many Hmong Njua in Vietnam and Thailand have converted to Christianity, there are relatively few Christian Hmong Njua/Qing Miao in China. Joshua Project, "Hmong Njua," accessed March 10, 2013, http://joshuaproject.net/people_groups/18495.

7. The false idea that Muslims do not eat pork because they believe the pig to be their forefather has its roots in anti-Muslim Chinese writing, dating back to the Yuan dynasty and has been conveyed to me on several occasions. Here, a similar idea appears in a minority people's version.

8. Similar reports of inflated numbers and "optimistic self-data" regarding evangelism in Latin America are reported in Jenkins 2011, 62.

9. Needless to say, the argument can be reversed. A major criticism of early Christian missionaries in China was that they paid converts or lured them through promises of heaven and the threat of hell. This was viewed as contrary to the true Chinese-Confucian ideal of doing right for its own sake, with no external benefit (Gernet 1985, 164).

10. Interestingly, unlike other American missionaries, Mark was far from being enamored with capitalism, "a system that nobody has been able to stand against," and often stressed the fact that Christianity should not be associated with any political or economic system.

11. Mark did not elaborate on the Yi subgroup he was referring to. The Yi residing in the region surrounding Tanhua Mountain in Dayao County have been noted as a society with vestiges of matriarchy (Yang Fuwang 1990). However, it is not clear if this was the group he had in mind.

12. The Lisu are mostly concentrated in the Nujiang River valley, on both sides of the Yunnan-Myanmar border. Due to the efforts of British missionaries in the colonial era, a majority of the Lisu on both sides on the border have accepted Christianity. The number of Lisu Christians today is estimated at three hundred thousand—approximately half of the Lisu population in China. Joshua Project, "Lisu in China," accessed July 1, 2015, http://joshuaproject.net/people_groups/13076/CH.

13. This seems to be the case with virtually all children of ethnically mixed couples I knew and is not particular to Christians. During research, I met couples who were Tibetan-Yi, Tibetan-Naxi, and Lisu-Dai. Their children always spoke Chinese only.

14. The Joshua Project divides the Dai of Dehong into two major groups: the Tai Nua (or Chinese Shan) and the Tai Pong. Despite reports of thirty-four Tai Nua who converted to Christianity in 1993 after encountering a Taiwanese mission group, the percentage of Christians in both subgroups does not exceed 0.22 percent of the population. For the Tai Nua, see Joshua Project, "Tai Nua in China," accessed January 11, 2015, http://joshuaproject.net/people_groups/15193/CH; for the Tai Pong, see Joshua Project, "Tai Pong in China," accessed January 11, 2015, http://joshuaproject.net/people_groups/18691/CH.

Chapter 3

1. Business as Mission, "The Future of Business as Mission in China," October 12, 2010, https://www.chinasource.org/resource-library/articles/the-future-of-business-as-mission-in-china/.

2. The entire series can be found online: China Soul for Christ Foundation website, accessed May 11, 2014, http://www.chinasoul.org.

3. According to Blum, the Dai minority are the exception to the rule, as they are associated with an exaggerated form of cleanliness (2001, 77).

4. Others have noted a number of fairly minor analogies between Tibetan Buddhism and Christianity, such as the "Tibetan reverence for the spoken word" (Sy 1987, 28).

5. It is interesting to note that the image of Tibetan masculinity shared by missionaries and other expats living in Shangrila stands in direct contrast to the common image of Tibetans in the West as peaceful and complaisant. Thus, Jeff relayed how the editor of the book he has written on the region strongly objected to the representation of Tibetans as anything other than smiling pacifists (interview, August 10, 2010).

6. The feminine image of Christianity may also be related to the fact that the majority of Christians throughout China are women (Hunter and Chan 1993, 173–74; Lim 2013a, 2).

7. ChinaForbiddenNews, "Christianity Spread Internationally and Tolerated in China," NTDTV news report, YouTube, February 24, 2013, https://www.youtube.com/watch?v=yOmpOrgyG28.

Chapter 4

1. The use of "wonders" such as healing and exorcism as a method of proselytizing is less common among missionaries but still very much present among local Christians, particularly in Pentecostal house churches (J. Ma 2011, 194).

2. It may be of some significance that the representatives of Western knowledge in this case were not Western themselves but rather ethnically Chinese from Hong Kong.

3. Yunnan Foreign Affairs Office, http://www.yfao.gov.cn (no longer online).

4. Yunnan Public Security Bureau Department for NGO Management, "Institutional Registration Announcement," accessed February 21, 2023, http://www.jwfzfzz.yn.gov.cn/gsgg/jgdjgs/index.html. For an interactive map based on the same data, see China NGO Project, "Registered Foreign NGO Representative Offices Interactive Map and Filterable Table," accessed February 22, 2023, https://www.chinafile.com/ngo/registered-foreign-ngo-offices-map-full-screen.

5. MSI Professional Services, home page, https://www.msips.org.

6. St. Stephan's is an organization founded by the famous British missionary Jackie Pullinger, who has been working in Hong Kong since the 1960s. The organization is closely related to the Vineyard Movement, a relatively new Christian evangelical denomination.

7. A similar example, in the realm of education, can be found in the brochure of The Anchor, a center for extracurricular activities for homeschooled children. The brochure clearly states that its goal is "to serve the expatriate community in Yunnan Province" and more specifically to deal with "the attrition rate of m's," i.e., missionaries.

8. Since this research was conducted, the central government has declared a healthcare reform including a gradual move toward a "treatment first, payment later" model. However, it is not clear to what extent and how quickly the new policy will be implemented (R. Lu 2013).

9. The video no longer appears on the website and was sent to me in a private communication with the main office of BCI.

10. The Mosuo institution of "walking marriage" is famous in this regard (Gladney 1994; Hyde 2007).

11. At the time of my research, US President Barack Obama was attempting to pass a bill on universal health coverage. Many of the American Christians I spoke to strongly opposed this as a "socialist policy" (with "socialist" used in a derogatory way).

Chapter 5

1. *The Jesus Film* is a portrayal of the gospel translated into numerous languages and considered a basic tool of missionary work. In Paul Hattaway's *Operation China* (2000), special attention is given to the number and percentage of Christians in a given group and the Christian materials available, including specific reference to the availably of *The Jesus Film* in the language of any given ethnic group in the world.

2. "China," in *Ethnologue: Languages of the World*, accessed October 25, 2014, https://www.ethnologue.com/country/CN.

3. In fact, Shih notes that some schools pose as bilingual, providing minimal and insubstantial instruction of the ethnic language to be eligible for special government grants (2002, 169).

4. A similar yet somewhat more ambivalent case can be made for traditional Judaism, with its general distrust of translation. Orthodox Jewish law allows for certain prayers to be recited in languages other than Hebrew, but this is considered a compromise of the ideal and is seldom practiced today in Orthodox synagogues. Furthermore, while translating the Bible is not prohibited, the day of the completion of the very first translation the Greek Septuagint ordered by King Ptolemy

of Egypt was declared by the sages as a day of mourning (*Masechet Sofrim*, 1.7).

5. It should be noted that my surprise at the way verses were reduced to their skeletal form reflects my own religious preconditioning. In Orthodox Judaism, the text of the Bible is perceived as holy in and of itself, with every word considered intrinsically meaningful. Omitting words from the text while reciting it would be inconceivable.

6. All quotes are from the International Mission Board website, https://www.imb.org/sub-saharan-africa/#.

7. T4T Online, "The Creation to Christ Story," accessed November 17, 2013, http://t4tonline.org/wp-content/uploads/2011/02/2-Creation-to-Christ-Story.pdf.

8. SIL International, home page, accessed April 18, 2012, http://www.sil.org.

9. All quotes are taken from the SIL East Asia website: "Zero Barrier: Zero Barrier Bilingual Education Concept," accessed January 12, 2015, http://www.eastasiagroup.net/en/zero-barrier (no longer online).

10. Pinyin is the official system of transliteration of Chinese characters into Latin letters.

11. SIL East Asia, "Zero Barrier Bilingual Education Photo Book," accessed November 18, 2013, http://www.eastasiagroup.net/content/zero-barrier-bilingual-education-photo-book (no longer online).

12. Interestingly, Sean pointed out that the parallel project among the Xishuangbanna Dai has encountered other problems. The Dai retain a strong ethnic identity and attachment to the Dai language. However, unlike the Bai, they do not place great emphasis on secular education and are reluctant to send their children to school, regardless of the language spoken.

13. The Bouyei, or Bouyi, of Guizhou number two and a half to three million people and are a group virtually indistinguishable from the Zhuang of Guanxi. Joshua Project, "Bouyei in China," accessed July 1, 2015, http://joshuaproject.net/people_groups/18421/CH; "The Bouyei Ethnic Minority," China.org.cn, accessed July 1, 2015, http://www.china.org.cn/e-groups/shaoshu/shao-2-bouyei.htm.

14. Simon preferred to define himself as nondenominational but was deeply involved in Pentecostal practices such as visions, dreams, and "speaking in tongues." Despite Wycliffe Bible Translation's reputation as a relatively conservative organization, in recent years, it has come under severe criticism for translations of basic Christian terms made to attract Muslims. Wycliffe's critics claim that the translations distort the basic Christian concept of the Trinity by using terms like "Messiah" instead of "Son" and "Lord" instead of "Father" (Breen 2012).

Chapter 6

1. Yan and his fiancée could attend an official Three Self church together. However, like many missionaries, Yan was severally critical of the TSPM's relationship with the state.

2. In fact, missionary attempts to avoid being identified with a foreign religion preceded the colonial experience. Ricci and the other Jesuits, for example, appeared in public with Buddhist and later Confucian robes (Gernet 1985, 16). Likewise, Hudson Taylor insisted on dressing in Chinese-style clothing and instructed his missionaries to do the same (Reinders 2004, 198).

3. Despite being Chinese, James and Cathy introduced themselves with their English names, hence my choice to use non-Chinese pseudonyms.

4. I heard old English-style hymn singing in a large Yi church in Sanyingpan, north of Kunming. The singing had clearly been imported by missionaries prior to 1949 and is still in use today.

5. Pray for China, accessed October 10, 2013, http://www.prayforchina.com (no longer online).

6. The verses cited at the end of each line are to be used in the given prayer.

7. For a discussion on the Guizhou Miao funeral rites and their relationship to concepts of geography and cosmology, see Huang Jin 2013.

Chapter 7

1. The centrality of Soviet influence over the classification project has been challenged by a number of scholars, who point out that the importance of local and historical considerations far outweighed that of the Soviet

theoretical model (Bin 2009; Mullaney 2010, 11; Tapp 2002, 67).

2. The official policy is not always applied. According to Francis Khek Gee Lim, 14 percent of Chinese Christians are members of the Chinese Communist Party (2013a, 2).

3. Tripadvisor, "Yunnan Nationalities VillageBenzilam," accessed February 21, 2023, http://www.tripadvisor.com/Attraction_Review-g298558-d379323-Reviews-Yunnan_Nationalities_Village-Kunming_Yunnan.html.

4. OMF International, "The Lisu of China," accessed February 21, 2023, https://omf.org/us/resources/people-and-places/famous-missionaries/james-o-fraser/lisu-people/. According to the Joshua Project, the number is closer to 80 percent. Joshua Project, "Lisu in China," accessed March 12, 2014, https://joshuaproject.net/people_groups/13076/ch.

5. See, for example, Wiki China, "Miao Ethnic Group," accessed December 25, 2013, http://wiki.china.org.cn/wiki/index.php/Miao.

6. Despite the fact that the Mosuo are officially a sub-group of the Naxi, the park contains a separate Mosuo compound. This contradiction with official ethnic classification is never explained. It may be theorized that the Mosuo are considered particularly exotic, largely due to their unique matriarchic society.

7. Yunnan Nationalities Village, "Jingpo People," accessed February 22, 2023, http://www.ynmzc.com/view/cnPc/22/71/view/325.html.

8. The spelling of "Bouyei" varies and can also be written "Bouyi" or "Buyi."

9. Joshua Project, "Bouyei in China," accessed December 11, 2013, http://www.joshuaproject.net/people_groups/18421/CH.

10. The use of the term "Christianity" for Protestantism reflects a problem of translation. The term (*jidu jiao*) can be translated either as "Protestantism" or as "Christianity." It is used to denote the official status of Protestantism, which is recognized as a separate religion from Catholicism (*tianzhu jiao*).

11. The version of the webpage cited in the text is no longer online. For the current page, see Yunnan Nationalities Village, "Miao People," accessed February 22, 2023, http://www.ynmzc.com/view/cnPc/22/71/view/313.html.

12. The famous Han-Mongolian singer Sa Dingding released a song featuring a Christian Miao choir, filmed in Yunnan: SadingdingVEVO, "Sa Dingding—Something like a Shadow Is Following You," YouTube, June 17, 2013, https://www.youtube.com/watch?v=8_xEZphoQzo.

13. The entire series is available online: China Soul for Christ Foundation website, accessed January 28, 2014, http://www.chinasoul.org/index.php?option=com_virtuemart&page=shop.browse_cg&category_id=5&Itemid=52&lang=en-gb.

14. Cheng Mengen website, accessed December 11, 2013, http://chengmengen.org/html.

Conclusion

1. I have refrained from revealing the Yi subgroup that Peter and Rebecca worked with, the name of their organization, or their location, for their privacy and protection.

2. A short piece of the concert can be seen here: happymittens, "Beijing International Christian Fellowship," YouTube, April 7, 2008, https://www.youtube.com/watch?v=QILlv1D1eWM.

3. Also known as the "Church of Almighty God," the "Eastern Lightning" cult was founded in Henan in 1990. Adherents believe that God has returned to Earth in the shape of a woman by the name of Yang Xiangbin. The group is on the Chinese list of cults and is widely condemned by human-rights organizations and mainstream Christians for using violence (Aikman 2003, 254–59). The Mentuhui are a Christian millenarian group founded in Shaanxi in 1989 by Ji Sanbu, who claimed to be Jesus (Lambert 2006). It is on China's cult list and has been severely persecuted (Su and Zhang 2014).

4. The film can be seen here: "From Xian to Zion," YouTube, July 18, 2014, https://www.youtube.com/watch?v=qX2EatMlj5k.

References

Abel, Andrew. 2006. "Favor Fishing and Punch Bowl Christians: Ritual and Conversion in a Chinese Protestant Church." *Sociology of Religion* 67 (2): 161–78.

Aikman, David. 2003. *Jesus in Beijing: How Christianity Is Transforming China and Changing the Global Balance of Power.* Washington, DC: Regnery.

———. 2006. *Jesus in Beijing: How Christianity Is Transforming China and Changing the Global Balance of Power.* First paperback ed. Washington, DC: Regnery.

Anderson, Allan. 2004. "Writing the Pentecostal History of Africa, Asia and Latin America." *Journal of Beliefs and Values* 25 (2): 139–51.

Anderson, Peter Stafford. 2006. "Communicating the Good News in China Today: Realistic Expectations for Foreign Believers." MA thesis, South African Theological Seminary, Rivonia, South Africa.

Austin, Alvyn. 2007. *China's Millions: The China Inland Mission and Late Qing Society, 1832–1905.* Grand Rapids, MI: Eerdmans.

Balmer, Randall. 2004. *Encyclopedia of Evangelicalism.* Waco, TX: Baylor University Press.

Banks, Nicola, and David Hulme. 2012. "The Role of NGOs and Civil Society in Development and Poverty Reduction." Working Paper 171. Brooks World Poverty Institute, June 1. http://papers.ssrn.com/sol3/papers.cfm?abstract_id=2072157.

Baranovitch, Nimrod. 2010. "Others No More: The Changing Representation of Non-Han Peoples in Chinese History Textbooks, 1951–2003." *Journal of Asian Studies* 69 (1): 85–122.

Barnett, Robert. 1992. "Saving Tibet from Satan's Grip: Present-Day Missionary Activity in Tibet." *Lungta* 11:36–41.

Barnett, Suzanne Wilson. 1972. "Protestant Expansion and Chinese Views of the West." *Modern Asian Studies* 6 (2): 129–49.

Barnett, Suzanne Wilson, and John King Fairbank. 1985. *Christianity in China: Early Protestant Missionary Writings.* Cambridge: Harvard University Press.

Bauman, Zygmunt. 1998. *Globalization: The Human Consequences.* Oxford, UK: Polity.

Bays, Daniel H. 1996. *Christianity in China from the Eighteenth Century to the Present.* Stanford: Stanford University Press.

———. 2003. "Chinese Protestant Christianity Today." *China Quarterly* 174:488–594.

———. 2009. "American Public Discourse on the Church in China." *China Review* 9 (2): 1–16.

———. 2011. *A New History of Christianity in China.* Hoboken, NJ: Wiley-Blackwell.

Bell, Daniel A. 2007. "From Marx to Confucius: Changing Discourses on China's Political Future." *Dissent* 54 (2): 20–28.

Benewick, Robert, and Stephanie Donald. 2009. *The State of China Atlas: Mapping the World's Fastest Growing Economy.* Berkeley: University of California Press.

Benge, Janet, and Geoff Benge. 1998. *Hudson Taylor: Deep in the Heart of China.* Seattle: YWAM.

Beyer, Peter. 1994. *Religion and Globalization.* London: Sage.

Billard, Liz, and Brian Billard. n.d. "Practical Research on Preschool Bilingual Education in Remote Minority Areas in Yunnan: A Report of the ChiME

Cooperative Program 2014–2019." https://www.sil.org/system/files/reapdata/15/66/19/156619378630126816520 53105865166171427/ChiME_Topics_A_G_EN.docx.

Bin Yang. 2009. "Central State, Local Government, Ethnic Groups and the Minzu Identification in Yunnan (1950s–1980s)." *Modern Asian Studies* 43 (3): 741–75.

Blum, Susan D. 2001. *Portraits of "Primitives": Ordering Human Kinds in the Chinese Nation*. Lanham, MD: Rowman and Littlefield.

———. 2002. "Margins and Centers: A Decade of Publishing on China's Ethnic Minorities." *Journal of Asian Studies* 61 (4): 1287–1310.

Bonk, Jonathan. 1993. "Globalization and Mission Education." *Theological Education* 30 (1): 47–95.

Borchert, Thomas. 2005. "Of Temples and Tourists: The Effects of the Tourist Political Economy on a Minority Buddhist Community in Southwest China." In *State, Market and Religion in Chinese Societies*, edited by Joseph Tamney and Fenggang Yang, 87–111. Leiden: Brill.

Borchigud, Wurlig. 1995. "The Impact of Urban Ethnic Education on Modern Mongolian Ethnicity, 1949–1966." In *Cultural Encounters on China's Ethnic Frontiers*, edited by Steven Harrell, 278–300. Seattle: University of Washington Press.

Boubacar, Diarra. 2004. "Village Doctor Training / Community Rehab in SW China, Project Grace." In *A Biblically Wholistic Approach to Health Missions: Global Health Missions Pre-Conference*, November 11. http://www.wlringdude.com/medsend/Conference_Book/17%20Hong%20He%20Village.pdf.

Bourne, Lisa. 2018. "Chinese Catholic Bishop Cedes Office to Government Backed Cleric at Pope's Request." *LifeSiteNews*, December 17. https://www.lifesitenews.com/news/chinese-catholic-bishop-cedes-office-to-govt-backed-cleric-at-popes-request.

Bowie, Julia, and David Gitter. 2018. "The CCP Plan to 'Sinicize' Religions." *The Diplomat*, June 14. https://thediplomat.com/2018/06/the-ccps-plan-to-sinicize-religions.

Brandner, Tobias. 2011. "Trying to Make Sense of History: Chinese Christian Traditions of Countercultural Belief and Their Theological and Political Interpretation of Past and Present History." *Studies in World Christianity* 17 (3): 216–36.

Branigan, Tania. 2013. "China's Anti-Prostitution Policies 'Lead to Increase of Sex Abuse.'" *Guardian*, May 14. http://www.theguardian.com/world/2013/may/14/china-prostitution-increase-abuse-workers.

Breen, Tom. 2012. "Wycliffe Bible Translation Criticized over Trinity Word Substitution in Muslim Countries." *Huffington Post*, April 26. http://www.huffingtonpost.com/2012/04/26/bible-translator-trinity_n_1455982.html.

Bresciani, Umberto. 2001. *Reinventing Confucianism / Xian dai xin rujia: The New Confucian Movement*. Taipei: Taipei Ricci Institute for Chinese Studies.

Brewington, Carla. 1995. "Lion of Judah on the Move in Tibet: Intercessors Ploughing up the Ground in the Heart of Darkness." *International Journal of Frontier Missions* 12 (1): 21–22.

Briggs, Magen. 2019. "New Chinese Translation of the Bible Seeks to Snuff Out Western Influence." *Church Leaders*, March 12. https://churchleaders.com/news/346272-the-sinicization-of-the-church-in-china.html.

Bulag, Uradyn E. 2003. "Mongolian Ethnicity and Linguistic Anxiety in China." *American Anthropology* 105 (4): 753–63.

Buruma, Ian. 1999. "The Pilgrimage from Tiananmen Square." *New York Times Magazine*, April 11. http://www2.kenyon.edu/Depts/Religion/Fac

/Adler/Reln270/TAM-Christianity.htm.

Cai Congxin. 2019. "Foreign Missionaries Deported from China for 'Violating Laws.'" *Bitter Winter*, December 21. https://bitterwinter.org/foreign-missionaries-deported-from-china-for-violating-laws.

Cao, Nanlai. 2008. "Boss Christians: The Business of Religion in the 'Wenzhou Model' of Christian Revival." *China Journal* 59:63–87.

———. 2017. "Spatial Modernity, Party Building, and Local Governance: Putting the Christian Cross Removal Campaign in Context." *China Review* 17 (1): 29–52.

Chambon, Michel. 2017. "The Action of Christian Buildings on Their Chinese Environment." *Studies in World Christianity* 23 (2): 100–121.

Chan, Kam Wing. 2012. "Internal Labor Migration in China: Trends, Geography and Policies, United Nations Population Division." In *Population Distribution, Urbanization, Internal Migration and Development: An International Perspective*, by United Nations, Department of Economic and Social Affairs, Population Division, 81–102. New York: United Nations. http://www.un.org/esa/population/publications/PopDistribUrbanization/PopulationDistributionUrbanization.pdf.

Chan Kei Thong and Charlene L. Fu. 2009. *Finding God in Ancient China: How the Ancient Chinese Worshiped the God of the Bible*. Grand Rapids, MI: Zondervan.

Chan, Kim-kwong. 2004. "Accession to the World Trade Organization and State Adaptation." In *God and Caesar in China: Policy Implications of Church-State Tensions*, edited by Jason Kindopp and Carol Lee Hamrin, 58–74. Washington, DC: Brookings Institution Press.

———. 2005. "Religion in China in the Twenty First Century: Some Scenarios." *Religion, State and Society* 33 (2): 87–119.

———. 2009. "The Christian Community in China: The Leaven Effect." In *Evangelical Christianity and Democracy in Asia*, edited by David Halloren Lumsdaine, 43–86. Oxford: Oxford University Press.

Chan, Kim-kwong, and Tetsunao Yamamori. 2002. *Holistic Entrepreneurs in China: A Handbook on the World Trade Organization and New Opportunities for Christians*. Pasadena, CA: William Carey International University Press.

Chang, Maria Hsia. 2004. *Falun Gong: The End of Days*. New Haven: Yale University Press.

Chen Cunfu and Huang Tianhai. 2004. "The Emergence of a New Type of Christians in China Today." *Review of Religious Research* 46 (2): 183–200.

Chen Li. 2012. "Duihua shi yu xia de jidujiao yu zhongguo wenhua de rongtong" [Study on accommodation of Christianity and Chinese culture in perspective of dialogue]. *Hunan Shifan Daxue Shehui Kexue Xuebao* [Hunnan University Social Studies Journal] 41 (6): 119–22.

Cheung, Siu Woo. 1995. "Millenarianism, Christian Movements, and Ethnic Change Among the Miao in Southwest China." In *Cultural Encounters on China's Ethnic Frontiers*, edited by Steven Harrell, 217–47. Seattle: University of Washington Press.

China Aid Association. 2006. "Massive Arrest of Church Leaders Including Americans in Yunnan Province: CAA Issues Heartbreaking True Stories on Persecution inside China." April 19. http://www.chinaaid.org/2006/04/massive-arrest-of-church-leaders.html.

———. 2013. "Yunnan Province Christian Threatened by TSPM Church, Banned from Holding Gatherings in Home." September 17. http://www.chinaaid.org/2013/09/yunnan-province-christian-threatened-by.html.

Chu, Cordia Ming-Yeuk. 1980. "Menstrual Beliefs and Practices of Chinese Women." *Journal of the Folklore Institute* 17 (1): 38–55.

Clark, Kelly James. 2005. "The Gods of Abraham, Isaiah and Confucius." *Dao: A Journal of Comparative Philosophy* 5 (1):109–36.

Clarke, Gerald. 1998. "Non-governmental Organizations (NGOs) and Politics in the Developing World." *Political Studies* 46 (1): 36–52.

Clarke, Samuel. (1915) 2009. *Among the Tribes in South-West China*. Hong Kong: Caravan.

Cohen, Paul. 1961. "The Anti-Christian Tradition in China." *Journal of Asian Studies* 20 (2): 169–80.

———. 1966. "The Roots of the Anti-Christian Tradition in China." In *Christian Missions in China: Evangelists of What?*, edited by Jessie G. Lutz, 34–41. Boston: D. C. Heath.

Coleman, Simon. 2000. *The Globalization of Charismatic Christianity*. Cambridge: Cambridge University Press.

———. 2009. "The Protestant Ethic and the Spirit of Urbanism." In *When God Comes to Town: Religious Traditions in Urban Contexts*, edited by Rik Pinxten and Lisa Dikomitis, 31–44. New York: Berghahn Books.

Covell, Ralph R. 1995. *The Liberating Gospel in China: The Christian Faith Among China's Minority Peoples*. Grand Rapids, MI: Baker Books.

———. 2001. "Christianity and China's Minority Nationalities—Faith and Unbelief." In *China and Christianity: Burdened Past, Hopeful Future*, edited by Stephan Uhalley and Xioaxin Wu, 271–82. Armonk, NY: M. E. Sharpe.

———. 2010. "Christian Communities and China's Ethnic Minorities" In *Handbook of Christianity in China*, vol. 2, *1800–Present*, edited by R. G. Tiedman, 717–32. Leiden: Brill.

Cox, Harvey. 1995. *Fire from Heaven: The Rise of Pentecostal Spirituality and the Reshaping of Religion in the Twenty-First Century*. Cambridge, MA: Da Capo.

Davidson, Helen. 2020. "Inner Mongolia Protests at China's Plan to Bring in Mandarin-Only Lessons." *Guardian*. September 1. https://www.theguardian.com/world/2020/sep/01/inner-mongolia-protests-china-mandarin-schools-language.

Davis, Sara. 2003. "Premodern Flows in Postmodern China: Globalization and the Sipsongpanna Tais." *Modern China* 29 (2): 176–203.

———. 2006. "Dance or Else: China's 'Simplifying Project.'" *China Rights Forum* 4:38–46.

Diamond, Norma. 1995. "Defining the Miao: Ming, Qing and Contemporary Views." In *Cultural Encounters on China's Ethnic Frontiers*, edited by Steven Harrell, 92–116. Seattle: University of Washington Press.

———. 1996. "Christianity and the Hua Miao: Writing and Power." In *Christianity in China from the Eighteenth Century to the Present*, edited by Daniel Bays, 138–57. Stanford: Stanford University Press.

Dirlik, Arif. 2002. "Modernity as History: Post-Revolutionary China, Globalization and the Question of Modernity." *Social History* 27 (1): 16–39.

Dong Min. 2003. "Chuan dian qian yizu tong jidujiao de chongtu yu tiaoshi" [The conflict and harmony between Christianity and Yi nationality in Sichuan, Yunnan, and Guizhou]. *Bijie Shifan Gaodeng Zhuanke Xuexiao Xuebao* [Journal of Teachers College] 21 (2): 25–30.

Doyle, G. Write. 2014. "Is Christianity a 'Chinese' Religion?" *Christian Daily*, July 9. http://www.christiandaily.com/article/g.wright.doyle.is.christianity.a.chinese.religion/49115.htm.

Dreyer, June. 1968. "China's Minority Nationalities in the Cultural Revolution." *China Quarterly* 35:96–110.

Duan Qi Ming. 1998. "Shilun zongjiao yu shehui zhuyi xiang shiying de jiben neihan" [Basic content of the mutual accommodation between religions and socialism]. *Zhongguo Zongjiao* [Religions in China] 18:23–26.

Duan Yunxue. 2001. "Jindai zhongguo shaoshu minzu de fan yangjiao douzheng" [The anti-Christianity struggles of ethnic groups in modern China]. *Yunnan Minzu Xueyuan Xuebao* [Yunnan Minority College Journal] 18 (4): 19–21.

Duara, Prasenjit. 1995. *Rescuing History from the Nation: Questioning Narratives of Modern China*. Chicago: University of Chicago Press.

DuBois, Thomas David, and Chi Zhen. 2014. "Opiate of the Masses with Chinese Characteristics: Recent Chinese Scholarship on the Meaning and Future of Religion." Asia Research Institute Working Paper 213. Asia Research Institute / National University of Singapore.

Dunch, Ryan. 2001. "Protestant Christianity in China Today: Fragile, Fragmented, Flourishing." In *China and Christianity: Burdened Past, Hopeful Future*, edited by Stephan Uhalley and Xioaxin Wu, 195–216. Armonk, NY: M. E. Sharpe.

———. 2002. "Beyond Cultural Imperialism: Cultural Theory, Christian Missions, and Global Modernity." *History and Theory* 41 (3): 301–25.

Dunn, Emily. 2008. "The Big Red Dragon and Indigenizations of Christianity in China." *East Asian History* 36:73–85.

Dwyer, Arienne M. 1998. "The Texture of Tongues: Languages and Power in China." *Nationalism and Ethnic Politics* 4 (1–2): 68–85.

Economist. 2009. "Health Care in China: Will Patients Be Rewarded?" April 16. http://www.economist.com/node/13496687.

———. 2011 "China Coming Down the Tracks: Integrating South-East Asia." January 22, 61–62.

Embassy of the People's Republic of China in the United States of America. 1997. "White Paper: Freedom of Religious Belief in China." http://www.china-embassy.org/eng/zt/zjxy/t36492.htm.

Feng, Emily. 2021. "China Is Removing Domes from Mosques as Part of a Push to Make Them more 'Chinese.'" NPR, October 24. https://www.npr.org/2021/10/24/1047054983/china-muslims-sinicization.

Feuchtawang, Stephan, and Wang Mingming. 1991. "The Politics of Culture or a Contest of Histories: Representation of Chinese Popular Religion." *Dialectical Anthropology* 16:251–72.

Forney, Mathew. 2001. "Positioning Missionaries." *Time*, February 19. http://www.time.com/time/world/article/0,8599,99019,00.html.

Frick, Michael. 2007. "Where the Sky Is High and the Hospital Is Faraway: Strategies for Rural Public Health Education in Yunnan, China." Independent Study Project (ISP) Collection 221. https://digitalcollections.sit.edu/isp_collection/221.

Fung, Patrick. 2004. "China's Medical Missionary Work—A Catalyst for Research Development." *China Insight*, September–October.

———. 2008. *Live to be Forgotten: D. E. Hoste*. Hong Kong: OMF.

Gan, Nectar. 2019. "Official Head of China's Protestant Churches Says Religions Must Be Purged of 'Western Influences.'" *South China Morning Post*, March 12. https://www.scmp.com/news/china/politics/article/3001240/official-head-chinas-protestant-churches-says-religions-must-be.

Gao Zhiying, and Sha Li'na. 2014. "Zongjiao Zuqiu yu jijin lidong yi zhongmian bianjing diqu Xinyang jidujiao kuajingminzu weige'an" [Religious pursuits and cross-border mobility: A case study of the ethnic Christian groups at the China-Myanmar border]. *Shijiezongjiao yanjiu* [Studies in World Religions] 6:108–16.

REFERENCES

Gernet, Jacques. 1985. *China and the Christian Impact.* Cambridge: Cambridge University Press.

Ghimire, Krishna, and Zhou Li. 2001. "The Economic Role of National Tourism in China." In *The Native Tourist: Mass Tourism in Developing Countries,* edited by Krishna Ghimire, 86–108. Abingdon, UK: Earthscan.

Giddens, Anthony. 2000. *Runaway World: How Globalization Is Reshaping Our Lives.* New York: Routledge.

Gladney, Dru. 1994. "Representing Nationality in China: Refiguring Majority / Minority Identities." *Journal of Asian Studies* 53 (1): 92–123.

———. 2004. *Dislocating China: Muslims, Minorities and Other Subaltern Subjects.* London: Hurst.

Goodman, Jim. 2009. *Yunnan: China South of the Clouds (Odyssey Guides).* Hong Kong: Airphoto International.

Groff, Stephan. 2012. "Supporting Sustainable Urbanization." *China Daily,* April 9. http://yunnan.chinadaily.com.cn/2012-04/09/content_15240326.htm.

Guenther, Bruce. 2005. "The 'Enduring Problem' of Christ and Culture." *Direction* 34 (2): 215–27.

Guo Shuhan. 2010. "Christian Group Sings Songs of Their Faith." *China Daily,* February 23. http://www.chinadaily.com.cn/cndy/2010-02/23/content_9486376.htm.

Gustafson, Bjorn, and Li Shi. 2003. "The Ethnic Minority-Majority Income Gap in Rural China During Transition." *Economic Development and Cultural Change* 51 (4): 805–22.

Hamrin, Carol Lee. 2003. "Faith-Based Organizations: Invisible Partners in Developing Chinese Society." Presentation at issues roundtable "To Serve the People: NGOs and the Development of Civil Society in China," Congressional-Executive Commission on China (CECC), Washington, DC, March 24. https://www.cecc.gov/sites/chinacommission.house.gov/files/documents/roundtables/2003/CECC%20Roundtable%20Testimony%20-%20Carol%20Lee%20Hamrin%20-%203.24.03.pdf.

———. 2007. "Engaging a Global Chinese Society and Culture." Gordon College. Accessed June 19, 2011. http://www.gordon.edu/ccs/usaspeakers/carolleehamrin.

———. 2008. "China's Protestants: A Mustard Seed for Moral Renewal?" *Tocqueville on China,* American Enterprise Institute, May 14. http://www.aei.org/publication/chinas-protestants.

Han Junxue. 2000. *Jidujiao yu Yunnan shaoshu minzu* [Christianity and Yunnan's nationalities]. Kunming: Yunnan Renmin Chubashe.

Hansen, Mette Halskov. 1999. *Lessons in Being Chinese: Minority Education and Ethnic Identity in Southwest China.* Seattle: University of Washington Press.

Harrell, Steven. 1990. "Ethnicity, Local Interests and the State: Yi Communities in Southwest China." *Comparative Studies in Society and History* 32 (3): 515–48.

———. 1996. "Introduction: Civilizing Projects and the Reaction to Them." In *Cultural Encounters on China's Ethnic Frontiers,* edited by Steven Harrell, 3–36. Seattle: University of Washington Press.

Harrell, Steven, and Bamo Ayi. 1998. "Chinese Nationalism in Minority Language Textbooks: The Case of the Nuosu (Yi) of Liangshan." *Bulletin of the Concerned Asian Scholars* 30 (2): 62–71.

Harris, Paul W. 1991. "Cultural Imperialism and American Protestant Missionaries: Collaboration and Dependency in Nineteenth-Century China." *Pacific Historical Review* 60 (3): 309–38.

Hartch, Todd. 2006. *Missionaries of the State: The Summer Institute of Linguistics, State Formation and Indigenous Mexico, 1935–1985.* Tuscaloosa: University of Alabama Press.

REFERENCES

Harwood, Russell. 2014. *China's New Socialist Countryside: Modernity Arrives in the Nu River Valley*. Seattle: University of Washington Press.

Hattaway, Paul. 2000. *Operation China: Introducing All the Peoples of China*. Carlisle, UK: Piquanet.

———. 2003. *Back to Jerusalem*. Carlisle, UK: Piquanet.

Heberer, Thomas. 2000. "Some Considerations on China's Minorities in the Twenty-First Century: Conflict of Conciliation?" Duisberg Working Papers on East Asian Studies 31. https://www.uni-due.de/oapol/wordpress/wp-content/uploads/Heberer_Some-Considerations-on-Chinas-Minorities-in-the-21st-Century1.pdf.

He Ming and Zhongli Yue. 2007. "Jidujiao xinyang xia de shaoshu minzu nongcun hexie shehui jianshe yanjiu" [The construction of a harmonious society in ethnic villages with Christianity: A case study of three Miao ethnic villages of Yunnan]. *Xueshu Tansuo* [Academic Exploration] 5:107–12.

Hesketh, Theresa, Wu Dan, Linan Mao, and Nan Ma. 2012. "Violence Against Doctors in China." *BMJ* 345:e5730. http://www.bmj.com/content/345/bmj.e5730.

Hiebert, Paul G. 2007. "Western Images of Other and Otherness." In *This Side of Heaven: Race, Ethnicity and Christian Faith*, edited by Robert Priest and Alvaro Nieves, 97–110. Oxford: Oxford University Press.

Hillman, Ben. 2005. "Monastic Politics and the Local State in China: Authority and Autonomy in an Ethnically Tibetan Prefecture." *China Journal* 54:29–53.

Hillman, Ben, and Lee Anne Henfry. 2006. "Macho Minority: Masculinity and Ethnicity on the Edge of Tibet." *Modern China* 32:251–72.

Hirono, Miwa. 2008. *Civilizing Missions: International Religious Agencies in China*. London: Palgrave Macmillan.

Homer, Lauren B. 2010. "Registration of Chinese Protestant House Churches under China's 2005 Regulation on Religious Affairs: Resolving the Implementation Impasse." *Journal of Church and State* 52 (1): 50–73.

Horth, Roberta. 2004. "Tourism in the Girl's Kingdom." In *Yunnan Through Foreign Students*, vol. 2, *Ethnic Minority Issues in Yunnan*, edited by Sam Mitchell, 182–93. Kunming: Yunnan Normal University.

Hu Zimo. 2021. "Religious Books Publicly Burned, DVDs Bulldozed in Yunnan." *Bitter Winter*, July 21. https://bitterwinter.org/religious-books-publicly-burned-dvds-bulldozed-in-yunnan.

Huang Jin. 2013. "Qian xibei Yi Miao diqu zongjiao bianqian yu zuqun xing" [Yi and Miao regions of Northwest Guizhou Province, religious change and ethnicity]. *Guizhou Minzu Yanjiu* [Guizhou Minority Research] 5 (34): 191–94.

Huang, Jingbo, and Fenggang Yang. 2005. "The Cross Faces the Loudspeakers: A Village Church Preservers Under State Control." In *State, Market, and Religions in Chinese Societies*, edited by Fenggang Yang, 41–62. Leiden: Brill.

Huang Xing. 1992. "On Writing Systems for China's Minorities Created by Foreign Missionaries." *International Journal of the Sociology of Language* 97:75–85.

Hui, Echo. 2014. "Faithful Rally to Save New Sanjiang Church in Wenzhou from Demolition." *South China Morning Post*, April 7. http://www.scmp.com/news/china/article/1466548/faithful-rally-save-new-sanjiang-church-wenzhou-demolition.

Hunter, Alan and Kim-kwong Chan. 1993. *Protestantism in Contemporary China*. Cambridge: Cambridge University Press.

Hvalkof, Soren, and Peter Aaby. 1981. *Is God an American? An Anthropological Perspective on the Missionary Work of the Summer Institute of Linguistics*. Copenhagen: IWGIA / SI.

Hyde, Sandra Teresa. 2007. "Sex Tourism and the Lure of the Ethnic Erotic." In *China's Transformations: The Story Behind the Headlines*, edited by Lionel Jensen and Timothy Weston, 216–39. Lanham, MD: Rowan and Littlefield.

ILO (International Labor Organization) / IPEC (International Program on the Elimination of Child Labor). 2002. "Yunnan Province China, Situation of Trafficking in Children and Women, a Rapid Assessment." International Labor Office, Bangkok.

Information Office of the State Council of the People's Republic of China. 2001. "White Paper on Tibet's March Towards Modernization." http://chicago.china-consulate.gov.cn/eng/zt/wp/200310/t20031023_5425387.htm.

Iredale, Robyn, Naran Bilik, Wang Su, Fei Guo, and Caroline Hoy. 2001. *Contemporary Minority, Migration, Education and Ethnicity in China*. Northampton, MA: Edward Elgar.

Jenkins, Philip. 2011. *The Next Christendom: The Coming of Global Christianity*. Oxford: Oxford University Press.

Jia Xijin. 2017. "China's Implementation of the Overseas NGO Management Law." Translated by Cameron Carleson and Gabriel Corsetti. *China Development Brief*, March 6. http://www.chinadevelopmentbrief.cn/articles/chinas-implementation-of-the-overseas-ngo-management-law.

Jia Zhongyi. 2006. *The Marriage Customs Among China's Ethnic Minority Groups*. Beijing: China Intercontinental Press.

Jiang, Rong. 2008. *Wolf Totem*. New York: Penguin.

Jochim, Christian. 1992. "Confucius and Capitalism: Views of Confucianism in Works on Confucianism and Economic Development." *Journal of Chinese Religions* 20:135–56.

Johnson, Ian. 2012. "Jesus vs. Mao? An Interview with Yuan Zhiming." *New York Review of Books*, September 4. http://www.nybooks.com/blogs/nyrblog/2012/sep/04/jesus-vs-mao-interview-yuan-zhiming.

———. 2014. "Church State Clash in China Coalesces Around a Toppled Spire." *New York Times*, May 29. http://www.nytimes.com/2014/05/30/world/asia/church-state-clash-in-china-coalesces-around-a-toppled-spire.html.

Johnson, Todd. 2010. "Globalization, Christian Identity and Frontier Missions." *International Journal of Frontier Missiology* 27 (4): 165–69.

Jordan, David K. 1993. "The Glyphomancy Factor: Observation on Chinese Conversion." In *Conversion to Christianity: Historical and Anthropological Perspectives on a Great Transformation*, edited by Robert W. Hefner, 285–304. Berkley: University of California Press.

Juergensmeyer, Mark. 2007. "The Church, the Mosque and Global Civil Society." In *Global Civil Society 2006/7*, edited by Marlies Glasius, Mary Kaldor, and Helmut Anheier, 144–58. London: Sage.

Junio, Diana. 2017. *Patriotic Cooperation: The Border Services of the Church of Christ in China and Chinese Church-State Relations, 1920s–1950s*. Leiden: Brill.

Kaiman, Jonathan. 2013. "Going Undercover, the Evangelists Taking Jesus to Tibet." *Guardian*, February 21. http://www.theguardian.com/world/2013/feb/21/going-undercover-christian-evangelists-tibet.

Kalir, Barak. 2009. "Finding Jesus in the Holy Land and Taking Him to China: Chinese Temporary Migrant Workers in Israel Converting to Evangelical Christianity." *Sociology of Religion* 70 (2): 130–56.

Kang, C. H., and Ethel R. Nelson. 1979. *The Discovery of Genesis: How the Truths of Genesis Were Found Hidden in the Chinese Language*. St. Louis: Concordia.

Katz, Paul. 2014. *Religion in China and Its Modern Fate*. Waltham: Brandeis University Press.

REFERENCES

Kaup, Katherine Palmer. 2000. *Creating the Zhuang: Ethnic Politics in China.* Boulder, CO: Lynne Rienner.

Kepler, A. R. 1966. "Christianity as a Social Gospel." In *Christian Missions in China: Evangelists of What?*, edited by Jessie G. Lutz, 16–21. Boston: D. C. Heath.

Kindopp, Jason. 2004. "The Politics of Protestantism in Contemporary China: State Control, Civil Society, and Social Movement in a Single Party-State." PhD diss., George Washington University.

Kipnis, Andrew B. 2001. "The Flourishing of Religion in Post-Mao China and the Anthropological Category of Religion." *Australian Journal of Anthropology* 12 (1): 32–46.

Koesel, Karrie. 2017. "Religion and the Regime: Cooperation and Conflict in Russia and China." *World Politics* 69 (4): 676–712.

Kolas, Ashild. 2003. "Teaching Tibetan in Tibet: Bilingual Education Is Survival." *Cultural Survival Quarterly Magazine* 27 (3): 67–71. https://www.culturalsurvival.org/publications/cultural-survival-quarterly/teaching-tibetan-tibet-bilingual-education-survival.

Kolas, Ashild, and Monika Thowsen. 2005. *On the Margins of Tibet: Cultural Survival on the Sino-Tibetan Frontier.* Seattle: University of Washington Press.

Komlosy, Anouska. 2009. "Feminization, Recognition and the Cosmological in Xishuangbanna." In *Marginalization in China: Recasting Minority Politics*, edited by Siu-Keung Cheung, Joseph Tse-Hei Lee, and Lida V. Nedilsky, 123–43. New York: Palgrave.

Kui, Shin Voo, and Larry Hovee. 1999. "The Lamb of God Hidden in the Ancient Chinese Characters." *CEN Technical Journal* 13 (1): 81–91.

Lai, Hongyi Harry. 2003. "The Religious Revival in China." *Copenhagen Journal of Asian Studies* 18:40–64.

Laliberté, André,. 2011. "Buddhist Revival Under State Watch." *Journal of Current Chinese Affairs* 40 (2): 107–34.

———. 2012. "Buddhist Charities and China's Social Policy an Opportunity for Alternate Civility?" *Archives de sciences sociales des religions* 158:95–117.

Lam, Nuala Gathercole. 2018. "NGOs at a Crossroads: A Q&A with Li Dan, Founder of the Crossroads Center." *The China NGO Project*, ChinaFile, February 5. http://www.chinafile.com/ngo/latest/ngos-crossroads.

Lambert, Tony. 1994. *The Resurrection of the Chinese Church.* Wheaton, IL: OMF/Shaw.

———. 1999. *China's Christian Millions.* Oxford, UK: Monarch Books.

———. 2001. "The History of Religion in Yunnan." *China Insight*, May–June. http://omf.org (no longer online).

———. 2005. "'Gospel Valley': An Extended Review." *China Insight*. April/May. Accessed July 3, 2012. http://omf.org (no longer online).

———. 2006. "Children at Risk! Chinese Cults Target Youth." *China Insight*, April–May. http://omf.org (no longer online).

———. 2011. "The Gospel in Tibet's Darkness." *China Insight*. http://omf.org (no longer online).

Lap, Yan Kung. 2002. "What to Preach? Christian Witness in China, with Reference to the Party's Policy of Mutual Accommodation." *Studies in World Christianity* 8 (2): 207–27.

Lee, Joseph Tse-Hei. 2007. "Christianity in Contemporary China: An Update." *Journal of Church and State* 49 (2): 277–305.

Lefebvre, Henri. 1991. *The Production of Space.* Translated by Donald Nicholson Smith. Hoboken, NJ: Wiley-Blackwell.

Leibold, James. 2010. "The Beijing Olympics and China's Conflicted National Form." *China Journal* 63:1–24.

———. 2013. "Ethnic Policy in China: Is Reform Inevitable?" *East West Center*

Policy Studies 68. http://www.east-westcenter.org/system/tdf/private/pso68.pdf.
Lemoine, Jacques. 1989. "Ethnicity, Culture and Development Among Some Minorities of the People's Republic of China." *New Asian Academic Bulletin: Special Issue on Ethnicity and Ethnic Groups in China* 8:1–10.
Leung, Beatrice. 2005. "China's Religious Freedom Policy: The Art of Managing Religious Activity." *China Quarterly* 184:894–913.
Li Hongjun and Mei Ying. 2007. "Qian xi jidujiao dui yunnan shaoshu minzu shehui jiaoyu de yinxiang" [Briefly on the impact of Christianity in minority education in Yunnan]. *Lincang Shilang Gaodeng Zhuanke Xuexiao Xuebao* [Journal of Lincang Teachers College] 16 (2): 12–15.
Li, Huanhuan. 2013. "Shimenkan xianxiang yanjiu zongshu" [Research review of Shimenkan phenomena]. *Lincang Shilang Gaodeng Zhuanke Xuexiao Xuebao* [Journal of Lincang Teachers College] 23 (3): 36–39.
Li Huiyu. 2005. "Zhong hua jidujiao hui zai xinan shaoshu minzu diqu de wenhua chuanbo yanjiu" [Culture propaganda of the Chinese Christian Church in southwestern ethnic areas]. *Guizhou Minzu Yanjiu* [Guizhou Minority Research] 25 (102): 65–71.
Li, Jianhua, Toan Ha, Cunmin Zhang, and Hogjie Liu. 2010. "The Chinese Government's Response to Drug Use and HIV/AIDS: A Review of Policies and Programs." *Harm Reduction Journal* 7 (4): 1–6. http://www.harmreductionjournal.com/content/7/1/4.
Li Ping Min, and Ma He Lan. 2010. "Jidujiao yu 'hexie shijie' de sixiang" [Christianity and 'harmonious world' thinking]. *Lishi Jiaoxue Wenti* [Issues in the Instruction of History] 2:26–34.
Li Yinqing, and Guo Anfei. 2013. "Power Grid Now Covers all Yunnan's Households." *China Daily*, January 29. http://www.chinadaily.com.cn/china/2013-01/29/content_16185604.htm.
Lim, Francis Khek Gee. 2013a. "Shields of Faith: Christianity in Contemporary China." In *Christianity in Contemporary China: Socio-cultural Perspectives*, edited by Francis Lim, 1–15. London: Routledge.
———. 2013b. "'To the People': Christianity and Ethnicity in China's Minority Areas." In *Christianity in Contemporary China: Socio-cultural Perspectives*, edited by Francis Lim, 105–20. London: Routledge.
Lin, Christina. 2011. "China's New Silk Road to the Mediterranean: The Eurasian Land Bridge and Return of Admiral Zhen He." *ISPSW Strategy Series: Focus of Defense and International Security* 165:1–23.
Lin Meilian. 2014. "Plateau Enlightenment." *Global Times*, April 23. http://www.globaltimes.cn/content/856367.shtml.
Lin-Liu, Jen. 2005. "At Chinese Universities, Whispers of Jesus." *Chronicle of Higher Education*, June 10. https://www.chronicle.com/article/at-chinese-universities-whispers-of-jesus/.
Litzinger, Ralph. 2000. *Other China: The Yao and the Politics of National Belonging*. Durham: Duke University Press.
Liu Daixia. 2008. "Bijie Miaozu Juju qu jidujiao chuanbo xianzhuang yu goujian hexie shehui" [The spread of Christianity and the construction of a harmonious society among the Bijie Miao]. *Bijie Xueyuan Xuebao* [Bijie College Journal] 6 (26): 108–11.
Liu, Jifeng, and Chris White. 2019. "Old Pastor and Local Bureaucrats: Recasting Church-State Relations in Contemporary China." *Modern China* 45 (5): 564–90.
Liu, Lin. 2011. "Christianity Development in China Today." *Asia-Pacific Science and Culture Journal* 1 (1): 43–48.
Lu, Rachel. 2013. "Will Chinese Hospitals Allow Treatment First and Payment Later? Not So Fast." *Tea Leaf Nation*,

February 26. http://www.tealeafnation.com/2013/02/will-chinese-hospitals-allow-treatment-first-and-payment-later-not-so-fast.

Lu Yaoming. 2011. "Ziyou yu hexie de tongyi—Zhongguo shehui zhuyi shichang jingji de yige zhogyao tedian: Jiyu jidujiao de ziyou sixiang yu rujia hexie sixiang dui Zhongguo zhehui shichang jingji yinxiang de fenxi" [The unification of freedom and harmony: One important feature of socialism market economy in China: Analysis on influence by the free thought of Christianity and the Confucian thought of harmony]. *Kexue, Jingji, Shehui* [Science, Economy, Society] 29 (2): 76–80.

Luo Zhufeng. 1991. *Religion Under Socialism in China*. Translated by Donald E. MacInnis and Zheng Xi'an. Armonk, NY: M. E. Sharpe.

Lutz, Jessie. 2001. "China and Protestantism: Historical Perspectives, 1807–1949." In *China and Christianity: Burdened Past, Hopeful Future*, edited by Stephan Uhalley and Xiaoxin Wu, 179–83. Armonk, NY: M. E. Sharpe.

———. 2008. *Opening China: Karl F. A. Gutzlaff and Sino-Western Relations, 1827–1852*. Grand Rapids, MI: Eerdmans.

Ma Huacheng. 2010. "When a Religion Reaches 200 or 300 Million, Can It Be Controlled?" Translated by Tony Lambert. *China Insight*, March–April.

Ma, Jungja. 2011. "Pentecostal Challenges in East and South-East Asia." In *The Globalization of Pentecostalism: A Religion Made to Travel*, edited by Murray W. Dempster, Byron D. Klaus, Douglas Peterson, 183–202. Eugene, OR: Wipf and Stock.

Mackerras, Colin. 2003. *China's Ethnic Minorities and Globalization*. London: Routledge Curzon.

Madsen, Richard. 2000. "Chinese Christianity: Indigenization and Conflict." In *Chinese Society: Change, Conflict and Resistance*, edited by Elizabeth J. Perry and Mark Selden, 257–78. London: Routledge Curzon.

———. 2010. "Back to the Future: Pre-Modern Religious Policy in Post-Secular China." Templeton Lecture on Religion and World Affairs. http://www.fpri.org/publications/e-notes.

———. 2011. "Religious Renaissance in China Today." *Journal of Current Chinese Affairs* 40 (2): 17–42.

———. 2013. "Signs and Wonders: Christianity and Hybrid Modernity in China." In *Christianity in Contemporary China: Socio-cultural Perspectives*, edited by Francis Lim, 17–30. London: Routledge.

———. 2021. *The Sinicization of Chinese Religions: From Above and Below*. Leiden: Brill.

Makinen, Julie. 2014. "China Demolition of Church in Wenzhou Leaves Christians Uneasy." *Los Angeles Times*, May 5. http://www.latimes.com/world/asia/la-fg-china-church-20140506-story.html.

Makley, Charlene. 2010. "Minzu, Market and the Mandala: National Exhibitionism and Tibetan Buddhist Revival in Post-Mao China." In *Faiths on Display: Religion, Tourism and the Chinese State*, edited by Tim Oakes and Donald Sutton, 127–56. Lanham, MD: Rowman and Littlefield.

Manji, Firoze, and Carl O'Coill. 2002. "The Missionary Position: NGO and Development in Africa." *International Affairs* 78 (3): 567–83.

Marcus, George. 1995. "Ethnography in/of the World System: The Emergence of Multi-sited Ethnography." *Annual Review of Anthropology* 24:95–117.

Martin, David. 1999. "The Evangelical Upsurge and Its Political Implications." In *The Desecularization of the World*, edited by Peter Berger, 37–50. Grand Rapids, MI: Eerdmans.

Maxey, James. 2010. "Bible Translation as Contextualization: The Role of Orality." *Missiology* 38 (2): 173–83.

Mazard, Mireille. 2014. "Stéphane Gros, *La Part manquante: Échanges et pouvoirs chez les Drung du Yunnan*" [The missing share: Exchange and power among the Drung of Yunnan]. *China Perspectives* 3:63–64. http://chinaperspectives.revues.org/6547.

McAlister, Elizabeth. 2005. "Globalization and the Religious Production of Space." *Journal for the Scientific Study of Religion* 44 (3): 249–55.

McCarthy, Susan. 2004. "Gods of Wealth, Temples of Prosperity: Party-State Participation in Minority Cultural Revival." *China: An International Journal* 2 (1): 28–52.

———. 2007. "Mao, Metta and Muhammad: Faith-Based Civil Society in Contemporary China." Paper submitted for the 2007 annual meeting of the Western Political Science Association, March 8–10, Las Vegas.

———. 2009. *Communist Multiculturalism: Ethnic Revival in Southwest China*. Seattle: University of Washington Press.

———. 2017. "In Between the Divine and the Leviathan: Faith-Based Charity, Religious Overspill and the Governance of Religion in China." *China Review* 17 (2): 65–93.

McLeister, Mark. 2012. "A Three-Self Protestant Church, the Local State and Religious Policy Implementation in a Coastal Chinese City." In *Christianity in Contemporary China: Socio-cultural Perspectives*, edited by Francis Lim, 234–46. London: Routledge.

Menuge, Angus J. L. 1999. "Niebuhr's *Christ and Culture* Reexamined." In *Christ and Culture in Dialogue*. St. Louis: Concordia. https://www.issuesetcarchive.org/articles/bissar26.htm.

Meyer, Birgit. 1999. "Commodities and the Power of Prayer: Pentecostalist Attitudes Towards Consumption in Contemporary Ghana." In *Globalization and Identity: Dialectics of Flow and Closure*, edited by Birgit Meyer and Peter Geschiere, 151–76. Oxford, UK: Blackwell.

Millward, James, and Dahlia Peterson. 2020. "China's System of Oppression in Xinjiang: How It Developed and How to Curb It." Brookings Institute, September. https://www.brookings.edu/wp-content/uploads/2020/09/FP_20200914_china_oppression_xinjiang_millward_peterson.pdf.

Morgan, Timothy. 1998. "China's Dynamic Church: Eyewitness Reports of Repression and Revival." *Christianity Today* 42 (8): 30–40.

Morse, Eugene. 1974. *Exodus to a Hidden Valley*. New York: Readers Digest Press.

Mueggler, Eric. 2001. *The Age of Wild Ghosts: Memory, Violence, and Place in Southwest China*. Berkeley: University of California Press.

Mullaney, Thomas S. 2004. "Ethnic Classification Writ Large: The 1954 Yunnan Province Ethnic Classification Project and Its Foundation in the Republican Era Taxonomic Thought." *China Information* 18 (2): 207–41.

———. 2010. *Coming to Terms with the Nation: Ethnic Classification in Modern China*. Berkeley: University of California Press.

Najarian, Nishan. 1982. "Religious Conversion in Nineteenth-Century China: Face-to-Face Interaction Between Western Missionaries and Chinese." In *Social Interaction in Chinese Society*, edited by Sidney L. Greenblatt, Richard W. Wilson, and Amy Aurbacher Wilson, 67–111. New York: Praeger.

Nam, Cuo Kyi. 2009. "Jidujiao zai Xizang chuanbo jubuweijian yuanyin zhi chuyi" [On the reasons of the difficult status of Christianity missionary in Tibet]. *Xizang Daxue Xuebao* [University of Tibet Journal] 24 (2): 79–82.

Niebuhr, Richard. 1956. *Christ and Culture*. New York: Harper and Row.

Nordstorm, Dwight, and Ryan Muir. 2010. "The Future of Business as Mission in China." *China Source*. https://www

.chinasource.org/resource-library/articles/the-future-of-business-as-mission-in-china/.

Northrup, Bernard. 1997. "Genesis Chronology According to the Miao People of South China." Lambert Dolphin's Library. http://www.ldolphin.org/miao.html.

Notar, Beth E. 2006. "Authenticity Anxiety and Counterfeit Confidence: Outsourcing Souvenirs, Changing Money, and Narrating Value in Reform-Era China." *Modern China* 32 (1): 64–98.

Nyiri, Pal. 2006. "The Yellow Man Burden: Chinese Migrants of a Civilizing Mission." *China Journal* 56:83–106.

Oblau, Gotthard. 2005. "Pentecostal by Default? Contemporary Christianity in China." In *Asian and Pentecostal: The Charismatic Face of Christianity in Asia*, edited by Allan Anderson and Edmond Tang, 411–36. Costa Mesa, CA: Regnum Books.

Olson, James. 1998. *An Ethnohistorical Dictionary of China*. Westport, CT: Greenwood.

Ong, Aihwa. 1997. "Chinese Modernities Narratives of Nation and of Capitalism." In *Underground Empires: The Cultural Politics of Modern Chinese Transnationalism*, edited by Aihwa Ong and Donald Nonini, 171–202. New York: Routledge.

Ortner, Sherry. 1973. "On Key Symbols 1." *American Anthropologist* 75 (5): 1338–46.

Ostrov, Benjamin C. 2005. "Something of Value: The Religious Response to De-Maoization in China." *Social Science Journal* 42:55–70.

Overmyer, Daniel L. 2009. "Protestant Christianity in China: Perspectives from the History of Chinese Religions and Early Christianity in the Roman World." *China Review* 9 (2): 41–61.

Palmer, David A. 2004. "Cyberspace and the Emerging Chinese Religious Landscape: Preliminary Observations." In *Cyber China: Reshaping National Identities in the Age of Information*, edited by Françoise Mengin, 37–50. Waterloo: University of Waterloo.

Peale, John. 2005. *The Love of God in China*. Lincoln, NE: iUniverse.

People's Daily Online. 2000. "Foreign Volunteers in Southwest China Province." November 16. http://english.people.com.cn/english/200011/16/eng20001116_55295.html.

People's Republic of China, State Council. 2017. "China Revises Regulation on Religious Affairs." September 7. http://english.gov.cn/policies/latest_releases/2017/09/07/content_281475842719170.htm.

Phillips, Tom. 2014. "Thousand Christians Forced from Church as Demolition Campaign Spreads." *Telegraph*, May 19. http://www.telegraph.co.uk/news/worldnews/asia/china/10841738/Thousand-Christians-forced-from-church-as-demolition-campaign-spreads.html.

Pickard, David. 1999. "From the General Director of OMF International." In *China's Christian Millions*, edited by Tony Lambert, 9–12. Oxford, UK: Monarch Books.

Ping, He. 1995. "Perception of Identity in Modern China." *Social Identities* 1 (1): 127–54.

Pippin, Tina, and Randel Bailey. 1996. "Introduction: Race, Class, and the Politics of Biblical Translation." *Semeia* 76:1–6.

Poa, Dory, and Randy J. LaPolla. 2007. "Minority Languages of China." In *The Vanishing Languages of the Pacific*, edited by Osahito Miyaoka and Michael E. Krauss, 337–54. Oxford: Oxford University Press.

Poewe, Karla. 1994. *Charismatic Christianity as a Global Culture*. Columbia: University of South Carolina.

Potter, Pitman. 2003. "Belief in Control: Regulation of Religion in China." *China Quarterly* 174:11–31.

Qian, Ning. 2000. "Jidujiao zai yunnan shaoshu minzu shehui zhong de chuangbo he yinxiang" [The dissemination and influence of Christianity in the ethnic minority society of Yunnan Province]. *Shijie Zongjiao* [World Religions] 3:18–28.

Qin Heping. 2014. "20 shiji 80 nian dai yi lai wazu diqu jidujiao huodong qinkuan shulun" [Narration of Christian activities in the areas of Wa ethnic minority group since the 1980s]. *Minzu Xuekan* [Minority Research] 6 (8): 12–24.

Rabinow, Paul. 1984. "Facts Are a Word of God: As Essay Review of James Clifford's *Person and Myth: Maurice Leenhardt in the Melanesian World*." In *Observers Observed: Essays on Ethnographic Fieldwork*, edited by George W. Stocking, 196–207. Madison: University of Wisconsin Press.

Reardon, Lawrence. 2015. "The Party Giveth and the Party Taketh Away: Chinese Enigmatic Attitudes Towards Religion." In *Religious Transformation in Modern Asia: A Transnational Movement*, edited by David W. Kim, 26–49. Leiden: Brill.

Reinders, Eric. 2004. *Borrowed Gods and Foreign Bodies: Christian Missionaries Imagine Chinese Religion*. Berkeley: University of California Press.

Reny, Marie-Eve. 2018. *Authoritarian Containment: Public Security Bureaus and Protestant House Churches in Urban China*. New York: Oxford University Press.

Rodgers, Ann. 2006. "Hearts Join over Plight of Tibetan Children." *Pittsburgh Post Gazette*, March 5. http://www.post-gazette.com/news/health/2006/03/05/Hearts-join-over-plight-of-Tibetan-children/stories/200603050235.

Rosenbaum, Kathryn. 2004. "In Search of the Truth: Modern Church-State Relations in Yunnan Province." Independent Study Project (ISP) Collection 535. http://digitalcollections.sit.edu/isp_collection/535.

Ross, Heidi, 2005. "China Country Study." Paper commissioned for the EFA Global Monitoring Report 2006, *Literacy for Life*, UNESCO. http://unesdoc.unesco.org/images/0014/001461/146108e.pdf.

Roy, Oliver. 2004. *Globalized Islam: The Search for a New Ummah*. New York: Colombia University Press.

———. 2010. "Religious Revivals as a Product and Tool of Globalization." *Le religioni nelle relazioni internazionali* 12:22–34.

Saich, Tony. 2000. "Negotiating the State: The Development of Social Organizations in China." *China Quarterly* 161:124–41.

Sanneh, Lamin. 2008. *Translating the Message: The Missionary Impact on Culture*. New York: Orbis.

Santos, Lean Alfred. 2016. "Charity Law Signals Growing Role for NGOs in China." *Devex*, April 11. https://www.devex.com/news/charity-law-signals-growing-role-for-ngos-in-china-87998.

SARA (State Administration for Religious Affairs). 2000. "Rules for the Implementation of the Provisions on the Administration of Religious Activities of Aliens Within the Territory of the People's Republic of China." http://www.sara.gov.cn/gb/zcfg/gz/20100423-01-948ea802-0a1c-11da-9f13-93180af1bb1a.html.

Sautman, Barry. 1998. "Affirmative Action, Ethnic Minorities and China's Universities." *Pacific Rim Law and Policy* 7 (1): 77–116.

———. 1999. "Ethnic Law and Minority Rights in China: Progress and Constraints." *Law and Policy* 21 (3): 283–314.

Schak, David. 2011. "Protestantism in China: A Dilemma for the Party State." *Journal of Current Chinese Affairs* 40 (2): 71–106.

Schein, Louisa. 1997. "Gender and International Orientalism in China." *Modern China* 23 (1): 69–98.

———. 2000. *Minority Rules: The Miao and the Feminine in China's Cultural Politics*. Durham: Duke University Press.

Scott, James. 2009. *The Art of Not Being Governed: An Anarchist History of*

REFERENCES

Upland Southeast Asia. New Haven: Yale University Press.
Sebag-Montifiore, Clarissa. 2013. "Good Lord: In China, Christian Fundamentalists Target Tibetans." Time, March 8. http://world.time.com/2013/03/08/good-lord-in-china-christian-fundamentalists-target-tibetans.
Shao, Hua Liu. 2010. Passage into Manhood: Youth Migration, Heroin and AIDS in Southwest China. Stanford: Stanford University Press.
Shen Dingping and Zhu Weifang. 1998. "Western Missionary Influence on the People's Republic of China: A Survey of Chinese Scholarly Opinion Between 1980 and 1990." International Bulletin of Missionary Research 22 (4): 154–58.
Shen Hong. 2006. Shi Men Kan Wen Hua Bai Nian Xing Shuai: Zhong Guo Xi Nan Yi Ge Shan Cun De Xian Dai Xing Jing Li [Modernity through grassroots lens: The cultural transformation of an ethnic community in southwestern China]. Shenyang: Wang Juan Publishing.
Shen Xinran. 2019. "World's Largest Cliff-Carved Guanyin Statue Demolished." Bitter Winter, March 1. https://bitterwinter.org/worlds-largest-cliff-carved-guanyin-statue-demolished-video.
Shih, Chih-yu. 2002. Negotiating Ethnicity in China: Citizenship as a Response to the State. New York: Routledge.
Shue, Vivienne. 2002. "Global Imaginings, the State's Quest for Hegemony and the Pursuit of Phantom Freedom in China: From Heshang to Falun Gong." In Globalization and Democratization in Asia: The Construction of Identity, edited by Catarina Kinnvall, 210–29. New York: Routledge.
Shu-li, Huang. 2014. "From Millenarians to Christians: The History of Christian Bureaucracy in Ahmao (Miao/Hmong) Society, 1850s–2012." PhD diss., University of Michigan.

———. 2017. "The Ahmao (Miao) Schism: The Problem of Spiritual Agency in Encounters Between Church and State in Southwest China." Asian Ethnicity 18 (2): 218–35.
SIL East Asia. 2009. Bai Project Report: Bai Han Shuang Yu Jiao Xiangmu Jian Jie [Bai-Chinese bilingual education summary report]. https://www.sil.org/about/news/china%E2%80%99s-bai-bilingual-education-project-evaluation.
Slack, James. 2011. "Practices in Orality: The Existence, Identification and Engagement of a People's Worldview." China Source, May 3. http://www.chsource.org/en.
Smalley, William Allen. 1991. Translation as Mission: Bible Translation in the Modern Missionary Movement. Macon: Mercer University Press.
Smyer Yu, Dan. 2012. The Spread of Tibetan Buddhism in China: Charisma, Money, Enlightenment. New York: Routledge.
Solinger, Dorothy. 1977. "Minority Nationalities in China's Yunnan Province: Assimilation, Power and Policy in a Socialist State." World Politics 30 (1): 1–23.
South China Morning Post. 2013. "China Needs to Make Reforms in Dealing with Prostitution." May 20. http://www.scmp.com/comment/insight-opinion/article/1241497/china-needs-make-reforms-dealing-prostitution.
Spence, Jonathan. 1996. God's Chinese Son: The Taiping Heavenly Kingdom of Hong Xiuquan. New York: Norton.
Spiegel, Mickey. 2004. "Control and Containment in the Reform Era." In God and Caesar in China: Policy Implications of Church-State Tensions, edited by Jason Kindopp and Carol Lee Hamrin, 40–57. Washington, DC: Brookings Institution Press.
Spittler, Russel. 1994. "Are Pentecostals and Charismatics Fundamentalist? A Review of American Uses of these Categories." In Charismatic

Christianity as a Global Culture, edited by Carla Poewe, 103–16. Columbia: University of South Carolina Press.

State Council. 1994. "Regulations Governing the Religious Activities of Foreign Nationals Within China." Signed by Premier Li Peng. January 31. http://host.uniroma3.it/progetti/cedir/cedir/Eventi/Cina_Reg-Act.pdf.

Stoltz, Christina. 2007. *Opposition to Evangelism in India, Tibet and China*. MA thesis, Florida State University, College of Arts and Sciences, Tallahassee. http://diginole.lib.fsu.edu/cgi/viewcontent.cgi?article=4854&context=etd.

Su Zhou and Zhang Yan. 2014. "Crackdown on Cults Continues with Arrests." *China Daily*, June 12. http://www.chinadaily.com.cn/china/2014-06/12/content_17581071.htm.

Sudworth, John. 2015. "China's Super Rich Communist Buddhists." *BBC News*, January 29. http://www.bbc.com/news/magazine-30983402.

Sugirtharajah, S. R. 1996. "Textual Cleansing: A Move from the Colonial to the Postcolonial Version." *Semeia* 76:7–19.

Sullivan, Christopher. 2011. "Ethnicity and Income Inequality in China." Paper prepared for the annual conference of the Population Association of America, Washington, DC, March 31–April 2.

Sun Haoran. 2013. "Yunnan shaoshu minzu zongjiao wenhua de xiandai chuancheng yu fazhan" [The inheritance and development of Yunnan ethnic religious culture]. *Xueshu Tansuo* [Academic Exploration] 6:96–100.

Sun, Little. 2007. "The Power of Love: Dispelling the Thick Fog in Wu-meng Mountainous Areas." *Shining Light Newsletter* 8. https://www.shine.org.hk.

Swain, Margaret Byrne. 1995. "Pere Vial and the Gni P'a: Orientalist Scholarship and the Christian Project." In *Cultural Encounters on China's Ethnic Frontiers*, edited by Steven Harrell, 140–85. Seattle: University of Washington Press.

Sy, Caris Faith. 1987. "A Study of Tibetan Culture and Religion and of Redemptive Analogies Which Would Heighten the Tibetan's Receptivity of Christianity." MA thesis, International School of Theology, Fontana, CA.

Tai Lai Yong. 2009. *Two Ears but Only One Mouth: Lessons from Yunnan, Insights from Proverbs*. Singapore: Kuo Chuan Presbyterian Secondary School and CHIJ Katong Convent.

Tamney, Joseph, and Linda Hsueh-Ling Chiang. 2002. *Modernization, Globalization and Confucianism in Chinese Societies*. New York: Praeger.

Tapp, Nicholas. 2002. "In Defense of the Archaic: A Reconsideration of 1950s Ethnic Classification Project in China." *Asian Ethnicity* 3 (1): 63–84.

Tenzin Jinba. 2014. *In the Land of Eastern Queendom: The Politics of Gender and Ethnicity on the Sino-Tibetan Border*. Seattle: University of Washington Press.

Thomassen, Bjorn. 2009. "The Uses and Meanings of Liminality." *International Political Anthropology* 2 (1): 5–27.

Tian Bin Shen and Wang Yan Shin. 2000. "Yunnan bufen shaoshu minzu jidujiao yinxiang de shehui zuo yong fenxi" [An analysis of the social function of Christian belief of some ethnic groups in Yunnan]. *Sixiang Zhanxian: Yunnan Daxue Renwen Shehui Kexue Xuebao* [The Ideological Front: Yunnan University Social Sciences Journal] 4 (26): 77–79.

Tien, Ju K'ang. 1993. *Peaks of Faith: Protestant Mission in Revolutionary China*. Leiden: Brill.

Tomlinson, John. 1999. *Globalization and Culture*. Cambridge, UK: Polity.

Tong, Davy, and Raymond Paul Petzholt. 2002. "The True Spiritual Roots for All Chinese." Davy Tong's website. https://www.ocf.berkeley.edu/davytong/publications.

REFERENCES

Tsung, Linda, Ge Wang, and Qunying Zhang. 2012. "Bilingual Education in China: The Case of Yunnan." In *Chinas Assimilationist Language Policy: The Impact on Indigenous/Minority Literacy and Social Harmony*, edited by Gulbahar H. Beckett and Gerard A. Postiglione, 105–20. Abingdon, UK: Routledge.

Tu, Weiming. 1999. "The Quest for Meaning: Religion in the People's Republic of China." In *The Desecularization of the World*, edited by Peter Berger, 85–102. Grand Rapids, MI: Eerdmans.

Tuttle, Grey. 2005. *Tibetan Buddhists in the Making of Modern China*. New York: Columbia University Press.

Uhalley, Stephen, Jr., and Xiaoxin Wu. 2001. *China and Christianity: Burdened Past, Hopeful Future*. Armonk, NY: M. E. Sharpe.

UNESCO Bangkok. 2006. "Yunnan Province of China, HIV/AIDS Profile." http://www.unescobkk.org/?id=5379.

Unger, Jonathan. 1997. "Not Quite Han: The Ethnic Minorities of China's Southwest." *Bulletin of Concerned Asian Scholars* 29 (3): 67–78.

UNHCR / Immigration and Refugee Board of Canada. 2009. "China: Wither Proselytizing Is Legal in China." http://www.unhcr.org/refworld/country,,IRBC,,CHN,,4b8631d828,0.html.

Vala, Carsten. 2017. *The Politics of Protestant Churches and the Party-State in China*. London: Routledge.

Varutti, Marzia. 2010. "The Politics of Imagining and Forgetting in Chinese Ethnic Minority Museums." *Outlines-Critical Practice Studies* 2:69–82.

Wade, Geoff. 2011. "Could ASEAN Drift Apart?" *Asia Sentinel*, March 2. http://www.asiasentinel.com/index.php?option=com_content&task=view&id=3027&Itemid=367.

Wallace, Nathan. 2005. "The Political Economy of Giving: Legitimacy, Welfare, and the Influence of Foreign NGOs in China." Independent Study Project (ISP) Collection 479. http://digitalcollections.sit.edu/isp_collection/479.

Wang, Amber. 2021. "China's Latest Crackdown on Religion Bans Foreigners from Spreading Church and Spiritual Content Online." *South China Morning Post*, December 22. https://www.scmp.com/news/china/politics/article/3160689/chinas-latest-crackdown-religion-bans-foreigners-spreading.

Wang, Xiaoying. 2002. "The Post-Communist Personality: The Specter of China's Capitalist Market Reforms." *China Journal* 47:1–17.

Wang, Yanan. 2018. "Beijing Demands Christians Infuse Faith with 'Chinese Characteristics' amid Crackdown on Religion." *Washington Post*, August 7. https://www.washingtontimes.com/news/2018/aug/7/china-moves-sinicize-christianity-chinese-characte.

Waters, Malcolm. 1995. *Globalization*. London: Routledge.

Watts, Jonathan. 2006. "Outrage at Chinese Prostitutes Shame Parade." *Guardian*, December 6. http://www.guardian.co.uk/world/2006/dec/06/china.jonathanwatts/print.

Weber, Max. (1905) 2003. *The Protestant Ethic and the Spirit of Capitalism*. New York: Dover.

Wei, Jing, Heide Otten, Leonie Sullivan, Laurie Lovell-Simons, Martine Granek-Catarivas, and Kurt Fritzsche. 2013. "Improving the Doctor-Patient Relationship in China: The Role of Balint Groups." *International Journal of Psychiatry in Medicine* 46 (4): 417–27. http://www.dcap.de/wp-content/uploads/2014/09/Improving-the-doctor-patient-relationship-in-china.pdf.

Wenger, Jacqueline. 2004. "Official Versus Underground Protestant Churches in China: Challenges for Reconciliation and Social Influence." *Review of Religious Research* 46 (2): 169–82.

White, Dob. 1992. "The Position and Role of Minority Languages and Their Writing Systems in China." *International

Journal of the Sociology of Language 97:47–57.

Whitefield, Brent. 2009. "Chinese Protestants and the West Since 1949." *China Source*. http://www.chsource.org/en.

Wielander, Gerda. 2011. "Beyond Repression and Resistance—Christian Love and China's Harmonious Society." *China Journal* 65:119–35.

———. 2013. *Christian Values in Communist China*. New York: Routledge.

Xiao Yao Hui and Liu Ding Yin. 2007. *Yunnan Jidujiao Shi* [Christianity in Yunnan]. Kunming: Yunnan Publishing House.

Xi, Lian. 2010. *Redeemed by Fire: The Rise of Popular Christianity in Modern China*. New Haven: Yale University Press.

Xie, Philip Feifan. 2001. *Authenticating Cultural Tourism: Folk Villages in Hainan, China*. PhD diss., University of Waterloo.

Xinhua. 2007. "Foreign Experts Win Friendship Award in China." July 17. http://news.xinhuanet.com/english/2007-07/17/content_6386622.htm.

———. 2009. "Health Care in China." http://www.gov.cn/jrzg/2009-04/06/content_1278721.htm.

———. 2012. "HIV/AIDS Cases in Yunnan Exceeds 100,000." November 27. http://news.xinhuanet.com/english/china/2012-11/27/c_132002862.htm.

———. 2014. "New Synthetic Drugs Challenge Yunnan's Anti-Drug Efforts." June 24. http://www.china.org.cn/china/Off_the_Wire/2014-06/25/content_32771734.htm.

Xu, Yihua. 2004. "'Patriotic' Protestants: The Making of an Official Church." In *God and Caesar in China: Policy Implications of Church-State Tensions*, edited by Jason Kindopp and Carol Lee Hamrin, 107–21. Washington, DC: Brookings Institution Press.

Yamamori, Tetsunao, and Kim Kwong Chan. 2000. *Witnesses to Power: Stories of God's Quiet Work in a Changing China*. Waynesboro, GA: Paternoster.

Yan, Xiao, Sibylle Kristensen, Jianping Sun, Lin Lu, and Sten H. Vermund. 2007. "Expansion of HIV/AIDS in China: Lessons from Yunnan Province." *Social Science and Medicine* 64 (3): 665–75. https://www.ncbi.nlm.nih.gov/pmc/articles/PMC2730760/.

Yang, Fenggang. 2004. "Between Secularist Ideology and Desecularizing Reality: The Birth and Growth of Religious Research in Communist China." *Sociology of Religion: A Quarterly Review* 65 (2): 101–19.

———. 2005. "Lost in the Market, Saved at McDonald's: Conversion to Christianity in Urban China." *Journal for the Scientific Study of Religion* 44 (4): 423–41.

———. 2006. "The Red, Black, and Gray Markets of Religion in China." *Sociological Quarterly* 47:93–122.

———. 2007. "Cultural Dynamics in China: Today and in 2020." *Asia Policy* 4:41–52.

———. 2018. "The Failure of the Campaign to Demolish Church Crosses in Zhejiang Province, 2013–2016." *Review of Religion and Chinese Society* 5 (1): 5–25.

Yang Fuwang. 1990. "Dayao Tanhua Yizu muquangzhi canyu tantao [An inquiry into the remnants of matriarchy among Yi in Tanhua]. *Yizu Wenhua* [Yi Culture]: 117–40.

Yang Jihong. 2013. "Kuajing minzu de zongjiao xinyang yu koutou chuantong guanxi—yi yunnan lisu zu wei ge'an" [Religious belief and oral cultural transmission of the cross-border ethnic groups: A case study of Lisu people in Yunnan]. *Baoshan Xueyuan Xuebao* [Baoshan College Journal] 1:1–7.

Yang, Mayfair Mei-Hui. 2004a. "Goddess Across the Taiwan Strait: Matrifocal Ritual Space, Nation-State and Satellite Television Footprint." *Public Culture* 16 (2): 209–38.

———. 2004b. "Spatial Struggles: Postcolonial Complex, State Disenchantment, and Popular Reappropriation of Space in Rural Southeast China." *Journal of Asian Studies* 63 (3): 719–55.

Yang Zhong. 2013. "Between God and Caesar: The Religious, Social and Political Values of Chinese Christians." *Problems of Post Communism* 60 (3): 36–48.

Ye Xiaowen. 2005. "China's Religions: Retrospect and Prospect." *Chinese Journal of International Law* 4 (2): 441–53.

Yeh, Emily. 2013. *Taming Tibet: Landscape Transformation and the Gift of Chinese Development*. Ithaca: Cornell University Press.

Yeung Yue Man. 2005. "The Pan-PRD and ASEAN-China FTA as Agents of Regional Integration in Pacific Asia." Keynote address, forum on *A Tale of Two Regions: China's Pan-PRD and ASEAN*, Hong Kong, November 4.

Yi, Yang. 2020. "Yunnan Dai Ethnic Minority Village Banned from Converting to Christianity." *China Christian Daily*, September 11. http://chinachristiandaily.com/news/church_ministry/2020-09-11/yunnan-dai-ethnic-minority-village-banned-from-converting-to-christianity_9566.

Ying, Fuk-tsang. 2009. "The Regional Development of Protestant Christianity in China: 1918, 1949 and 2004." *China Review* 9 (2): 63–97.

You Bin, Wang Aiguo, and Gong Yukuan. 2004. "Christianity in a Culture of Ethnic Pluralism: Report on Christianity Among the Minorities of Yunnan." *Chinese Theological Review* 19 (3): 100–124.

Yu, Anthony. 2005. *State and Religion in China: Historical and Textual Perspectives*. Chicago: Open Court.

Yu, Cissy. 2014. "Around Town: St. John Gospel Church." *GoKunming*, July 4. http://www.gokunming.com/en/blog/item/3261/around_town_st_john_gospel_church.

Yu, Verna. 2015. "'Sinicize' Religion to Combat 'Hostile Forces' Chinese Official." *South China Morning Post*, June 16. https://www.scmp.com/news/china/policies-politics/article/1822607/sinicise-religion-combat-hostile-f.

Zhang Danfeng. 2003. "Jindai jidujiao zai yunnan shaoshu minzu diqu xuanbu he yinxiang" [Dissemination and cultural impact of Christianity in the living places of Yunnan ethnic groups]. *Baoshan Shizhuan Xuebao* [Journal of Baoshan Teachers College] 22 (6): 15–19.

Zhang Guanbai, Heng Jiang, Jiucheng Shen, Pinyuan Wen, Xuebing Liu, and Wei Hao. 2018. "Estimating Prevalence of Illicit Drug Use in Yunnan, China, 2011–2015." *Front Psychiatry* 9:256. https://www.ncbi.nlm.nih.gov/pmc/articles/PMC6010540.

Zhang Shuang. 2011. "Guizhou shimenkan miaozu jiaoyi renlei xue tianye kaocha" [An ethnography of the history of education of the Shimenkan Miaos of Guizhou]. *Xuejiao Wenhua Luntan* [Education and Culture Forum] 3:101–8.

Zhang Weiwen and Zeng Qingnan. 1993. *In Search of China's Minorities*. Beijing: New World.

Zhang Xiao Qiong. 2002. "Jidujiao zai yunnan shaoshu minzu zhong chuanbo tezheng tanzi" [Clash and mix: Disseminative features of Christianity among ethnic minorities of Yunnan in the late nineteenth century]. *Yuxi Xueyuan Xuebao* [Yuxi College Journal] 21 (1): 25–30.

Zhao Hongyi. 2010. "Prostitutes or Fallen Women?" *Beijing Today*, December 10. http://www.beijingtoday.com.cn/debate/prostitutes-or-fallen-women.

Zhao Wenjuan. 2008. "Qingmo min chu jidujiao chuanjiao shi zai minzu diqu de xuanjiao huodong: Yi xun dao gonghui chuanjiao shi bai ge li wen ge'an" [Missionary work of Christian missionaries in ethnic area of southwest China during late Qing dynasty and early republic of China period—A case study of Samuel Pollard]. *Xibei di er Minzu Xueyuan Xuebao* [Journal of the Second Northwest University of Nationalities] 1 (79): 96–99.

Zhao Yuezhi. 2002. "The Rich, the Laid Off and the Criminal in Tabloid Tales: Read All About It!" In *Popular China: Unofficial Culture in a Globalizing Society*, edited by Perry Link, Richard Madsen, and Paul G. Pickowicz, 111–35. Lanham, MD: Rowman and Littlefield.

Zhou, Minglang. 2003. *Multilingualism in China: The Politics of Writing Reforms for Minority Languages, 1949–2002*. Berlin: De Gruyter.

Zimmerman-Liu, Teresa, and Teresa Wright. 2013. "Making Sense of China's State-Society Relations: Unregistered Protestant Churches in the Reform Era." In *Christianity in Contemporary China: Socio-cultural Perspectives*, edited by Francis Lim, 220–33. London: Routledge.

Index

abortions, 75, 210
Adam, James, 24–25, 28
Aikman, David, 4, 10, 11, 12, 13, 52, 67, 74, 172
animal sacrifice, 55, 85, 204, 206
animism, 55, 83, 170, 182–83, 199, 203
ancestor worship, 21, 42, 141–43, 150, 183, 204, 212
Anning, 48–50, 60, 155
Arabic, 95, 125
assimilation, 14, 27, 45, 49, 120–24, 137, 140, 181
atheism, 5, 35, 165

Bai nationality, 86, 132–34, 137–38, 142, 175, 176, 218n12
Baoshan, 181
batik art, 175, 189–90, 198
baptism, 101, 165
bible, 4–5
    confiscation of, 9, 12
    evangelical perception, 18–19, 37
    in minority languages, 139–40, 143, 193, 195, 198
    lack of, 53
    similarities with minority mythology, 85, 192–93
    study, 4, 42–43, 56, 62, 69–70, 80, 85, 95, 100, 115, 165
    translation, 4, 9, 21, 57, 120–23, 125–28, 131, 135–36, 144, 193, 198, 208, 217n4, 218n5, 218n14
    values, 37, 74–5, 78
bilingual education, 121, 124, 131–37, 142, 217n3
Bless China International, 98, 107–8, 112, 117–18, 162
blood, 81–82
Bouyei Nationality, 54, 108–9, 131, 138–44, 170, 183, 204, 218n13
Boxer Rebellion, 25, 210
Brazil, 27, 38, 163
Buddhist monks, 57, 68–69, 83, 86, 88, 90, 153, 181
burial rites, 15, 170
Burma. *See* Myanmar
Business as Mission, 62, 64–65

Catholicism, 29, 73, 125, 178, 183, 185, 187, 192, 209, 215n1, 219n10
China Inland Mission, 21, 98, 204, 215n1
Chinese Communist Party, 22, 103, 148, 158, 178, 208, 219n2
Christ-Culture conflict, 33–35, 52, 59
Christianity
    growth in reform era China, 6, 10, 23, 64, 69, 172
    foreign origin, 22, 59, 72, 148, 183, 190, 192–93, 201, 208, 211, 218n2
    indigenization, 59, 61, 192, 209, 212–13
    internationalism, 172, 189, 205
Christian identity, 31, 34–37, 39, 55, 59, 98, 108, 205
Christian NGOs, 13–14, 93–94, 95, 98, 130, 156
church construction, 8, 14, 147, 149, 154, 159, 167, 203
civilizing project, 7, 24, 26, 28, 30, 33, 50, 63, 65, 68, 77, 82, 89, 122, 172, 206
Clarke, Samuel, 24–29, 49, 91, 142
colonialism, 10, 11, 22, 77, 96–97, 153, 188, 190, 198, 208–9, 218n2
Communist Revolution, 2, 11–12, 22, 55, 73, 152, 189
Confucianism, 20, 21, 52, 76, 77, 81, 85, 92, 102, 162, 211, 216n9, 218n2
    civilizing mission, 50, 79
    state sponsored revival, 63, 80, 83, 90, 93, 174, 178, 198, 209–10
conversion to Christianity, 12, 15, 17, 19, 29, 34, 39, 42, 45, 50, 54, 57, 60, 65, 68, 73–76, 86–87, 131, 141, 144, 145, 149, 168
    compatibility with the free market, 76–79, 82, 96
    conflict with Tibetan identity, 70–73
    in Chinese history, 21–31, 37–38, 55
    mass conversion, 22, 24–29, 40, 45, 190, 194, 215n5
    missionary criticism of, 51–53, 55, 60
    motivations, 66–67
    personal stories, 5, 37, 138–39
    rates, 111, 116
    rehabilitation process, 92, 99–103
corruption, 74, 85, 113
Covid19, 9–10, 208

INDEX

Creation to Christ (C2C) 126–27
Cross, The, 73–75, 88, 89, 92
cultural imperialism, 4, 128
Cultural Revolution, 10, 23, 114, 154, 178

Da Hua Miao. *See* Miao Nationality
Dai nationality, 55–59, 82, 92, 101, 132, 152–53, 175–76, 181–82, 216n14 (chap. 2), 216n3 (chap. 3), 218n12
Dali, 87, 132–33, 176
Daoism, 10, 158, 169, 178, 181, 193, 211
decolonization, 30, 96
Dehong, 55–58, 104, 118, 181, 216n14
democracy, 74, 97, 102
demons. *See* Devil Worship
Deng Xiaoping, 49–50, 63
Deqin, 13, 15, 70, 72, 81
devil worship, 15, 83, 85, 155, 168–69, 211
Disciples (*Mentuhui*), 207, 219n3
doctor-patient relationship, 109–11
drug addiction. *See* substance abuse
drug rehabilitation, 13, 14, 62, 92–93, 95, 96, 99–106, 117–18, 156, 207, 210
Dulong Nationality, 180, 215n5

Eastern lightning, 207, 219n3
economic prudence, 63, 76, 88, 90
English language, 13, 17, 56–57, 59, 67, 70, 73, 92, 94–95, 111, 133, 136, 137, 206
ethnic classification, 122, 177–79, 184, 188, 218n1
ethnic identity, 4, 7, 9, 13–15, 24–25, 31, 32–33, 35, 39, 41, 44–45, 50, 54, 60–61, 72, 79, 91, 121, 123, 134, 137–38, 144–46, 171–72, 176, 179, 193, 199, 202–5, 218n12
ethnic relations, 44, 171, 197–98
ethnic stereotypes, 8, 25, 63, 78–79, 145, 153, 174, 177, 182, 189
evangelical theology, 7–8, 17–18, 21, 23–24, 45, 48, 51, 55, 77, 121, 125, 127–28
   de-culturized (pristine) faith, 13, 32–35, 59, 148–49, 162
   de-territorial religion, 7, 32, 34, 148–49, 154, 167–69, 171
   hostility towards traditionalism, 37, 71, 141
   individually based faith, 5, 7, 23, 28, 33, 37–39, 40, 50–52, 55–56, 71, 138, 141, 162, 166, 170, 205
   "keys and bridges", 127, 145, 211

"face" (*mianzi*), 52, 92, 211
Falun gong, 89, 106

family life, 8, 63, 73–75, 77–79, 87–88, 90, 100–103, 138
family planning. *See* one child policy
fengshui, 196
festivals, 28, 33, 54, 56, 58, 133, 177, 182, 183, 202–3, 215n4
fidelity, 67, 75, 88, 209
Fraser, James, 24, 28, 56–57, 130, 139, 204
free market capitalism, 8, 53, 64, 67, 112, 137, 154, 205–6

gambling, 67, 77, 86, 90
Gansu Province, 135–36
global era religion, 34
gods, 15, 85, 101, 150, 170, 180
Golden Triangle, 104
Great Leap Forward, 123, 129, 150, 152
Guizhou, 16, 24–25, 29, 41, 45–47, 108, 131, 132, 140, 155, 170, 190, 215n2, 218n13 (chap.5), 218n7 (chap.6)
Gutzlaff, Karl, 29

Haiti, 167–69
Hani, 6, 16, 138, 170, 177
Hanization, 8, 27, 59, 61, 86, 133, 139–40, 143
harmonious society, 14, 44, 63, 67, 73, 76–79, 83
health care, 29, 63, 89, 106–12
Henan Province, 22, 44, 162, 176, 219n3
HIV/AIDS, 14, 91–92, 105, 113, 116
heterodoxy, 20, 26, 51, 156, 188, 194
Hmong. *See* Miao
Hong Kong. 43, 65, 98, 103, 106, 109, 115, 135, 162, 195, 207, 217n2, 217n6
house Churches, 6, 9, 10, 13, 23–24, 55, 59, 62–63, 68, 78, 154, 156, 164–67, 194, 207–8, 211, 217n1
Hui nationality, 45, 49–50, 87, 95, 135, 176, 181–82, 185, 189
hygiene, 63, 65, 77

ideological vacuum, 27, 64, 154
Inner Mongolia Province, 87, 124
inter-ethnic marriages, 43–45, 48–49
internal orientalism, 87, 172, 174–75, 177, 199
international clinic, 106–12
Islam, 9, 32, 35, 93, 95, 125, 167, 178, 182, 185, 186, 189, 208–9, 211, 216n7, 218n14

Jesuit mission, 20, 29, 52–53, 106, 211–12, 218n2
Jesus film, 121, 143–44, 217n1
Jianchuan school, 132–37, 142, 145
Jiang Zemin, 2, 174, 199

INDEX

Jingpo nationality, 26, 168, 182–83, 186
Joshua Project, 37–39, 167, 183
Journey to the West, 212
Judaism, 4–6, 43–45, 69, 160–61, 165, 202

Korean nationality, 124
Kunming
    missionary Center, 2–4, 11
    modernization, 112, 117, 167, 207–8
    neighborhoods, 16, 36
    Southeast Asian commercial hub, 99, 153
Kunming International Academy, 35, 161
Kuhn, Isobel and John, 24

Lahu nationality, 24, 26, 183, 185, 187
lamas, 69–70, 73, 84–86, 177, 186
languages
    endangered, 123
    preservation, 120–22, 131, 136, 142, 145
    state policy, 123–24
Laos, 43, 57, 153
Lefebvre, Henri, 14, 149–50, 152, 166, 184
leprosy, 13, 71–72
literacy, 27, 121, 129–32, 134, 137
Lhasa, 68, 84, 88–89
Lijiang, 6, 16, 44, 132, 142, 176
Lisu nationality, 7, 24, 26, 28, 37–38, 50, 54–59, 60, 70, 99, 134, 139, 143, 144, 181, 183, 185, 186, 187, 194, 205, 215n5, 216n12, 216n13, 219n4
Lisu (Fraser) script, 50, 56, 130, 139

machismo, 86–87
Manchu nationality, 181
Mandarin Chinese. *See* Putonghua
Maoist era, 10, 12, 14, 22–23, 63, 69, 123–25, 151, 154, 197
marginalization of ethnic minorities, 8, 22, 25–27, 42, 47, 50, 72, 77, 140
Marxism, 8, 77, 85, 98, 153, 178
Masai (Kenya), 139
masculinity, 87–90, 174, 216n5
mass conversions, 25–28, 40, 45, 190, 215n5
materialist philosophy, 5, 174, 196
matriarchy, 54, 79, 180, 216n11, 219n6
Miao nationality, 5, 15–16, 37, 39, 55, 57, 181, 215n2
    choir singing, 54, 189, 219n12
    conflict with the Chinese state, 25–26, 42
    contemporary communities, 39–51, 60, 66, 78, 129–30, 205
    conversion in the early 20th century, 24–30, 142, 156, 162
    Miao missionaries, 43

nationalities village compound, 173–75, 179, 182–200, 205
Qing Miao, 48–50, 155, 216n6
migrant workers, 46, 48, 106, 108–9, 111, 140, 148, 155, 206
migration, 63, 65, 154–55
missionaries
    agricultural projects, 13, 94, 95, 107
    African, 70, 162
    American, 2, 3, 6, 35, 51–52, 55, 60, 67, 94, 96, 160, 189, 196, 216n10, 217n11
    Baptist, 26, 202
    children's education, 35
    criticism, 30, 40, 78, 187
    destruction of ceremonial artifacts, 28, 30
    definition, 17
    dissemination of tracts, 2, 17, 21, 96, 195–96
    ethnic Chinese, 3, 54–55, 60, 66, 79, 85–86, 189
    ethnographic writing, 24
    European, 1, 3, 71, 160, 162, 193, 202
    interest in Israel, 4–5, 36, 43, 44, 46, 160, 165, 202
    Korean, 3, 43, 141
    legality, 2–3, 7, 10–12, 21, 23, 26, 57, 92, 95, 103, 109, 131, 134–35, 141, 155–57, 165, 167, 206
    opportunities for employment, 65–66
    protection of converts, 6, 26
    size of communities, 40
modernization, 9, 29–31, 48, 60, 65, 68, 77, 84, 87, 112, 117, 152–55, 158, 167, 177, 204, 207–8, 213
Mojiang, 16, 138, 177
Mongolian nationality, 87, 124, 136
monogamy, 77–78, 90, 206
monotheism, 28, 43, 51, 85, 191–93, 195, 196, 211–12
Morison, Robert, 21
Morse family, 24
mosques, 94, 158, 181, 185, 188, 208
Mosuo, 182, 217n10, 219n6
Myanmar, 22, 26, 55, 57, 113, 130, 152–53, 216n12

Nationalities Park, Beijing, 173, 179, 180, 183
Naxi Nationality, 6, 7, 16, 142, 175, 176, 216n13, 219n6
Neo-Confucian, 63, 198, 209–10
non-governmental organizations (NGOs), 11, 14, 64, 81, 92, 93–94, 95, 97–99, 130, 133, 135, 137, 141, 145, 156, 160, 207, 217n4
Niebuhr, Richard, 33–35, 215n1
nominal Christianity, 33–40, 51, 54–55, 60, 204

INDEX

Nujiang Valley, 37, 38, 55, 77, 118, 139, 181, 216n12
Nuoso Yi, 152

one child policy, 65, 75, 178
opium trade and production, 11, 14, 91, 104, 187
Opium war, 21

patriotism, 78, 189, 208
Pentecostalism, 18–19, 23, 34, 101, 125, 139, 201, 217n1, 218n14
persecution, 12, 32, 53
Pollard, Samuel, 24–25, 27–28, 41, 43, 46, 50, 129–30, 190, 193, 196, 198, 204
Pollard script, 27, 42, 45, 47, 50, 129- 130, 190
polyandry, 63, 79, 86
polygamy, 63, 79, 90
Post-Maoist era. *See* Reform era
prayer, 1, 18, 23, 27, 40, 67, 80, 85, 100–103, 111, 112, 115, 126, 144, 158, 159–69, 188, 196, 201–3, 217n4, 218n6
prison, 104–5, 113–14, 164
privatization, 91, 94, 97, 99, 106, 116–17, 133
prostitution, 8, 14, 91–93, 112–17, 206
Protestant reformation, 21, 145
Public Security Bureau, 6, 41, 46, 98, 104, 114, 203
putonghua, 14, 46, 123–24, 132, 134, 178

Qing Dynasty, 22, 25, 41
Qinghai province, 89, 90

Reform era
    Confucianism, 209–10
    economic liberalization, 8, 64, 91, 106, 118, 133, 205
    ethnic and cultural revival, 42, 49–50, 57, 72, 123–24, 149, 152–53, 171, 177, 178, 207
    religious revival, 10, 23, 57, 74, 149, 208
    social problems, 14, 63, 75, 91, 106, 118
religious syncretism, 18, 42, 53
Republican era, 118, 123, 153
Ricci, Mateo, 52–53, 164, 191, 193, 211–12, 218n2
riots of 2008, 68, 89
ritual territoriality, 15, 148- 152, 167, 171, 207

Sani Yi, 29–30, 140, 192, 215n3
Sanyingpan, 5, 44, 208n4
second coming of Christ, 194–96
sexuality, 28, 54, 56, 74, 78, 84, 88, 113
Shangdi, 2, 44, 126, 166, 191–92, 211
Sichuan, 1, 3, 16, 40, 98, 168, 201–3
Singapore, 80, 106, 110, 162

Sinicization of religion, 9, 208
shame parades, 114–17
Shangrila, 15, 16, 40, 44, 66–73, 81, 86–87, 176, 216n5
Shaxi, 133
Shenzhen, 47, 48, 114, 179
Shimenkan, 5, 16, 27, 29, 45–48, 57, 60, 129, 156, 190, 205
Southeast Asian development, 99, 117, 153
speaking in tongues, 18–19 101, 119, 125, 218n14
Spirit of capitalism, 14, 88, 90, 205–6
State Administration of Religious Affairs (SARA), 2, 74
state religious policy, 9, 199
    definition of orthodoxy and heterodoxy, 20, 156, 188, 194
    Maoist era, 22–23, 31, 114, 154
    takeover of Christian organizations, 105
state space production, 14–15, 150, 152–53, 157–59, 167, 169
substance abuse, 8, 14, 28, 30, 63, 65, 67, 71, 75–78, 87, 90–91, 93, 97, 99–106, 116–17, 206
Summer Institute of Linguistics (SIL), 13, 124, 130–38, 141, 143–45
superstition (*mixin*), 14, 56, 58, 77, 84, 90, 141–42, 145, 153, 155, 169, 172, 188
Suzhi (quality) 65

Taiping Rebellion, 22, 192
Taylor, Hudson, 21, 98, 100, 204, 215n1, 218n2
televangelist, 188–89, 193, 200
Thailand, 26, 57, 152–53, 216n6
Theravada Buddhism, 55–56, 152, 181, 186
Three Self Patriotic Movement (TSPM), 22–24, 62–63, 68, 135, 156, 157, 160, 165, 194, 208, 218n1
Tiananmen protests, 74, 171
Tibet, 45, 68, 73, 84, 90, 124, 171, 177, 178
Tibetan Buddhism, 69, 72–73, 83–86, 89, 168, 177, 181, 182, 185, 210, 216n4
Tibetan nationality, 7, 13, 15, 16, 40, 67–73, 79, 81–90, 173, 176, 184, 204, 205, 215n4, 216n3
    language, 69, 124, 135, 136
    masculinity, 86–90, 216n5
    relationship with missionaries, 73, 83- 89
tourism, 31, 54, 153, 175–77, 182
translatability, 120, 122–23, 125–26, 145

Uighur nationality, 87
unity of nationalities (*minzu tuanjie*), 44, 197–98
urbanization, 155

Vatican, 209

Vial, Paul, 24, 29-30, 140, 192, 193, 215n1
Vietnam, 43, 113, 216n6

Wa nationality, 24, 26, 78
Weber, Max, 14, 64, 77, 88, 90
Weining, 45-47
Wenhua, 27, 41, 45, 87, 121, 129
Wenzhou, 155, 157-58, 167, 171, 206
World Trade Organization, 11, 65, 97, 200
writing systems, 8, 26- 27, 42, 44-45, 47, 50, 56, 58, 60, 120-21, 128-30, 132, 136, 139, 145, 156, 190, 198, 204
Wuding, 5, 16, 25, 41-51, 54-55, 57, 60, 129, 185, 189-90, 205
Wycliffe Bible Translations, 128, 131, 138, 143-44, 218n14

Xinjiang, 124, 171, 178, 209
Xi Jinping, 9, 12, 96, 178, 208, 210, 213
Xishuangbanna, 82, 152, 176, 218n12

Yao Nationality, 181
Yi nationality, 5, 7, 16, 25-26, 40, 44, 45, 54, 71, 85, 104, 126-27, 134, 152, 164-65, 170, 185, 187, 192, 193, 201-3, 215n3, 216n11, 218n4, 219n1
Young, William, 24
Youth with a mission (YWAM), 64, 160
Yuan Zhiming, 73-74, 92
Yunnan
    Development, 8, 64, 93, 99, 112, 117, 118, 153, 207-8
    tolerance of missionary work, 2-3, 7-9, 10-13, 35, 40, 57, 68, 93, 94, 102-5, 115-17, 135, 147, 149, 156, 174, 195, 200, 203, 208-9

Zhejiang Province, 157-58
Zhongdian. *See* Shangrila
Zhuang nationality, 171, 182, 218n13

www.ingramcontent.com/pod-product-compliance
Lightning Source LLC
Chambersburg PA
CBHW022048290426
44109CB00014B/1020